An Invisible Rope

AN INVISIBLE ROPE

portraits of
Czesław Miłosz

Edited by Cynthia L. Haven

Ohio University Press • Athens

Swallow Press / Ohio University Press, Athens, Ohio 45701
www.ohioswallow.com

© 2011 by Ohio University Press

Front cover photo: © Zygmunt Malinowski

Printed in the United States of America
Swallow Press / Ohio University Press books
are printed on acid-free paper ♾ ™

17 16 15 14 13 12 11   5 4 3 2 1

Library of Congress Cataloging-in-Publication Data
An invisible rope : portraits of Czesław Miłosz / edited by Cynthia L. Haven.
    p. cm.
Includes bibliographical references and index.
ISBN 978-0-8040-1132-7 (hc : alk. paper) — ISBN 978-0-8040-1133-4 (pb : alk.
paper)
    1. Miłosz, Czesław—Criticism and interpretation. 2. Authors, Polish—20th
century—Biography. I. Haven, Cynthia L.
PG7158.M5532I58 2010
891.8'58709—dc22

2010037732

Contents

Contents

Contents

Preface

The time was right to do this book: we will not, for long, be able to collect the memories of those who knew Miłosz in the 1930s and 1940s; we are lucky to have a few of them here. Two of our contributors, Leonard Nathan and Morton Marcus, have died since offering their essays for this book. Even Miłosz's youngest friends have memories that will dim with the years or be displaced as they conform to other, more prominent accounts.

This book is the inspiration of Natalie Gerber, who, at the time I met her, was Miłosz's personal assistant. She arranged my interview with him in 2000, a few months before he was to move permanently to Kraków. She encouraged me as I gathered interviews for *Czesław Miłosz: Conversations*. For a subsequent book—this one—she had suggested that I focus on the lesser-known people in his life, those whose memoirs might not have a predestined outlet in the pages of literary journals or newspapers. I have included a few of those—diplomat John Foster Leich, who knew Miłosz at the time of the poet's defection, comes to mind—but for the most part, such an aim proved impractical. Lesson learned: if you want writing, it's best to go to writers. (Some of the contributors did indeed have a predestined outlet—publishing their contributions elsewhere before we went to press.) I did, however, gather those whose less-celebrated memories might be confined to a brief time of his life and could therefore offer snapshots rather than a movie—for example, poetry instructor Judith Tannenbaum, who had a day with the poet at her class in San Quentin.

The urgency of the task is underscored by the corruptibility of memory. Already, contradictions abound in the memories collected here: for example, people have described Miłosz's hair as red, silver, black, or brown. Those are among the more superficial contradictions. Others are at variance in ways that are more substantive—of course, different years, different days, different observers could account for many of these discrepancies. I have left most of the inconsistencies and incongruities "as is." In some cases, memories conflict openly with facts—I have let the author have the final say, even in at least one case in which the errors are egregious. Essays are arranged in a very rough chronological order, according to when the particular contributor entered Miłosz's long life or what era contained the bulk of the contributor's memories.

What emerged is an astonishing range of material. Nonetheless, certain themes are evident: the overwhelming loneliness of Miłosz's pre-Nobel years; his passionate and often conflicted friendships; his love-hate relationship with his home in exile, America; his dedication to the Polish language; his fight against oblivion.

My goal was to be as inclusive as possible, of as many perspectives as possible. Perhaps I, too, have been infected by Miłosz's desire not to lose anything. As Miłosz said, accepting the Nobel Prize in Literature on December 8, 1980: "Those who are alive receive a mandate from those who are silent forever. They can fulfill their duties only by trying to reconstruct precisely things as they were, and by wresting the past from fictions and legends."

I hope I have done so.

Acknowledgments

A book of this nature is necessarily a collaborative effort, and I have benefited greatly from the encouragement, creativity, and advice of many. I must thank first of all the thirty-two contributors to this volume, who have waited patiently for its birth after a long gestation.

This work was supported in its early stages by a grant from the Kościuszko Foundation, for which I am grateful. I am also deeply grateful for the Milena Jesenská Fellowship, which sponsored my research in Poland and at the Institut für die Wissenschaften vom Menschen in Vienna.

A number of individuals, as well, should be singled out for especial thanks. Natalie Gerber suggested the book idea nearly a decade ago. Agnieszka Kosińska and Adam Zagajewski offered much-needed guidance to literary Kraków during my Milena Jesenská Fellowship in the summer of 2008. Anna Frajlich has been a touchstone on the Polish language, history, culture, literature, and customs. Her patience and perseverance have been exemplary. Alla Makeeva-Roylance labored over several translations for this book out of the kindness of her heart and out of her personal devotion to the Polish language, as she did in 2006 for *Czesław Miłosz: Conversations.*

Ohio University Press has offered outstanding support. Gillian Berchowitz has been an advocate and advisor for this project since its inception, and, as my Virgil through the Purgatorio of complicated editing and copyright procedures, I would like to thank Rick Huard.

Especial thanks to photographer Zygmunt Malinowski for allowing us to reprint his historic photos and to the Miłosz Estate for its generosity.

Finally, I must thank the father of the feast, Czesław Miłosz, "in gratitude for all the gifts."

Chronology

1911   On June 30, CM is born in the family's former manorial village, Szetejnie (in Lithuanian, Šateiniai, in the Kedainiai District), on the banks of the Niewiaża River, in the Grand Duchy of Lithuania, to Weronika (née Kunat) and Aleksander Miłosz. His family is part of the Polish-speaking gentry of Lithuania.

1914–18   Aleksander Miłosz is drafted into the czar's army as a highway engineer after the outbreak of World War I. As a combat engineer officer, he builds bridges and fortifications in front-line areas. His wife, CM, and CM's younger brother, Andrzej, join him in his constant travels around Russia. The family is in the Russian town of Rzhev, on the Volga, at the outbreak of the 1917 October Revolution. The Miłosz family returns to Lithuania in 1918.

1921–29   For his secondary education, CM attends the Zygmunt August High School in Vilnius (Wilno in Polish; Vilna in Russian), which had become part of Poland during these years.

1929   CM enters the Law Department at Stefan Batory University in Vilnius; he is active in the Polish Studies Literary Club.

1930   CM publishes his first poems in the university student periodical, *Alma Mater Vilnensis.*

1931   CM is cofounder of the literary group Żagary, whose bleak political outlook and symbolism gave them the nickname "the school of catastrophists." He is also active in the Vagabonds Club and participates in summer travels to Western Europe with other students. On his first trip to Paris, he meets his kinsman Oscar Milosz, the French poet, who was to become a major influence.

1933   The Polish Studies Club of Stefan Batory University publishes CM's first volume of poetry, *Poemat o czasie zastygłym* (Poem on frozen time). With Zbigniew Folejewski, he coedits *Anthology of Social Poetry,* also published in Vilnius.

1934   CM receives a master of law degree from Stefan Batory University; in Vilnius, he receives the first Philomath Literary Award from the Polish Writers' Union (Związek Literatów Polskich) for his poetry. A grant from the National Cultural Fund allows him to spend a year in France; he leaves for Paris in the fall.

1935   In Paris, CM studies at the Alliance Française and audits lectures on Thomism at L'Institut Catholique. He continues his conversations with Oscar Milosz. Among other poems, he writes "Hymn" and "Gates of the Arsenal." He returns to Vilnius in December.

1936   CM begins work as a literary programmer at Polish Radio in Vilnius. With help from the Polish Writers' Union, he publishes his second volume of poetry, *Trzy zimy* (Three winters).

1937   CM is dismissed from his broadcasting job for his leftist views and his willingness to allow Jews to broadcast; he travels to Italy. On his return, he takes a job as a programmer for Polish National Radio in Warsaw. He publishes poems and articles in literary periodicals.

1938   CM receives a prize in a competition, sponsored by the journal *Piony,* for his novella *Obrachunki* (Reckonings). As the first translation of a poem by CM, Oscar Milosz's translation of CM's "A Song" ("Un chant") appears in the French journal *Cahiers du Sud.*

1939   During the first days of the war, CM is sent to the front as a radio operator.

1940   In January, CM returns to Vilnius and is trapped when Soviet tanks arrive in the city. In July, CM escapes into Nazi-

occupied Warsaw, where he joins the socialist resistance; en
route, he steals across four borders guarded by Soviet and
German security troops. He will not see his native Lithuania
again for more than forty years. In Warsaw, he publishes a
volume of poetry, *Wiersze* (Poems), in mimeograph form
under the pen name of Jan Syruć, a pseudonym taken from
his maternal grandmother's maiden name, acknowledging his
Lithuanian origins.

1941   CM takes a job as a janitor at the Warsaw University Library,
making ends meet with some black market trading.

1942   CM's anthology of anti-Nazi poems, *Pieśń niepodległa*
(Invincible song), and his translation of Jacques Maritain's
pro–de Gaulle "À travers le désastre" are published by
underground presses in occupied Warsaw.

1943   CM writes "The World: A Naïve Poem," a turning point
marking a departure from the catastrophism of his youth and
expressing a faith in the future, and the cycle "The Voices of
Poor People." He also translates Shakespeare's *As You Like It*
on commission from the Underground Theatre Council. CM
participates in clandestine poetry readings.

1944   During the Warsaw occupation, CM marries Janina Dłuska,
whom he had met when they both worked for the radio
station in the late 1930s. In August, after the failure of the
Warsaw Uprising and the destruction of the city, CM and his
wife spend a few months in Goszyce, near Kraków, in the
family home of his friend Jerzy Turowicz, where CM writes a
number of poems.

1945   CM's mother dies near Gdańsk during a typhus epidemic. A
volume of collected poems, *Ocalenie* (Rescue), comes out in
liberated Poland. CM moves to Kraków. He leaves for the
United States in December to assume a diplomatic post.

1946   Although not a member of the Communist Party, CM works
in the Polish consulate in New York as the cultural attaché.
His poems of this period include "Child of Europe."

1947   CM is transferred to Washington, D.C. He writes "Treatise on Morals." He is a correspondent for the literary press in Poland and translates poetry into Polish. CM's first son, Antoni, is born.

1948   "Treatise on Morals" is published in the journal *Twórczość*.

1949   CM makes a brief trip to Poland in the summer. He is shocked at the full dimension of the system's totalitarianism.

1950   CM is transferred to the post of first secretary of the Polish Embassy in Paris, while his family remains in the United States. In December, he travels to Warsaw on holiday and his passport is taken away, effectively imprisoning him in Communist Poland.

1951   The minister of foreign affairs, Zygmunt Modzelewski, at the insistence of his wife, Natalia Modzelewska, approaches Polish Communist leader Bolesław Bierut in January to ask that CM be given his passport. The passport is returned, and CM returns to Paris. On February 1, he asks the French government for political asylum. He moves to Maisons-Laffitte, near the Polish émigré publishing house Kultura. His first article as an émigré, "No," appears in the May issue of *Kultura*. Miłosz is denied a U.S. visa to rejoin his family because of his association with the Communist Polish government. Impoverished, separated from his family, and depressed, he begins work on *The Captive Mind*. CM's second son, Piotr, is born.

1953   *Zniewolony umysł/The Captive Mind*, CM's first book published by the Polish-language Instytut Literacki (the publishing house that sponsors *Kultura*) debuts in Paris, with concurrent translations in English and French. The publisher also issues *Światło dzienne* (Daylight), CM's first volume of poetry as an émigré. In desperate financial circumstances, CM writes *Zdobycie władzy* (Seizure of power), a fictional account of events in Poland from 1939 to 1950, and has it translated into French *(La prise du pouvoir)* to enter a competition sponsored by La Guilde du Livre in Switzerland. As a result, CM receives the Prix Littéraire Éuropéen. The prize gives CM the recognition and funds to bring his family to Paris.

1955   CM publishes his second novel, *Dolina Issy* (Issa Valley), a semiautobiographical account of his childhood in Lithuania, and his translation of Jeanne Hersch's philosophical essays *Politics and Reality. Zdobycie władzy* is published in Polish.

1957   Instytut Literacki publishes *Traktat poetycki* (Treatise on poetry) as a book; it receives *Kultura*'s annual literary prize.

1958   CM publishes a volume of his essays and his translations of poetry, *Kontynenty* (Continents), and his translation of the selected writings of Simone Weil into Polish. He receives the award of the Union of Polish Émigré Writers.

1959   CM's father dies. CM publishes his intellectual autobiography, *Rodzinna Europa* (published later as *Native Realm: A Search for Self-Definition*).

1960   CM moves to the United States to assume the position of visiting lecturer in the Department of Slavic Languages and Literatures at the University of California at Berkeley.

1961   CM receives a permanent appointment as professor and settles permanently in Berkeley.

1962   CM publishes *Król Popiel i inne wiersze* (King Popiel and other poems) and his study of Stanisław Brzozowski, *Człowiek wśród skorpionów* (Man among scorpions), with Instytut Literacki.

1965   CM translates and publishes his influential English anthology of Polish poetry, *Postwar Polish Poetry: An Anthology.* His seventh volume of poetry, *Gucio zaczarowany* (Bobo's metamorphosis), is published by Instytut Literacki.

1966   CM becomes a fellow of the Humanities Institute, Berkeley.

1967   Oficyna Poetów i Malarzy (Poets' and Painters' Press) in London publishes an extensive selection of CM's poems in a volume entitled *Wiersze* (Poems). He receives the Marian Kister Literary Award in New York.

1968   *Native Realm: A Search for Self-Definition* is published in the United States. CM receives the Alfred Jurzykowski Foundation award.

1969   CM publishes another volume of poetry, *Miasto bez imienia* (City without a name), and a collection of essays, *Widzenia nad zatoką San Francisco* (Visions from San Francisco Bay). His academic textbook, *The History of Polish Literature,* is published in the United States.

1970   CM becomes a U.S. citizen.

1972   Instytut Literacki publishes CM's collection of literary essays, *Prywatne obowiązki* (Private obligations). The volume wins a Radio Free Europe plebiscite for the best book of the year.

1973   Seabury Press in New York publishes the first volume of CM's poetry in English, *Selected Poems* (reissued in a revised version by Ecco Press in 1982), sparking the late recognition of CM as a poet rather than a political essayist and author of *The Captive Mind.*

1974   CM publishes a volume of poetry, *Gdzie wschodzi słońce i kędy zapada* (From the rising of the sun), for which he receives the I. Wandycz Award. The Polish PEN Club awards him its prize for his translations of Polish poetry into English.

1976   CM receives a Guggenheim Fellowship to pursue work on his own poetry and his poetry translations.

1977   The University of Michigan Slavic Publications (Ann Arbor) publishes an extensive selection of CM's poems in Polish in *Utwory poetyckie: Poems.* The university also confers an honorary doctorate on CM. Instytut Literacki publishes *Ziemia Ulro* (Land of Ulro). A collection of his essays in English translation, *Emperor of the Earth: Modes of Eccentric Vision,* and CM's English translation of Aleksander Wat's *Mediterranean Poems* are published in the United States. *Mój wiek: Pamiętnik* (My century), Wat's memoirs (transcripts of conversations with CM), is published in London.

1978   CM receives the Neustadt International Prize for Literature, presented under the auspices of Oklahoma State University. For his literary and academic merits, the University of California presents CM with its highest recognition the Berkeley Citation, as he retires and becomes professor emeritus. The second volume of his poetry in English translation, *Bells in Winter,* is published in the United States.

1979   Éditions du Dialogue in Paris publishes CM's translation of the Book of Psalms from Hebrew to Polish, for which he receives the Zygmunt Hertz Award. *Ogród nauk* (Garden of knowledge), a collection of essays and translations of foreign poetry into Polish, is published by Instytut Literacki.

1980   On October 9, CM is awarded the Nobel Prize in Literature, presenting his Nobel lecture on December 8. Éditions du Dialogue publishes CM's translation of the Book of Job from Hebrew into Polish. Instytut Literacki begins publishing a multivolume edition of CM's collected works.

1981   In June, CM visits Poland for the first time since his exile. He receives an honorary doctorate from Lublin Catholic University; he meets with Lech Wałęsa and other Solidarity leaders in Gdańsk. An exhibit devoted to his life and work opens at the Literary Museum in Warsaw. The Polish presses Wydawnictwo Literackie and Czytelnik publish the first volumes of CM's work available in Poland since 1945. Within days of his visit, the first official Polish publication of his poetry sells 150,000 copies. A bilingual, Polish-English edition of CM's Nobel lecture is published. CM holds the Eliot Norton chair at Harvard for the academic year 1981/82 and gives the six public Norton lectures on poetry. He is awarded an honorary doctorate by New York University. In December, martial law is declared in Poland; most of CM's work is again banned and circulated in samizdat.

1982   Instytut Literacki and Michigan Slavic Publications publish his tenth volume of poetry, *Hymn o perle* (Hymn of the pearl). Éditions du Dialogue publishes his translation of *The Books of Five Megiloth* (Lamentations, Ruth, Esther, Ecclesiastes, and Song of Songs).

1983   CM receives an honorary doctorate from Brandeis University. His 1980 Norton lectures are published as *The Witness of Poetry.*

1984   A new volume of poems, *The Separate Notebooks,* is published in a bilingual edition. *Nieobjęta ziemia* (Unattainable earth)—a collection of poetry (his own and others'), letters, and historical excerpts influential to his thinking from 1981 to 1984—is published in Polish by Instytut Literacki. Éditions du Dialogue publishes his translations, from the Greek, of the Gospel According to Mark and the Apocalypse.

1985   CM publishes *Poszukiwania: Wybór publicystyki rozproszonej, 1931–1983* (Explorations: Selected articles); *Zaczynając od moich ulic* (Beginning with my streets), a new volume of essays, is published by Instytut Literacki.

1986   *Unattainable Earth* is published in English. On April 17, CM's first wife, Janina, dies, after a decade-long illness.

1987   CM writes another volume of poems, *Kroniki* (Chronicles).

1988   CM's *Collected Poems, 1931–1987* is published in English, with translations by Robert Hass, Leonard Nathan, Robert Pinsky, and others.

1989   CM receives the National Medal of Arts. He publishes *Metafizyczna pauza* (Metaphysical pause). Communist rule is overthrown, and Poland becomes what is constitutionally known as the Third Polish Republic.

1990   CM publishes *Rok myśliwego* (Year of the hunter). He is admitted to the American Academy and Institute of Arts and Letters.

1991   CM publishes his new volume of poems, *Provinces,* in English. He returns to Lithuania for the first time since World War II and is granted honorary citizenship. *Beginning with My Streets* is published in English.

1992   CM marries Carol Thigpen, a historian and former associate dean for the College of Arts and Sciences at Atlanta's Emory

University. He publishes *Szukanie ojczyzny* (In search of a homeland).

1994   The president of Poland presents CM with the Order of the White Eagle.

1995   CM publishes a volume of poems about his return to Lithuania: *Facing the River.*

1997   CM publishes *Piesek przydrożny* (Road-side dog), a collection of thoughts. CM publishes the first of the two-volume memoir *Abecadło Miłosza* (Miłosz's ABC's) in a Polish genre called *abecadło* (an alphabetical arrangement of entries on people, places, and events in an individual's life).

1998   *Road-side Dog* is published in Robert Hass's English translation by Farrar, Straus and Giroux, and CM receives the 1998 Polish Nike Literary Prize for the volume. The second volume of Miłosz's abecadło—*Inne abecadło* (Further ABC's)—is also published.

1999   CM publishes *Zniewolony umysł* in Poland. With access to Kraków archives, the poet compiles an anthology of essays and reportage from 1937 to 1946, documenting the anti-Semitism that had been denied in subsequent years.

2000   CM moves to Poland permanently, after years of dividing his time between Kraków and Berkeley.

2002   On August 15, CM's second wife, Carol, dies of cancer. CM's final book of poems, *Druga przestrzeń* (Second space), is published in Kraków.

2004   On August 14, CM dies at his home in Kraków. *Second Space* is published in English in the fall.

2005   *Legends of Modernity* is published in English.

2006   *Selected Poems, 1931–2004* is published in English. *Wiersze ostatnie* (Last poems) is published by Znak in Kraków.

Introduction

From Devenir *to* Être

CYNTHIA L. HAVEN

Endurance comes only from enduring.
With a flick of the wrist I fashioned an invisible rope,
And climbed it and it held me.

—Czesław Miłosz, "Magic Mountain"

Though Czesław Miłosz often seemed austere and forbidding to Americans, those who knew the Nobel laureate found him warm, witty, and endlessly enriching. Of his poetry, the late Joseph Brodsky once said, "Even if one strips his poems of the stylistic magnificence of his native Polish (which is what translation inevitably does) and reduces them to the naked subject matter, we still find ourselves confronting a severe and relentless mind of such intensity that the only parallel one is able to think of is that of the biblical characters—most likely Job."[1] Moreover, his life, his knowledge, and his oeuvre are a through-the-looking-glass foray into a vanishing world of art, history, education, values, aesthetics.

The crown that Brodsky and others conferred sat uneasily on Miłosz's head—less a circle of laurels, perhaps, than a crown of thorns. While disavowing any kind of comforting spirituality, he nevertheless stands awkwardly, contestably, as one of the twentieth century's great souls, as well as one of the greatest poets of our times.

Miłosz's worldview, his sense of hierarchy and values, puts him squarely, if reluctantly, in a select spiritual salon. In our times, it is a lonely place to be. Miłosz has become an icon, his works canonical, but head-on-a-coin status can often be a substitute for real understanding. This is particularly true when those spending the coins never lived under the Generalgouvernement of the Gestapo. For Generation Y, the communism years (and communism itself) constitute only a tedious chapter in history textbooks. (See Natalie Gerber's "Missing Miłosz" in this volume for one young woman's attempt to describe Miłosz to the Millennials.) It may be a universal truth that a younger generation must try to distance itself from the seriousness of purpose in an older generation of giants.

This mileage provides a raison d'être for this book, as the distance stretches to the horizon's vanishing point and threatens with extinction the very values Miłosz endeavored to preserve. This statement is more than old fogeyism[2] or the specter of apocalypse—for Miłosz's peers are almost entirely gone (he would have been one hundred years old in 2011), and, moreover, the restlessness, the segmentation of attention, and the increasing difficulty in absorbing anything more than 140 characters long are not merely traits of the younger generation but affect us all. Few can deny the dizzying rate of social and technological upheaval in the information age, where we communicate in real time with Peru and Twitter back what we hear, yet human greed, cowardice, and power-lust remain essentially the same. That acceleration, juxtaposed with man's fallibility, is very much to the point.

One metric for measuring the chasm pertains to what Miłosz called *être* and *devenir*. (Or, to put a Thomist slant on it, he uses the Latin *esse* elsewhere.) When I interviewed him at his legendary Grizzly Peak home a decade ago, I asked him about *être* and *devenir*. He dodged the question: "My goodness. A big problem," he said.

After some hesitation, however, he elaborated. "We are in a flux, of change. We live in the world of devenir. We look at the world of être with nostalgia. The world of essences is the world of the Middle Ages, of Thomas Aquinas. In my opinion, it is deadly to be completely dissolved in movement, in becoming. You have to have some basis in being.

"In general, the whole philosophy of the present moment is post-Nietzsche, the complete undoing of essences, of eternal truths. Postmodernism consists in denying any attempt at truth."

Then he retreated to his initial reservations: "In truth, I am afraid of discussing this subject. The subject needs extreme precision. In conversation, it's not possible."

Time reveals what conversation could not. Rilke said we must live the question—at this late date, however, we must live the answer. We inhabit a world where history doesn't matter. The first victim in our technology age has been time, even more than space. The net effect isolates us in the "Little Now" of devenir. As a result, we lose the ability to think and learn from the past—the very past in which the "now" is invisibly rooted. We become walled off from the world, which comprises centuries as well as nations. Without such context, we only fetishize culture—extol it without understanding it, memorialize it without being able to profit from it.

Miłosz survived into the age of globalization—as literary scholar Valentina Polukhina describes it, "a period in which our long history has been put into single storage."[3] As a cause and effect of that storage, "Today's world is not monolithic: discrete events, fragmented thinking and perceptions, ideas of good and evil are so confused that the only proper response is apocalypse."[4]

There is a time-honored, if unpopular, way that goes beyond language to drive man back to the world of être. Suffering can be a man's personal sign of refusal. For Miłosz, it took him on his own psychological journey, a *via negativa* through despair, loneliness, abandonment, and doubt as the years of exile stacked up like empty bottles.

Ironic, then, that America holds the image of Miłosz as the Poet Triumphant—an image Miłosz honed and perfected. For example, I recall his last reading at Berkeley in 2000, in a standing-room-only crowd with students on stairwells and others peering between balustrades—or the first press photographs of the poet shyly backing away from his barely opened front door after the 1980 Nobel announcement. But the person who emerges in the pages of this book is more nuanced, more complex, and infinitely contradictory—these essays limn what Jerzy Illg of the Polish publishing house Znak called "Continent Milosz."

One of the most haunting images to emerge in these essays occurs in Morton Marcus's "Uneasy Exile." When Marcus meets Miłosz in the 1960s, the poet is literally weeping with loneliness. Others have commented on Miłosz's profound isolation in the three decades between defection and the Nobel, but perhaps no other account is so moving. Anna Frajlich, in her essay, recalls him telling her, "Nobody chooses loneliness."

On visiting Poland, I can better understand the intensity of Miłosz's sense of abandonment in the United States; as an American, I can also understand that the estrangement would necessarily reach its apogee in California, which represents a national extreme that is as foreign to many Americans as the Huli wigmen. With its dramatic coastline, California is the ultimate endpoint where American hopes and aspirations are extinguished in the infinite—the place where envisioning a landscape that

3

endures beyond mankind's journey is most possible. California is very much the land of Carmel poet Robinson Jeffers, who so fascinated and repelled Miłosz with his philosophy of "inhumanism."

But nowhere in America would have been home. The Polish landscape, the architecture, the familiar streets, the cafés, the old friends, and old jokes in his native tongue were gone. In America, he would always be the devotee of "some unheard-of tongue"[5]—although it is less unheard-of now, thanks to his indefatigable efforts (some of them chronicled in these pages). Nevertheless, the fire of literary amities, enmities, and conversations is something unmatched in America except, perhaps, in New York City. Even the Big Apple is a problematic comparison: the density and intensity of a language whose 40 million speakers are concentrated in 121,000 square miles cannot easily be likened to the world's new Latin, the imperial language with nearly ten times as many native speakers.

Miłosz's assistant, Agnieszka Kosińska, recalled his happy return to Poland in a way that underscored what had been missing in America: "These are the people with whom he had a thousand discussions, a thousand literary evenings." Polish literary friendships seem close and demanding; Americans would find them smothering. (It is hard for me to imagine anyone in Poland complaining, "I need space.") In America, getting far enough under the skin to explore the existential questions that were bread to Miłosz is relatively difficult—indeed, foreigners often complain that Americans seem to have no depths to plumb. Such contact must be sought and, when found, cultivated—not assumed as a given. (It is fitting that Facebook is now based in California. One can now have hundreds of friends without finding a real companion, just as we have hundreds of television channels with nothing to watch.) Consider this remark from Alexander Schenker in this volume: "America is not an easy country for foreigners to settle in. At first blush, Americans appear easygoing, even friendly, but closer encounters reveal that it is a country of social alienation. Interpersonal contacts outside the family are generally superficial and tend to be limited to a workplace or to a group of people who have similar interests but lack emotional ties."

Yes, surely, transmuting suffering into être was one strand of his invisible rope. Miłosz's story echoes Simone Weil's beloved fairy tale, the Grimms' "Six Swans," which was the subject of an essay while Weil was still a student at the École Normale. The princess, whose brothers have been turned into swans, must spend six years patiently weaving jackets of white anemones—to free her brothers of the spell that renders them powerless and mute, and to free herself from silence. "To make six shirts from anemones and to keep silent: this is our only way of acquiring power," Weil wrote. It might have been a page from Miłosz's book, except that he worked decades, not years, turning promising students into gifted translators. ("Why, this reads like the work of a *beginning* translator!" he reproached Lillian Vallee, who thought, "That sounded logical to me; that's exactly what I really was." She went on to translate his *Bells in Winter,* the book that brought him a Western audience for his poetry.) He ceaselessly gave over his own creative energies to create the miracle of Polish poetry in English through his books, essays, and translations. He also championed candidates for academic positions, created a chair at Columbia, financed writers and their work, and, in the case of Aleksander Wat, extended a most unusual brand of academic patronage.

The white anemones, patiently and tirelessly woven, created princes, just as miraculously as in the fairy tale—and a few princesses, too. Consider the remarkable cache of translators who flourished under his aegis: Robert Hass, Robert Pinsky, Bogdana Carpenter, Madeline Levine, Lillian Vallee, Peter Dale Scott, Richard Lourie, Leonard Nathan, Louis Iribarne, and others. The 1968 *Selected Poems* he translated with one of them, Peter Dale Scott, created the reputation of Zbigniew Herbert in America—years before Miłosz's own poetic voice would be recognized. He tirelessly wrote about the works of Anna Swir, Wisława Szymborska (long before her own 1996 Nobel), Miron Białoszewski, and others in his essays, in *Postwar Polish Poetry,* and in *The History of Polish Literature.* Meanwhile, colleagues, such as Schenker, reminded him of how important it was to have good English and Swedish translations of his work—the Nobel was already in their crosshairs. "The fact is the English translations of my poems played an enormous role," Miłosz himself told Adam Michnik.[6]

It was more than enough to encourage envy and resentment in Berkeley colleagues—and something of the same in a few students as well, to their profit. In his essay, "Love at Last Sight," Richard Lourie recalls being a Miłosz student in the 1960s, when Miłosz read his "rather well-written" essay that nevertheless "betrays a typical American lack of any feel for history."

Lourie, burning with shame, recalls his feelings: "To hell with him! I'll get one of those! I'll get a sense of history if it kills me! I vowed in the no-doubt-typical American belief that you can always get what you don't have. Later, I was much aggravated to learn that for Miłosz, as for Joyce, history had always been a nightmare from which he was trying to awaken, but by then it was too late." It's an acquired taste—a bitter, yet medicinal, infusion.

Hence this book. To understand, to move from devenir to être means to join him in retrieving memory from oblivion, to become, like him, one of time's ragpickers. For without memory, how can there be justice, and without justice, how can there be order? And without order—chaos and oblivion.

Clearly, then, the retrieval is more than a literary device and more than a reverence for history; it becomes an existential quest. As Hass said of Miłosz (in the interview included in this volume), "He truly thinks it's horrible that everything just passes away, into oblivion. He hates it. . . . There's that terrific sense of urgency, and one of the things that goes with it is: if he can't remember and get down on paper the hairstyle of his piano teacher who was crushed in a bombing when she was an old lady, if her life goes unmarked into oblivion—then oblivion won."

Miłosz articulated his feelings in "Antigone," a poem that, to my knowledge, has not been published elsewhere in English, other than the *Hungarian Quarterly* translation by one of this volume's contributors, George Gömöri (and Richard Berengarten):

> To accept what happens just as one accepts
> Seasons piling pell-mell on one another,
> And on our human world to cast the same
> Indifference as on mute Nature's transformations?
> So long as I shall breathe I shall say—No.
> Do you hear me, Ismene? I shall say—No.[7]

In "Antigone," he makes the critical link between this endeavor and what Lourie called the nightmare of history:

> Fools alone believe they can live easy
> By relegating Memory to the past.
> Fools alone believe one city falling
> Will bring no judgement down on other cities.[8]

Now it is Miłosz himself whose life and whose being we are trying to rescue in an America that, perhaps, never fully understood him.

Since the advent of New Criticism, the life of the writer has often been excessively devalued relative to the merits of the oeuvre itself—though, ironically, any introduction to Miłosz (or Constantine Cavafy or Osip Mandelstam) inevitably resorts to biographical data: that he was born in 1911 in Lithuania, a son of Polish-speaking gentry; that he survived the Warsaw Uprising; that he was a diplomat for the Communist regime who defected in Paris; that eventually he found a home in America. The New Criticism viewpoint, fervently embraced by his friend and fellow Nobel laureate Joseph Brodsky, is especially limited when approaching the poets of the former Soviet bloc, where poetry was often the national substitute for public discourse and where it performed a historic function as well as an aesthetic one. Miłosz, after all, is one of three figures on the Solidarity monument in Gdańsk, along with Lech Wałęsa and Pope John Paul II. Moreover, Polish poetry has always had a role intertwined with its national history. (Miłosz distanced himself from the prevalent nationalistic strains in Polish poetry despite, or because of, his firsthand experience of the war, the Nazi occupation, and Stalinism.) Only in the postmodern world are young Polish poets embracing the luxury of a "personal poetry." For Miłosz, whose Norton lectures, published as *The Witness of Poetry*, helped popularize the term so often used to limit him in recent years—"poet of witness"—his life, and the way he chose to live it, illuminates the poetry and also illuminates a chapter in our collective history. We have much to learn from it. We have much to learn, especially, from his profound and unshakeable sanity in an inhuman century, for Miłosz once described poetry as "a search for how man should behave in an untenable position."[9]

Miłosz wrote, "Endurance comes only from enduring."[10] The invisible rope he fashioned was not only twined from the fiber of his inner world: another strand was his unseen readers in Poland, the readers that, for decades, he did not dare to assume even existed. Yet another strand undoubtedly included the friendships he forged in America, particularly in Berkeley. Both halves of his bifurcated life, in Poland and in the United States, were vital to making Polish literature one of the richest and most widely recognized literary legacies of the twentieth century.

Miłosz's existential concerns always veer close to the theological—and the contradictions between them reverberated within the man himself. He once said, famously, that his central concerns were religious, but the dissonance between his Catholicism and his distinctly Manichaean leanings is legendary. Jane Hirshfield and Hass, in this volume, recollect that his struggle between yes and no, faith and doubt, continued to his death. Not everyone sees it quite that way, however. His confessor, Fr. Zbigniew Krysiewicz, recalled to me his own rapprochement with the poet, motivated by Miłosz's late-life search during his last years in Kraków. In the priest's view, Miłosz seems to have been seeking a kind of affirmation: "Let's say you had an experience with a great fire once—you have a vague memory of it. You have spent a lot of years trying to describe it, and read a lot of books describing it. What you remember is an echo of it. You search and look for someone who can testify about this fire—that it is real—who can testify beyond words, because we know that words are too weak."[11]

Joanna Zach, another contributor to this book, recalled to me one of her last meetings with Miłosz in the hospital, the morning after a blood transfusion. "He felt he had experienced a revelation," she said. "He said, 'I know what I'm going to write about when I go home from the hospital.' And that day he started to dictate to me a poem. He never finished that poem. It was a poem about his experience in the hospital—of compassion and how he experienced his body, and his contact with other people who were lying next to him—touching to the very core of humanity."[12]

This brings us back to the Poet Triumphant—but triumphant in a deeper and more enduring sense than his visible badges of success might offer, moving from obscurity and defeat to an ascendancy, not only in the world of poetry; he became, as mentioned earlier, one of the world's great souls, as well as one of the greatest poets of our times.

It's a picture hinted at during a conversation I had in Kraków with Dr. Anatol Roitman of Novosibirsk, his Russian translator, who recalls his pilgrimages to Miłosz's home on Bogusławskiego, as the ailing nonagenarian poet continued to write and supervise translations. Even in the last months, Roitman's translations of Miłosz's poems into Russian (a language Miłosz understood) would meet with Miłosz's famously explosive laughter and approval.

In the late fall of 2003, Roitman recalled sitting with Miłosz, with the powerful magnifying glass that accommodated the poet's deteriorating eyesight. Together, they were going over Roitman's translations of the poems from *Second Space,* the last collection Miłosz supervised. Then they reached the final poem in the volume, "Metamorphoses," with its epigraph from Ovid. Because of its rhyme and short meter, "Metamorphoses" had proved resistant to English translation, and Miłosz had decided not to include it in the American edition of *Second Space.* But what of the Russian?

"Whenever I heard his famous stentorian laughter, I knew he liked the translation," Roitman recalled. "But when we got to 'Metamorphoses,' his reaction was quite different."

"He was silent at first, and then quietly uttered one word: 'Victory.'"

Notes

1. Quoted in William Riggan, "Czesław Miłosz: Silence . . . Memory . . . Contemplation . . . Praise," *World Literature Today* 73 (Autumn 1999): 617.
2. The fictional Jesuit of Evelyn Waugh's *Brideshead Revisited,* speaking in the 1920s, sounds quaint and naïve to us now, in an era when scientists say technology is changing the very circuitry of our brains. Yet he's worth revisiting: "The trouble with modern education is you never know how ignorant people are. With anyone over fifty you can be fairly confident what's been taught and what's been left out. But these young people have such an intelligent, knowledgeable surface,

and then the crust suddenly breaks and you look down into depths of confusion you didn't know existed" (Evelyn Waugh, *Brideshead Revisited* [Boston: Little, Brown, 1945], 193). The confusion persists and even deepens, as we learn to think and approach the world in an utterly new way.

3. Valentina Polukhina, *Brodsky through the Eyes of His Contemporaries* (Boston: Academic Studies Press, 2008), 2:xxiv.

4. Ibid., 2:xxiii.

5. Czesław Miłosz, "Magic Mountain," in *New and Collected Poems, 1931–2001* (New York: Ecco, 2003), 336.

6. Adam Michnik, "'One Has to Rise Early in the Morning': A Conversation with Czesław Miłosz," in *Czesław Miłosz: Conversations*, ed. Cynthia L. Haven (Jackson: University Press of Mississippi, 2006), 217.

7. Czesław Miłosz, "Antigone," trans. Richard Berengarten (Burns) and George Gömöri, *Hungarian Quarterly* [Budapest] 42 (Winter 2001): 64.

8. Ibid., 66.

9. Czesław Miłosz, *Year of the Hunter* (New York: Farrar, Straus and Giroux, 1994), 217.

10. Czesław Miłosz, "Magic Mountain," in *New and Collected Poems*, 335–36.

11. Quoted in Cynthia Haven, "Poet Czesław Miłosz's Last Days," *Los Angeles Times*, October 5, 2008.

12. Ibid.

Way Back in Wilno . . .

ELIZABETH KRIDL VALKENIER

I first knew Czesław Miłosz when I was a child before World War II. He was a student of my father, Manfred Kridl, professor of Polish literature at the Stefan Batory University in Wilno.[1] After the war, as an adult, I knew him in the United States, where he worked first in the Polish diplomatic service and, after resigning that position, took up an academic career.

No matter how old or recent my memories, they invariably recall an outsider, someone who in his young adulthood insisted on asserting his own, separate identity and later came to believe in his special destiny.

In Wilno, he was not part of the small group of students who would visit my father and occasionally play with his two children. Come to think of it, the students who did come to our house were all women. Very aptly in his *Miłosz's ABC's* (a Polish literary genre loosely composed of short, alphabetically arranged entries devoted to people, events, or ideas that had influenced the author's life), Miłosz referred to the literature department as "a matrimonial department, populated almost exclusively by young women."[2] And that fact might have made this particular group unattractive to him, preventing him from joining the others. Even so, he did join a department picnic in 1936 at the medieval castle in Troki, outside of Wilno. However, a photograph of the group shows Miłosz standing apart—behind my father and others—about to make a funny face, or was it to be an ironic gesture? Miłosz is absent altogether from another snapshot of the same outing, with the group sitting in the picturesque ruins of the castle. And I cannot locate him in yet another photo of us all in a rowboat. This is not, however, how Miłosz chose to remember the event. Again in his ABC book, under the entry devoted to Kridl, he wrote, "We squeezed into a boat. . . . I am at the oars, rowing vigorously out beyond the island, to the open expanse of the lake."[3]

Despite the infrequent visits to our house, the bonds between professor and student must have been very strong. Both were leftists, opposed to the authoritarian government of the colonels in the late 1930s and also opposed to the traditional Polish patriotism, with its regrettable mixture of messianism and anti-Semitism. In addition, Miłosz was swept up in the innovative—and radical at the time—formalist analysis, or early structuralism, which Kridl introduced in his lectures and seminars.[4]

For his part, my father was supportive of the rebellious young poet and wrote a laudatory introduction for the anthology of progressive, social poetry Miłosz edited in 1933.[5] This is how he evaluated the young poet in a 1934 public lecture, shortly after the volume's publication:

> Czesław Miłosz should be numbered among the genuinely fresh
> and clearly defined talents of the young generation. . . . He has
> tried his hand at several styles, all of which have in common a
> striving for the mastery of lyricism, rigorous form and a break
> with traditional rhythm, rhyme, versification . . . replacing them
> with uneven, fragmented rhythms, non-rhyming verses and new
> metaphors that are completely divorced from reality. . . . But still
> it should be emphasized that the essence and value of Miłosz's po-
> etry lie not in experimentation. Even in his earliest poems he was
> capable of poetic formulations that conveyed a general sense of
> independence from this or that school. . . . From what Miłosz has
> already given us, there emerges a clearly defined poetic individual-
> ity that strives to formulate its own view of the world, its own
> imagery. As we had seen, he had accomplished a good deal toward
> that goal. We wish him continued and even greater success.[6]

Furthermore, Kridl defended Miłosz and a number of other leftist students, either at the university or in court, against accusations of subversive activities as alleged members of the Communist Party. I have no precise recollections, and there are no survivors to consult about the exact nature or venue of the trial. I just remember hearing vague references to it among adults. It could have been a "disciplinary investigation" at the university. As for my father's role, being an ardent democrat (among the founders of the Social Democratic Club in Wilno), he undoubtedly defended Miłosz with the freedom of speech argument.

After the war, they resumed contact in the United States, where another element entered their relationship. My father was the first to arrive in 1940 from Portugal, where he was stranded at the start of World War II, to teach at Smith College. (That job offer was a generous gesture that enabled my father to obtain an American visa.) Miłosz came in late 1945, first to serve briefly in the Consulate of the Polish People's Republic in New York City and then as a cultural attaché at the embassy in Washington, D.C. He broke with the Communist regime in 1951.

Both had become outsiders. Given his leftist convictions and reputation, Kridl could never feel comfortable with the right-leaning majority of the politically and culturally active Polish émigré community. Similarly, while Miłosz was in the diplomatic service of the Communist government, he was ostracized by that same community, which was solidly opposed to the new system in People's Poland. I remember Miłosz saying that when he lived in the United States, his friends among the émigré community tended to be either Polish or Polish Jewish leftists, both shunned by most émigrés for questioning the traditional national values. The émigré establishment's hostility continued after Miłosz's break with the Communist government. The persistent ostracism did concern him, and he explained in a 1954 letter to my father that his independent, leftist opinions on matters of Polish culture and politics "did not mean that I am in the least attracted to some internationalism or cosmopolitanism. I am steeped in Polish literature and want to remain faithful to it."

In the United States, Kridl and Miłosz conducted a warm correspondence and helped one another in various ways, beginning when father taught at Smith and then (from 1948 on) at Columbia. Most of these letters were recently published.[7] Their content reveals not only a close personal relationship—Kridl would address Miłosz as "Kochany," a term stronger than "Dear" in English, while Miłosz would refer to Kridl as "my Wilno guardian"—but also a common effort in the service of Polish culture, to which much space in these letters was devoted. This effort ranged from sending academic books for war-devastated Polish universities to getting scholarships for Polish students to arranging concerts of Polish music. It also included observances of the 150th anniversary of the birth of the greatest Polish romantic poet, Adam Mickiewicz (1798–1865), and the publication of a commemorative scholarly volume for which Miłosz contributed a chapter, "Mickiewicz and Modern Poetry," and secured a subsidy from the Polish Embassy.[8] As a cultural attaché, Miłosz was eager to speak in public on Polish literature or culture, and my father arranged for him to lecture at Smith College, where he taught at the time. I well remember one appearance in Northampton in 1947. Since Miłosz gave his talk in Polish, the audience consisted almost entirely of Polish American farmers from the neighborhood. The lecture did not go well. Some in the audience objected that the speaker concentrated on post–World War I innovative writers and failed to mention Henryk Sienkiewicz—a nineteenth-century author of popular historical novels with stirring descriptions of seventeenth-century Polish military exploits.[9] Miłosz did not take that criticism kindly, and in the privacy of our home, he fulminated against the narrow-minded ignorance of the "little peasants" *(chłopki)*.

He showed no more forbearance for our American friend Virginia Pickett, who offered to put up Miłosz and his first wife, Janka, during another lecture at Smith. A college graduate and well-off member of local society, Virginia tried to entertain the poet with some appropriately "elevated intellectual" conversation, steering their talk to some well-known names in music or literature. Again, rather than take this incident lightly and see its comical aspects, Miłosz expostulated to us on Virginia's attempts at "cultured talk" as unbearable middle-class pretense and banality.

However, also in Northampton, in our home, Miłosz had the good fortune to meet Jane Zielonko. An intelligent, lively free spirit and the daughter of a bishop in a breakaway Catholic group, the Polish National Catholic Church, in the United States,[10] she was at Smith to work with Hans Kohn on his studies of central European nationalism. Miłosz asked her to translate his political book, *The Captive Mind,* an analysis of what attracted Polish intellectuals to communism—his first success with a wide English-speaking audience. I was sorry to see that, for some reason, he failed to include Jane in his ABC book. Maybe he preferred to forget his political past. But they did become close friends, and her excellent translation played a large role in gaining Miłosz recognition abroad.

Miłosz's contempt for the routine and ordinary did play a role in my life when I was job hunting after getting an M.A. in Russian studies at Columbia. In 1951, I stayed with the Miłoszes in Washington soon after he had broken with the Warsaw government. They obviously had little to live on—the apartment was small, dark, and sparsely furnished. But their warmth and hospitality did not change, and they took an active interest in my interviews. Among the most interesting and lucrative job offers was one from the CIA—to investigate and report on the activities of Polish émigrés in London. When, with some pride, I told Miłosz about it, he responded with ill-disguised contempt: "So you want to be a bureaucrat?" His use of the Polish word *urzędniczka*—which has a strong connotation of office routine and low status—instantly obliterated my vision of a glamorous future in London, mixing with exiled politicians, generals, and writers. And so, thanks to Miłosz, I never became a "bureaucrat" and instead found a rewarding career in the academic world.

13

During 1947 and 1948, when the Warsaw government and Columbia University were negotiating an endowed chair for Polish literature, Miłosz loyally and regularly kept my father informed about the progress of the talks. All along, he strongly supported Kridl's candidacy and helped overcome various obstacles. For one, the Polish government, which financed the chair, insisted on naming its own candidate. Columbia, although eager and willing to accept money from the Communist regime, was just as eager to preserve its autonomy and insisted on its sole right to decide on the nominee. Initially, my father's name figured fourth on the Warsaw list. I can say without exaggeration that, in my opinion, Miłosz's efforts led to my father's eventually assuming the Adam Mickiewicz Chair. Kridl's appointment at Columbia met with considerable and vocal opposition from the Polish American community, creating some unpleasant publicity for the university as well as for its new president, Dwight Eisenhower.[11]

This is the way I remember the complicated, contentious story of the Polish literature chair at Columbia, a memory confirmed by the recent publication of the Miłosz-Kridl correspondence. However, this is not the way "Pan Czesio," as our family called him, remembered it. When I met Miłosz in Vilnius in 1999, he introduced me to his second wife, Carol, as the daughter of Manfred Kridl, who had occupied the Adam Mickiewicz Chair at Columbia, the first ever endowed chair of Polish literature in the United States—"which I had created." By then, Miłosz had won the Nobel Prize, turning from a nonconformist outsider into a world-famous personality with a strong sense of destiny.

In those last years, Miłosz would sometimes say that both he and his late wife, Janka, had believed—way back in the early 1950s—that someday he would become a Nobel laureate.

Notes

1. Now it is Vilnius, the capital of Lithuania—but between the two world wars Wilno was part of Poland and the seat of a major Polish university.

2. Czesław Miłosz, *Abecadło Miłosza* (Kraków: Wydawnictwo Literackie, 1997). Published in English as *Milosz's ABC's*, trans. Madeline G. Levine (New York: Farrar, Straus and Giroux, 2001), 173.

3. *Milosz's ABC's*, 176.

4. Formalism, or structuralism, was a new school of literary criticism that offered an objective, scientific analysis of literary texts, instead of the traditional approach, which concentrated on national identity, personal biography, or the social significance of texts. Manfred Kridl was one of its chief advocates in Poland. It was related to the Russian formalist school and was snuffed out by the Communist regime in the late 1940s.

5. Czesław Miłosz, *Antologia poezji społecznej, 1924–1933* [Anthology of social poetry] (Wilno: Koło Polonistów Słuchaczy Uniwersytetu Stefana Batorego, 1933).

6. The text of the June 30, 1934, lecture was reprinted in *Teksty drugie*, no. 5 (2003): 166–68.

7. Czesław Miłosz, *"Mój Wileński Opiekun": Listy do Manfreda Kridla (1946–1955)* ["My Wilno Guardian": Letters to Manfred Kridl (1946–1955)], ed. A. Karcz (Toruń: Uniwersytet M. Kopernika, 2005).

8. Manfred Kridl, ed., *Adam Mickiewicz: Poet of Poland* (New York: Columbia University Press, 1951).

9. Incidentally, Sienkiewicz was the first Pole to win the Nobel Prize in Literature.

10. [The Polish National Catholic Church (PNCC), founded in the United States by Polish Americans, is a dissident, breakaway group from the Roman Catholic Church. It differs from the Roman Catholic Church, however, on several important theological points. In November 2006, it had a membership of over 60,000. Its priests are allowed to marry.—Ed.]

11. As already indicated, Miłosz supported various cultural activities of the Adam Mickiewicz Chair during my father's tenure (1948–56). His interest assumed another form after the poet's break with the Communist government and departure from the United States. In December 1954, upon hearing of Kridl's impending retirement, he offered his own candidacy.

"Only a Pole Could Have
Been So Careless"

JOHN FOSTER LEICH

I first met Czesław Miłosz in September 1947, when he was the cultural attaché in the Polish Embassy in Washington, D.C. I remember the occasion very well. I had just been admitted into the U.S. foreign service and assigned to my first post as vice consul in Gdańsk.

It is customary for newly appointed consuls and diplomats to pay a call on the embassy of the nation to which they have been accredited. However, September 1947 was a low point in Polish-U.S. relations. Polish parliamentary elections had been held in January of that year, which resulted in the complete exclusion of the anti-Communist parties from the government.

So instead of the ambassador, I was the one who, it was agreed, would be received by the cultural attaché: Czesław Miłosz. The cultural attaché is the lowest-ranking foreign service officer in any embassy. In normal times, he or she is responsible for cultural and educational exchanges, student scholarships and the promotion of artistic exchanges, concert tours, and so forth. Because these were not at all normal times, none of this existed between Poland and the United States. Miłosz had very little to do and was probably quite bored.

We met in his office in the Polish Embassy in Washington. My recollection is of a pleasant but quite taciturn man who seemed unhappy with his embassy assignment. Because of the poor state of Polish-U.S. relations at the time, he did not want to seem too cordial—hence, perhaps, his taciturnity.

The chronology is also important here: Miłosz was sent to Washington by the Polish government of national unity, which had been created by

Roosevelt, Churchill, and Stalin at the Yalta Conference in 1945. They proposed a formula whereby the new Polish government would include representatives from the London government-in-exile, the wartime underground
parliament, and the Soviet-sponsored Lublin Committee. The wartime
Polish underground parliament represented clandestinely the government-
in-exile in London. The Lublin Committee was a protogovernment con-
sisting of Polish Communists and Socialists, appointed by the Soviets in
the Polish city of Lublin after it was liberated from the Germans in early
1944. This "national unity" government, which was to be neither pro- nor
anti-Communist, joined the United Nations and was recognized by most of
the world, except for Spain, the Vatican, and one or two other states, which
continued to recognize the government-in-exile in London. The first free
elections in an independent Poland in 1947 resulted in a defeat for the anti-
Communist parties, including those of Stanisław Mikołajczyk, the former
prime minister of the London government-in-exile and vice prime minister of the national unity government, and the underground leader, Stefan
Korboński, who had been the secret delegate of the London government in
Warsaw during the war. Both had escaped abroad on American and British
cargo ships and were urging the overthrow of the pro-Communist Polish
government from abroad. This is the backdrop for my meeting with Miłosz
in September 1947. Although I did not arrive in Poland until after the election, at a moment when Mikołajczyk and Korboński were on the point of
fleeing the country, Polish-American relations were clearly at a very low ebb.

Some years later, in the mid-fifties, Miłosz wrote about his time in Washington in the "Natura" section of *Treatise on Poetry.* There is a point in
the notes to which I would take exception: I do not think that anything in
the *Treatise* actually reflects a contemplation of the possibility of defecting
while still serving as cultural attaché in Washington, D.C. I think Miłosz is
merely contrasting the American lifestyle with the European. His Polish-
Lithuanian continuing identity crisis is the background to this and reflects
his admiration for (envy of?) the greatest of all Polish/Lithuanian poets,
Adam Mickiewicz.

According to the London *Guardian,*

> while [Miłosz] always had political doubts about the regime, they
> weren't crystallised until he returned home in 1949 and saw first-
> hand the direction the regime was taking. He attended a lavish
> evening function attended by most of Poland's ruling elite. On his
> way home, at about four in the morning, he has said that he came
> across some jeeps carrying newly arrested prisoners. "The soldiers
> guarding them were wearing sheepskin coats, but the prisoners

were in suit jackets with the collars turned up, shivering from the cold. It was then that I realised what I was part of."

I was not aware of his trip to Poland in 1949. I had been transferred out of the American Embassy in Poland to the Munich Consulate General, where I issued ten thousand visas to east European displaced persons in one year. I was totally disconnected from Poland and things Polish.

My recollection of Warsaw when I visited there from Gdańsk, and was briefly stationed there, in 1948, was of an immensely impressive ruin—cold, wet, a Hotel Bristol full of bedbugs, and mud everywhere. I had the feeling of being constantly watched. I remember work brigades of scantily clad German POWs being marched through the snowy, ruined streets, but not much more.

If, after 1947, when he was transferred to Paris, Miłosz was seriously contemplating defection, I think it would have come to the attention of the Free Europe Committee (the parent organization of Radio Free Europe), headquartered in New York, which I joined in the summer of 1950, as assistant director for exile relations and a specialist for Polish matters.

One of my tasks was to try to prevent distinguished writers, artists, musicians, and other exiles—people such as Miłosz—from returning to Poland and subjecting themselves to the control of the Communist regime. The Twentieth Congress of the Communist Party of the Soviet Union, with its denunciation of Stalin, set the stage for détente known in Poland as *odwilż*, or "thaw." The Polish government had been trying to persuade Polish writers and artists in exile to return to Poland and perform and publish there. This would mean subjecting themselves to Communist Party censorship; public diplomacy projects such as Radio Free Europe hoped to fight against this. We supported the publication and translation of their works and, in some cases, gave them a modest monthly allowance.

Miłosz defected in 1951 from the Polish Embassy in Paris. He was in a difficult position in France, where nothing like Free Europe existed—in fact, the French Foreign Office was cultivating their prewar friendship with Poland as a means of discouraging a revival of an aggressive Germany. Commenting on Miłosz's defection in Paris, I remember Burke Elbrick, the head of the Polish desk at the U.S. State Department, saying that "only a Pole would be so careless to defect in France rather than the United States, where he would have had a much better and safer life." It is my recollection that a few years later, Free Europe was of some assistance to Miłosz in the publication and distribution of *The Captive Mind*. Our sister organization, Free Europe Press, smuggled anti-Communist literature, such as *The Captive Mind*, into Poland and distributed it there.

The Free Europe Committee also had a branch office in Paris, which I used to visit on committee business. I remember calling on Miłosz around 1953 at his charming farm near Maisons-Laffitte, not far from the Polish émigré publishing house Kultura, which published a quarterly journal of the same name. Miłosz's writings were published with Kultura—in fact, *Kultura* published his essay "No," explaining his decision to defect. Jerzy Giedroyć, the publisher of *Kultura,* and Miłosz were strong personalities with a high opinion of their importance to the cold war.

I was invited to lunch by the Miłosz family, and it was very good. Mme Miłosz cooked lunch for us, and there were other family members or friends present. The conversation was lively and sociable, but I fear I cannot recall the precise topics discussed. Miłosz did most of the talking, as you would imagine. It was a very pleasant occasion all around. Bearing in mind that these talks took place about sixty years ago, the fact that I remember very few details indicates that we did not discuss anything memorable or important. I certainly did not discuss his defection either at the Polish Embassy, before it happened, or in Maisons-Laffitte. I remember in France offering him some financial help with his writing.

Many years later, when I wrote to congratulate him on receiving the Nobel Prize, he sent me a delightful holograph poem about bees buzzing at sunrise! A holograph poem is one that is reproduced or printed in the poet's own handwriting. In this case, Miłosz provided a typed transcription, fortunately—his handwriting was almost illegible. I had to reconstruct the Polish text!

Let me share with you the poem that he sent me as thanks for my congratulations on winning the Nobel Prize:

> Leaves glowing in the sun, zealous hum of bumblebees,
> From afar, from somewhere beyond the river, echoes of lingering voices
> And the unhurried sounds of a hammer gave joy not only to me.
> Before the five senses were opened, and earlier than any beginning
> They waited, ready, for all those who would call themselves mortals,
> So that they might praise, as I do, life, that is, happiness.

> —Czesław Miłosz 1980.

An Epistolary Friendship

GEORGE GÖMÖRI

I came across the work of Czesław Miłosz in the autumn of 1953. As a very young Hungarian poet and translator, I spent three months in Poland on a scholarship from the Hungarian Writers' Association. During a short visit in the seaside town of Sopot, I was shown a copy of a prewar collection of Miłosz's poetry. The person who showed it to me had treasured the book and told me in confidence that Miłosz was one of those Polish writers who "had chosen freedom" some years earlier and now lived in Paris. I liked some of the poems, but they did not make me particularly interested in the author.

In October 1956, I was very much involved in the Hungarian revolution—first as one of the organizers of the large student march in sympathy with the Poles that had kick-started events and later as an editor of the newspaper *Egyetemi ifjúság* (University Youth). Two weeks after the second Soviet intervention, in mid-November, I had to flee to Austria. My lucky star did not leave me, for by December I was already in Oxford, where as a member of St. Antony's College, I could continue my studies on a graduate scholarship. I chose post-1945 Polish and Hungarian poetry as the subject of my thesis and by 1957 was a regular reader of *Kultura,* the excellent Polish émigré review. That year, I was invited to the summer school of the Free Europe Committee in Château de Pourtalès in Strasbourg.

Miłosz was one of the speakers at the school, and although I understood only half of his lecture given in French (one year at the Alliance Française in Budapest was not enough for more), I introduced myself after the lecture. He was visibly elated by the fact that someone not of Polish origin could speak Polish as well as I did, and he encouraged me to write to him with any queries I might have on modern Polish poetry.

I took the opportunity and turned to him with various questions in early 1958. Miłosz answered in Polish, in a long and very interesting letter (dated Montgeron, February 8, 1958), stressing that he was not a traditional Polish nationalist: "[I]f I have ever written anything on Poland or about the Polish nation, it was almost always unintentional" (*jeżeli kiedykolwiek pisałem o Polsce, o narodzie polskim, to zawsze niejako mimowoli*). He went on, saying that he was not a "true" Pole, since he was born in Lithuania, which he said was comparable to someone living in Finland but writing in Swedish. While he had no objections to my translating his postwar poem "Naród" (Nation) into Hungarian, he wanted to avoid—as he always had done—attempts "to force every poet into the role of a National Bard" (*wieszcz narodowy*). He found the theme of my thesis (Polish and Hungarian poetry, 1945 to 1956) "extremely interesting" and foresaw the possibility of its eventual publication in book form, advising me to give it a "catchy title."[1]

In his second letter some months later (again written at Montgeron, dated June 22, 1958), Miłosz told me about his interest in the younger Polish poets, most of whom first came to notice in the Thaw of 1955–56. Among these, he found Miron Białoszewski and Zbigniew Herbert the most talented, adding, "I think that Herbert has stronger chances for future development than Białoszewski. . . . I have just read his collection *Hermes, pies i gwiazda*, which he gave me, as he is here, in Paris, for a couple of months. . . . I recommend this poet to you." In the autumn, I, too, met Herbert in Paris and obtained a copy of his new book; our long friendship began then, and we would meet from time to time and corresponded over many years.[2]

Discussing modern Polish prose writers in his letter, Miłosz made negative comments on Stefan Żeromski, "a very uneven writer," and suggested that I read Witold Gombrowicz. He also recommended S. I. Witkiewicz (who wrote under the pen name "Witkacy"), if I could find his out-of-print books, although Miłosz wondered whether I would be able to figure out Witkiewicz's complex and unusual style. I did manage to get hold of a copy of one of Witkiewicz's works. Although I read his novels properly only years later, I could already see then why Czesław Miłosz was fascinated by this enfant terrible and great political satirist of modern Polish literature.

Soon afterwards we met again in Paris. All I remember of this meeting, which took place in a bistro, was that we talked about current political developments and also about literature. I continued reading Miłosz's work and translating his best poems into Hungarian, but I lost contact with him for a while. (The first poem that I translated was "Naród" [Nation], published sometime in 1958 in the Munich-based Hungarian journal *Nemzetőr.*)

Our correspondence was renewed in 1962 when, having finished my B.Litt. thesis at Oxford, I was looking for a teaching job overseas, as Polish literature was taught at only three universities in the entire United Kingdom at that time. I must have written to Miłosz about the possibility of continuing my studies at Berkeley, where he had received a teaching post in 1960. I also mentioned my intention of writing a book on the nineteenth-century Polish poet Cyprian Norwid. In his encouraging reply, he wrote, "I would be very pleased if you came here to study. I will try to be helpful to the best of my ability." I was pleasantly surprised when some months later, in early 1963, I received an invitation from the University of California for a one-year teaching post at Berkeley. I did not know at the time that Miłosz was planning to spend a sabbatical semester in Paris in the autumn. At Berkeley, I was expected to teach Polish language as well as take over Miłosz's literature course, but my very first teaching job turned out to be rather different from what I had expected.

One of Miłosz's colleagues, a Polish lady, was already teaching the Polish language course at Berkeley, and when she heard that Miłosz was leaving for a sabbatical, she requested that his literature course should be assigned to her rather than to that "newcomer" from England. This deft move left me as a temporary lecturer in Polish whose task was merely to teach graduate students advanced Polish grammar—a veritable trap for anyone who was not Polish-born and not even a professional linguist. Never before or after in my life was I given a task so difficult, involving so much hard preparation. I somehow endured these first few months at Berkeley but was greatly relieved when Miłosz came back in December and we were able to talk about the literature course I was to give in the following semester.

At that stage, Miłosz could not do much about his compatriot's fait accompli, so I had to carry on with the grammar lessons. He also had to consider what duties to give to the poet Aleksander Wat, who had arrived in mid-December, as it was he who had arranged for Wat's invitation to Berkeley. I had met Wat before, in Oxford, and we had exchanged letters prior to his arrival in California;[3] however, I was not quite aware that his English was almost nonexistent. So when Miłosz suggested that Wat and I should give a graduate seminar titled "Postwar East European Literature," I agreed, although with some apprehension. Only a couple of brave students signed up for the seminar, and at the very first session, it turned out that Pan Aleksander could, alas, talk only in French or Russian—definitely not English. Also, after this first unusual seminar, he informed me that he was unable to continue teaching because he suffers from persistent splitting headaches.[4] At least I was able to continue teaching this course by myself. Wat's stay at Berkeley proved to be useful: after my departure, in 1964 and 1965, Miłosz recorded Wat's reminiscences, later published under the title *My Century (Mój wiek)*. This was not the only time that Miłosz helped to promote other Polish writers in the United States. His groundbreaking collection *Postwar Polish Poetry* (Doubleday, 1965) first established modern Polish poetry, including the work of Zbigniew Herbert, as an important part of the European cultural scene for American readers.

In the first half of 1964, during my teaching appointment for the academic year of 1963/64, I visited Miłosz several times in his house on Grizzly Peak Boulevard, at the top of the hill above Berkeley, with its magnificent view of San Francisco Bay. We also met and chatted often in the campus café near the Student Union and attended the 1964 University Charter Day together. As we sat next to each other during the ceremony, he told me of his utter puzzlement about America: a country of such immense contradictions! "One can hardly believe," he said, "that this university and Barry Goldwater exist in the same country!" He added that in his view, with the death of John F. Kennedy, America lost its only truly intelligent politician. We listened (in the Greek Theater) to Adlai Stevenson's speech, which pleased Miłosz, but both of us knew that unfortunately Stevenson was no longer a politician who really mattered. U Thant, the Burmese secretary-general of the United Nations, also spoke, rather boringly. "Asia," jotted down Miłosz on a piece of paper, which he handed over to me, and I understood what he meant: it was an Asiatic tradition to make long and flowery speeches without much substance.

That day, I asked Miłosz whether he'd ever thought of visiting Poland. He said yes, but immediately added that, as everything has political significance in Poland, his eventual visit and lectures would now also make the wrong political impression. So he was not contemplating such a visit for the time being, though he had been approached by some institution (perhaps the Catholic University in Lublin). At any rate, he was not completely persona non grata at the time—some of his prewar poems had been reprinted in Poland already in a 1962 anthology.

In the first semester of 1964, Miłosz gave two courses, one on Polish literature from its beginnings and another one on the history of the Polish theater. I attended both and took copious notes, which filled two small notebooks; I still have both in my possession. Most of the time I agreed with his views, but in a few instances I tried to challenge them. For example, I once told him that I thought he was unfair to Julian Tuwim, who after all was a good poet and only his political naïveté drove him into the embrace of the Communists. "No," said Miłosz, "Tuwim was not just a Russophile, he was a Russomaniac! Look how different was his attitude to Russia from Słonimski's!" Here he compared the attitude of a not-quite-assimilated Jewish Pole, Julian Tuwim, to that of an assimilated Jew whose family had lived for generations in Warsaw, that is, Antoni Słonimski. Most Jews who went from Russia to Poland favored Polish independence less than Jews born in Poland did.

During my time at Berkeley, Miłosz was working on an anthology of Polish poetry in English translation (the *Postwar Polish Poetry* mentioned earlier), and he asked my opinion about his selection of poets. I agreed with him about his choices for the anthology—for instance, he selected only Bogdan Czaykowski from the London-based Kontynenty group of poets, and I was pleased to see poems by Tadeusz Różewicz, Białoszewski, and Herbert included. "I tried to be objective," said Miłosz with a smile. "I have even translated a few poems by Przyboś, my archenemy!" (This was a nice gesture on his part; in a lecture sometime later, he called Julian Przyboś a "pompous ass"!)

On another occasion—dinner in Miłosz's house with his first wife, Janina, and my former wife, Gudrun, present—we spoke about regionalism in prewar Poland—how did the Lithuanian Poles regard Poles from Warsaw? They had a low opinion of them, said Miłosz, for most of those sent to Wilno (now Vilnius) were superficial characters, cynical careerists. I remarked that this prewar Polish Wilno reminded me of Transylvania during the war years when, from 1940 to 1944, its northern part was returned to Hungary. Janina was actually from Warsaw, but she was an exception to the above; as a matter of fact, she told us that she had never visited Wilno. My Austrian-born wife inquired whether she had liked Paris. "I just *hated* Paris," confessed Janina. Knowing the political circumstances after Miłosz's break with the Communist regime and the isolation of the Miłoszes while living there, I was not too much surprised, yet I could detect a certain difference of opinion on this issue between Czesław Miłosz and his wife.

Miłosz spoke fluent English, with a strong Polish accent. His Berkeley lectures were very entertaining, especially when he discussed contemporaries, people whom he had known personally. On such occasions, he became quite animated. For example, he told us with relish of a visit to Jarosław Iwaszkiewicz's country house during the German occupation where he got drunk in the company of Jerzy Andrzejewski and Włodzimierz Zagórski and then they risked their lives getting back to Warsaw during an official curfew. At another time, talking about Stanisław Wyspiański's play *Wesele*

(Wedding), he described the last scene with the hypnotic dance of the wedding guests who follow the rosebush that had come to life—then Miłosz jumped to his feet from the top of the desk where he was sitting and danced around the classroom, to the great amusement of his students.

I often discussed translation with Miłosz. I tried to cajole him into translating modern Hungarian poets, especially the very versatile Sándor Weöres,[5] but he was rather reluctant, for he did not like translating from languages that he did not know. He liked modern American poets, and we shared an admiration for Robinson Jeffers—not so much for the ideology of this great recluse but for his courage and his sonorous verse. Miłosz also told me that Jerzy Giedroyć, the editor of *Kultura,* wanted him to translate Russian poets such as Anna Akhmatova and Boris Pasternak into Polish, but he resisted. "They are too directly lyrical, I can't do that" was his verdict on that subject.

At one of our meetings, I tried to engage him in a discussion of contemporary European poetry. Miłosz had a fairly low opinion of French poets; yes, of course, he liked Jules Laforgue, but then Laforgue was writing in the nineteenth century. And then he said something that did not altogether surprise me, knowing his "historicist" vein: "There was only one truly great poet in this century: Cavafy!" A young American friend of mine, himself a poet, who was present at this conversation waxed enthusiastic— yes, that's what he thought as well. Miłosz, by the way, was clearly appalled by the ignorance of the average American. He told me that once, when he gave a talk at the Davis campus of the University of California, a student asked Miłosz, a survivor of the Second World War, "Could you please tell us, is it really better to live today on the campus of an American university than it was in a German concentration camp?"

As for my own work, Miłosz gave me good advice on the book I was planning on Norwid. First my ambition had been to write a large book on Norwid's philosophy, but Miłosz talked me out of it. "It's like a German scholar's project from the nineteenth century! You should write something shorter and more concise," he warned me. Fortuitously, soon afterward Miłosz was asked to write a book on Norwid by Twayne, an American publisher of monographs. He declined, saying he had no time, but he very generously recommended me as "a young lecturer who has already published an essay and is doing research on Norwid." Thanks to his mediation, I got a commission from Twayne in 1964. (My monograph, *Cyprian Norwid,* was published eventually in Twayne's World Authors Series in 1974.) On my behalf, Miłosz also wrote a letter of recommendation to Professor Wiktor Weintraub and the Harvard Russian Research Center.

Thanks to his effort, I received a senior research fellowship at Harvard for the academic year 1964/65.

Though I left Berkeley for Harvard in the summer of 1964, I continued to keep in touch with Miłosz. In March 1965, he sent me a copy of a letter he had written to the *New York Times,* which had declined to publish it. Miłosz was objecting to the newspaper's misrepresentation of a statement he had made at a meeting of Berkeley professors as well as to the *New York Times* report referring to him as "a defector," which he perceived as a negative term.

In the summer of 1965, I returned to England and accepted the first job on offer, a research fellowship-cum-librarianship at a research center of the University of Birmingham. In the autumn of 1966, I was commissioned by Charles Newman, editor of the *Tri-Quarterly Review,* to put together an "East European issue" of the magazine (excluding the literature of the Soviet Union). Remembering Miłosz's interest in Witkiewicz's work, I wrote to him for a contribution to the forthcoming special issue. In his letter dated October 24, 1966, written in English, Miłosz remarked that "the idea of writing an article on Witkiewicz is enticing" and went on to discuss the interest in Witkacy in the Bay Area. (He was referring, in particular, to Daniel C. Gerould, who later translated several of Witkiewicz's plays.) He also wrote a personal note in Polish at the end of the letter, which pleased me very much: *"Pana diariusz w 'Kulturze' ciekawy i dobrze pisany"* (Your diary printed in *Kultura* was interesting and well-written). He was referring to my diary of the Hungarian revolution of 1956, first published in Polish translation in Giedroyć's excellent journal (*Kultura* 10, no. 228 [1966]) and later published in English in *Kultura Essays,* an anthology edited by Leopold Tyrmand (Free Press, 1970). Miłosz, by the way, regarded Hungarians with special sympathy and in 1959 even translated from the French a collection containing a long essay and some poems entitled *Węgry* (Hungarians) for Instytut Literacki.

In his next letter, just after Christmas 1966, Miłosz said he had sent me under separate cover his essay on Witkiewicz. It was later published in the special Spring 1967 issue of *Tri-Quarterly* ("Tradition and Innovation in Eastern European Literature"). He also sent several translations of Polish poets. I included four in *TQ:* one poem each by Przyboś, Wat, and Mieczysław Jastrun, as well as one of Miłosz's own ("King Popiel"). As I heard later, the only thing that somewhat spoiled his satisfaction regarding this special issue was the inclusion of a review article on the translation of Polish poetry by Tymon Terlecki,[6] a (more conservative) Polish academic living in America, though other Poles may well have agreed with some of

Terlecki's critical remarks. This particular issue of *Tri-Quarterly* was quite a success—the *Times Literary Supplement* hailed it in a leading article; in the following year, it was published as a hardback by Quadrangle Publishers of Chicago.[7]

In April 1969, I inadvertently clashed with Czesław Miłosz after I reviewed his poems in the American literary magazine *Books Abroad*. It was a rather favorable review of his earlier work, but toward the end of my piece I posed a question that I thought was appropriate. As Miłosz had lately written much about his dreams and the memories of his childhood, did that mean that he had turned his back on history? Or had history bypassed him? The question stung Miłosz, and he replied in a long letter to the editor of *Books Abroad*. Apparently, he understood my question to mean that he had landed "in the dustbin of history" (a dismissive Marxist expression). Miłosz pointed out in his letter that "a poet is committed to the language" and that "the tactics of the poet change in accordance with the kind of historical dangers, threatening words with distortion of their meaning and with debasement." As I was a member of the editorial board of *Books Abroad* (and because the magazine normally did not publish letters), I was asked by the editor to approve publication. This prompted me to write a long letter to Miłosz, in which I agreed in principle with what he said but asked him to cut the "dustbin" phrase. The letter, however, remained unpublished, although I retained a copy.

Miłosz changed his mind on political engagement, however. After the March 1968 events and the "anti-Zionist-anti-Revisionist" campaign in Poland, he wrote a dramatic poem entitled "My Faithful Mother Tongue" (*Moja wierna mowo*). This marked the rebirth of Miłosz the political moralist. Although he consistently refused the traditional role of a "national bard," on more than one occasion he was forced to confront the wild twists and turns of history. One such "political" poem, from many years later, is "Sarajevo," which I, for one, hold as the best poetic comment on the Bosnian war.

I have several more letters from Miłosz from the 1970s and 1980s. One of these was a reply to my congratulations on his winning the Nobel Prize in Literature. Although I had always belonged to the fairly small circle of disciples and sincere admirers, news about the prize came as both a surprise and a cause for great joy—after all, Miłosz was the first Pole to win the Nobel since Władysław Reymont in 1924! In this letter, which Miłosz answered from Berkeley on November 21, 1980, I conveyed my publisher Carcanet's interest in publishing an English collection of his poems—but Miłosz wasn't interested, writing that there were already two collections in English, one of which Ecco Press was about to issue in paperback.[8]

The tone of this short letter, though, was quite friendly, ending with the words "Thank you very much for your congratulations and I hope that fate enables our paths to cross once more" (*że losy nas jeszcze zetkną*).

This, indeed, happened some years later in Oxford, where I was invited to give a paper at the "Polish-Jewish conference" in September 1984. By that time, Czesław Miłosz was a celebrated author not only in the United States and Western Europe but also in Poland, where his triumphant return in 1981 drew crowds of young people to his talks and readings. He was also the centerpiece of the Oxford conference held in Somerville College, which ended with his poetry reading in Yarnton Manor's Hebrew and Jewish Studies Research Centre. As far as I remember, "Campo dei Fiori," his great poem reflecting upon the 1943 uprising of the Warsaw ghetto, was also read; it was one of my favorites, and I translated it into Hungarian many years earlier. From the conversations with Miłosz in Oxford, I remember only one sentence in which he acknowledged my academic advancement and intellectual development—this, coming from him, gave me great satisfaction.

The very last letter that I received from Miłosz refers to his poem "Antigone," which he dedicated to the memory of the Hungarian revolution in 1956. However, the dedication of the poem (reprinted in his collection *Kontynenty*) makes it clear that this dialogue in verse between Antigone and her sister Ismene was written much earlier—in 1949—and that it refers in the first place to the "unburied dead" of the Warsaw Uprising of 1944: "I devote this fragment written in 1949 to the memory of Hungarian workers, students and soldiers" (*Pamięci węgierskich robotników, studentów i żołnierzy ten fragment, napisany w 1949 roku, poświęcam*).[9] As I intended to reproduce this poem in my anthology *Polscy poeci o węgierskim październiku* (Polish poets on the Hungarian October),[10] I asked Miłosz for his permission. He answered in a short handwritten letter granting the permission, on the condition that I make it clear that the poem was written *before*, not because of, the Hungarian revolution. This wish was easy to fulfill—all I had to do was to reproduce Miłosz's original dedication of the poem. Because he did not like this poem as much as others, it remained unselected for his first collections in English (it does not figure in any edition of his *Collected Poems*, and it was not until 2001 that Richard Berengarten [Burns] and I made an English version of it which was printed in the *Hungarian Quarterly* of Budapest).[11]

Nonetheless, "Antigone" remains eloquent proof of Czesław Miłosz's sympathy for Hungarians—a sympathy that has amply benefited me throughout my life. In appreciation of his poetry and as an expression of my gratitude, in 2001 I published a small collection of Miłosz's verse in Hungarian—translating forty-three poems into my native tongue.[12] Since then, I have also translated and partly published in Hungarian his last great cycle of poems, "Theological Treatise" (*Traktat teologiczny*), written in 2002 in Kraków, where he returned to live in his old age and to die. This cycle of poems is a summation of his faith and doubts about afterlife—a beautiful, moving farewell to a long and very fruitful life.

Antigone

—Czesław Miłosz

A fragment, written in 1949, which I dedicate to the memory of the workers, students, and soldiers of Hungary.

ANTIGONE:

To accept what happens just as one accepts
Seasons piling pell-mell on one another,
And on our human world to cast the same
Indifference as on mute Nature's transformations?
So long as I shall breathe I shall say—No.
Do you hear me, Ismene? I shall say—No.
Nor have I any need of consolation—
Your night-time flowers in springtime, nightingales,
Sunshine or passing clouds, familiar streams,
No, none of these. Let whatever is left
Be left to ripen, unquelled, uncontrolled.
All that is worth remembering is our pain.
See these rust-covered ruins, my Ismene?
They know it all. Death with its crow-black wings
Has masked or muffled all those years behind us
When we might have believed this land of ours
To be like any other, and our people just
Like those who live in any other land.
The curse of fate must lead to sacrifice
And sacrifice, in turn, to fate's next curse,
And when this fate fulfils itself, the time
To protect our petty lives is over.
This is no time to shed tears on ourselves.
There is no time. Let an immense catastrophe

Sweep across this entire pitiless Earth.
As for those laughing now at our despair,
Let them witness their own towns razed to dust.
Creon's law! Creon's rule! Who in the world
Is Creon when our world itself is crumbling?

ISMENE:

Indeed. But Mother and Father both lie dead
As do our brothers, and no revolt of yours
Will bring them back. So why keep looking back?
An old man with a stick in a silent city
Goes rummaging in vain for fallen sons.
Old women quietly mourn amidst the dust
Then pass on by, their wizened heads bowed down.
Yet even in bleak neighbourhoods, life greens again.
Nettle and wormwood creep across the rubble.
Like a slip of paper in a fire, a butterfly
Goes fluttering at the rock edge of a precipice.
Children in ragged clothes return to school,
Lovers' hands clasp each other's. In all this,
Believe me, powerful rhythms reassert themselves.
Sobs commingle again with celebration—
Persephone returns again to earth.

ANTIGONE:

Fools alone believe they can live easy
By relegating Memory to the past.
Fools alone believe one city falling
Will bring no judgement down on other cities.

ISMENE:

Do not belittle how hard it is, Antigone,
To go on suffering, forcing lips and hearts
To silence. For each of these small victories
Is victory too. This struggle gives us hope.

ANTIGONE:

Sister, I need no hope of yours. Remember,
I have seen the remains of Polynices
Beneath the steps of the destroyed Cathedral,
With tufts of light hair wafting from his skull

Like any little boy's. A crumpled handful
Of bones wrapped in a dark and rotting cloth.
The stench of a corpse. That was our own brother.
There was a time his heart beat just as strong
As yours and mine do. He knew joy, sang carefree
Songs—and knew the fear of death, since the same
Voices which call us now, called out in him
Towards bright vistas of a future life.
Yet, faithful to his word and pledge, he willingly
Made his choice to relinquish them, and die.
Twenty years old, a boy, handsome and gentle,
He had to quell whatever plans he'd nourished,
Works hardly started, reticent, shy thoughts,
And alone, force his will to face destruction.
And this is he who now, by Creon's command,
Is branded traitor, and his place some dark
Sand-blown corner out on the city's edge
Where wind goes whistling through his empty helmet.
Yet for the others, glory-peddlers, filchers,
Statues will be erected and young girls
Will lay out wreaths in all the broadest squares
And lights twinkle from torches on their names.
Here, though, nothing, but dark. The trembling hands
Of writers, impelled by debasing fear,
Will not stint in their praise for thieves of glory.
And so, those stripped of legend will pass down
Into the centuries' amnesia. Traitors? Heroes?

ISMENE:

By means of words, pain kindles into flame.
Who maintains silence, perhaps suffers more.

ANTIGONE:

These are not merely words, Ismene—not just words.
Creon shall never have the strength to build
His state upon our graves. Nor shall he found
Government upon sheer power of the sword.
The dead wield greater power—so great, no man
Can hide from it. Although on every side
He fences himself with countless guards and spies
Still they will find him out. The hours themselves

Await the ironic laughing dead to trample
Upon the madman who still disbelieves them.
Then, when he's called to settle his account,
An error, small at first, will trickle through
His calculations, tiny, as if from nowhere,
Then multiply and magnify a thousandfold,
And then, while treason torches towns and villages—
Enough—the flaw will ripen, swell to madness,
Crying, Blood! Blood! Too late by then for any
Red ink flowing from his hand to blot
That single error. It will be his end.
Does this wretched Creon think he'll govern us
As if ours were some land of brute barbarians,
As if each stone were not engrained with memories
Of its own tears of despair, tears of hope?

(Translated by Richard Berengarten and George Gömöri,
published in the *Hungarian Quarterly*
[Budapest] 42, no. 164 [Winter 2001].)

Notes

1. My thesis was eventually published in 1966 by Clarendon Press, Oxford.
2. Herbert's letters to me were published in *Twórczość*, no. 4 (2006): 74–83.
3. Wat's letters to me were published in *Twórczość*, no. 4 (2008): 91–97.
4. Wat, a prewar Communist, was taken by the Soviets and passed through eleven Soviet prisons during the Second World War. He returned to Poland after the war and left his native country for medical treatment in 1958. His headaches originated from his wartime sufferings.
5. My essay on Weöres was published in the East European poetry issue of *Books Abroad* 43, no. 1 (Winter 1969).
6. After the publication of *Zniewolony umysł* (*The Captive Mind*) and the verse collection *Światło dzienne* (Daylight), both in 1953, Czesław Miłosz became a regular author of Giedroyć's Instytut Literacki.
7. *New Writing of East Europe* (Chicago: Quadrangle Press, 1968).
8. The first American publisher of Miłosz's verse was Seabury Press, which in 1973 brought out a selection. Ecco published *Bells in Winter* in 1978.
9. Originally in *Kultura*, 1956/12, also in Czesław Miłosz, *Kontynenty* (Paris: Instytut Literacki, 1958), 363–66.
10. Translated and edited by George Gömöri (London: Polska Fundacja Kulturalna, 1986). The second, extended edition: London, 1996.
11. Czesław Miłosz, "Antigone," *Hungarian Quarterly* 42, no. 164 (Winter 2001): 61–67.
12. Czesław Miłosz, *Ahogy elkészül a világ: Válogatott versek* (Bratislava: AB-ART, 2001).

Half a Century with Miłosz

MAREK SKWARNICKI

My first encounter with Miłosz's poetry was in 1952 when, after three years in the Philology Department of Warsaw University, I was no longer able to continue my studies. The reason for my dismissal was politically motivated: I refused to join the Union of the Polish Youth, our equivalent of the Soviet Komsomol.

I found a position as an assistant to Stanisław P. Koczorowski, curator of the National Library in Warsaw. Before World War II, Koczorowski had been the director of the Polish Library in Paris. Although blind, the curator possessed exceptional knowledge of everything relating to books and libraries, knew six languages, and was a great scholar and erudite. I became the curator's eyes and hands. After the war, the National Library, while running its usual business, also became a repository for the collections that had lost their owners. Some of these private libraries came from the homes of aristocracy and landowners who were banished by the Communists; others were rescued when the army seized trainloads of books that Germans were shipping to their country. There was still another category of books, books that were—for political or ideological reasons—withdrawn by the Communists from public and school libraries. Our job was to sort through these books and evaluate whether they were to be included in the library's permanent collection or to at least make some sort of a record for the less valuable ones. This was how we came across several copies of Miłosz's poetry collection *Rescue;* the books had been removed from libraries after the author "had chosen freedom"—in the parlance of the times—in 1951. The curator let me keep one copy (it now carries the author's inscription "Kraków, 2002"—his home after returning to Poland).

The curator and I were working in the former building of the Krasiński Library. The Germans had incinerated much from the collections during the Warsaw Uprising, including almost all of Chopin's original sheet music. Under these circumstances, the title of Miłosz's book sounded comforting, and the poems encouraged one to keep faith in the humanistic dimension of mankind's destiny. No one dared to utter even a word about Miłosz's poetry at the Warsaw University.

My friend, the curator (now long-departed), recognized the sad state of my education resulting from years of Polish studies in a Marxist vein; he took me in as his student. He was an unusual old man, for even during the years of the greatest Stalinist terror in Poland, he was able to obtain, through mysterious sources (most likely through the French Embassy), the magazines and books of the Kultura publishing house in Paris. I must have pulled a lucky ticket in life, because I had constant access to its monthly *Kultura,* and I became one of the first Polish readers of Miłosz's *Daylight* and *The Captive Mind.* I was only twenty-three years old, but I had spent the war years in Warsaw, fought in the Warsaw Uprising, and later was deported to the Mauthausen concentration camp. I mention this because the very titles of the books—*Rescue* and *Daylight*—not only offered great comfort but also fortified one's spirit in resistance against totalitarianism, for the main merit of the poet's writing then was a call for fighting not against Russians or Germans but against totalitarianism itself. This may be the root of his conflict with Polish patriots, who often were quite nationalistic in their sentiments and, for all their nobility and courage, failed to recognize what kind of fight was unfolding in Europe and in the world after World War II. The value of his collection of essays, *Native Realm,* lies precisely in this understanding.

Because of the changes in the Soviet Union, Khrushchev coming to power and de-Stalinization, the year 1956 became pivotal in Polish political history. The publishing policies in my country experienced a "thaw," an easing up of the state censorship that used to control not only every printed word but also the size of periodical circulation and even the content of business cards. The name of Czesław Miłosz was now permitted to be mentioned in print. *Tygodnik Powszechny*—a general-interest, political, Catholic, sociocultural weekly—resumed its publication after a forced hiatus.

While still a student, I had written for the magazine under an assumed name. Later, I forged relations with the former editors and, in 1957 (because I myself had started writing poetry), my poem titled "A Letter from Warsaw" appeared in *Tygodnik Powszechny;* this poem was my way of thanking Czesław Miłosz for being the "daylight" of my young years and the "rescue" in Warsaw. Truth be told, the entire Communist press lashed out at me. Nevertheless, the poem was published.

On Christmas 1957, I received a letter from Paris. The envelope carried no return address. Inside was a white card with a red-and-white border. In the top left corner, there was a little Christmas tree and a handwritten inscription "Merry Christmas"; in the lower right corner, it was signed "from Czesław Miłosz." This was the beginning of our relationship, which deepened into a friendship between an older poet and a younger one (this is how Miłosz described it) and ended only with his death in Kraków. At about the same time, I received a job offer from *Tygodnik Powszechny* and moved with my family to Kraków. By then I was married; my wife was originally from Wilno. She, too, was a great fan of Miłosz. When we still lived in Warsaw, we copied many of his poems by hand and circulated them among friends. Miłosz was gaining popularity among the young intelligentsia; however, as I later discovered, he was completely unaware of it, especially when he lived in Berkeley.

My father was a professional officer in the prewar Polish Army; he had fought in the 1920 war against the Bolsheviks and was promoted to the rank of colonel. After the Second World War, he found himself in the West and could not return to Poland. He was granted political asylum in the United States and settled in Chicago. In 1964, he sent me an invitation, and after much ado, I received a passport and was able to visit him after twenty-five years apart. When I found myself in Chicago, I immediately wrote to Miłosz's address in Berkeley, which had been given to me by his friend and my boss, Jerzy Turowicz, editor in chief of *Tygodnik Powszechny*. Miłosz replied to me after a long delay, for he had been away on a vacation somewhere in the wilderness of the northern United States.

We did not get a chance to meet then, but he sent me a package, without telling me what was inside. The package got lost, to the great chagrin of us both, because I had changed addresses several times while in the States. The parcel mysteriously caught up with me in Kraków thirty-six years later. One day in 2002, Miłosz invited me over and handed me that long-lost thick notebook with a dozen or so handwritten poems. The autograph on the first page read, "These poems and sketches are a gift to Marek Skwarnicki, September 1964." Miłosz told me that this poetical copybook had been found in the personal archive of his brother, who had died two weeks before. This unusual gift included a draft of an unknown poem and a great number of pieces from the then-unpublished "Gucio Enchanted," in a somewhat different form. There were also translations of works by Walt Whitman and Robinson Jeffers and English translations of Zbigniew Herbert. This collection was released in the fall of 2008 at the Bertelsmann Polska publishers as a facsimile edition with my introduction and editorial notes.

In later years, I was able to travel beyond the Iron Curtain more often, first as a representative of the Polish Catholic laity. Later, as a *Tygodnik Powszechny* reporter, I covered the trips of Pope John Paul II to Mexico, the Philippines, Japan, and other countries, including European ones. Every time I found myself anywhere outside the Iron Curtain, as long as it existed, I would always send Miłosz my Western addresses where he could write to me (letters sent to Poland could be censored by the postal service). This is how our correspondence started, and it lasted many years; fragments of it appear in the book *My Miłosz*, published in Kraków. However, we did not meet in person until 1973.

And this is how it happened. In 1972, I was invited to spend the 1972/73 academic year with the International Writing Program, founded by the poet Paul Engel at the University of Iowa. I arrived late because of some passport complications. During the winter, I received a questionnaire from Washington. Among other questions, I was asked what places I would like to visit and whom to meet during my stay. In addition to visits to Chicago, Denver, San Francisco, Los Angeles, New Orleans, and Phoenix, I requested a meeting with Czesław Miłosz in Berkeley.

In Berkeley, I stayed at the University Club, which doubled as a hotel for visitors. The club was built of wood, and the log house reminded me of peasant huts in the Polish highlands. The elegance and originality of this wooden structure stood out against the backdrop of the surrounding architecture. It was very pleasing to me.

The time came when, with my heart beating wildly, I went down to the lobby to meet my favorite author and a living legend. Recently, *Tygodnik Powszechny* (Miłosz was a regular reader) published my poem "Tree"—another poem that mentioned Miłosz. Surprisingly, it had passed the censors:

> Well, even Miłosz above his ocean,
> Which changes colors every minute,
> Turns off his exhausted lamp in the early hours
> And returns to his nameless town.
> And when layers of dream peel away, one by one,
> He sees underwater forests and the depths of wilderness.

Miłosz promptly informed me that he does not work by night. But the poem turned out well.

After the meeting in the club, Miłosz took me for a tour around the Berkeley campus. Among other places, we ascended to the top of the bell tower, modeled after the campanile on St. Mark's Square in Venice. A wide vista opened up from there. The university occupied a relatively small area; the Golden Gate Bridge loomed behind it. On the eastern side—behind the school building, the sports center, and the Greek Theater—one could see undulating hills with specks of dwellings here and there.

Later, we returned to his home. His first wife, Janka, was still alive, and the younger Miłoszes were also there. After so many years, I don't remember what we had for dinner, but we certainly drank plenty of whisky. The evening came, and the fire was started in the fireplace. During our conversation, we did not speak much about Poland. Rather, we talked about America. Miłosz considered Berkeley to be the modern Athens, although he also talked with resentment about the escapades of the local beatniks and leftist groups. "I escaped from commies, but Lenin managed to catch up with me here," Miłosz said. At that time, the spirit of the revolution swept though many American campuses. It germinated in Berkeley. Suddenly, students from several departments insisted on creating special student-run committees, which would dictate to professors what and how to teach. Exactly the same thing had happened at Warsaw University in 1949, during Stalin's times. Berkeley even witnessed some confrontations with the police. Communes were sprouting all over rural California: some were set up by weirdly dressed potheads, but there were also others that drew youthful idealists who wanted to escape the cities in pursuit of a deeper spiritual life.

In this "new Athens," different theories and philosophical trends arose and clashed: here jazz was developing in new directions and, most importantly, the atomic civilization was taking root. On the surface, it appeared that in so remote a place, closer to Japan than to Athens, everything was only of local importance. However, as we know now, its importance was rather global. At the same time, hippies were appearing in Kraków, Warsaw, and Rome.

Within this human beehive lived a poet who had come from a Lithuanian estate, had graduated from Stefan Batory University in Wilno, had survived the German occupation and the Warsaw Uprising—the harrowing existence of a leftist who could not yield to the pressures of the Stalinist regime in his country and escaped as far as he could to a place where he could create freely, paint a picture of the modern world, and teach Slavic literatures to Americans. The beauty of America manifested itself for him in Berkeley, through its open and firm defense of human freedom and dignity, even if it took the shape of an adolescent anarchy.

During our conversations, Pan Czesław, who was greater than me both in age and in talent, mentioned Jack London several times, perhaps because the great American writer was born in nearby Oakland, and Miłosz derived pleasure from that fact. Besides, I am sure, my older friend-to-be valued the masculinity and courage of London, who was born poor in Oakland in 1873. London later became a sailor; he traveled around the world and, in his later years, settled in Sonoma, near San Francisco. Miłosz took me to visit the country house of the author of *White Fang* and *Martin Eden*. London, too, was one of the strongest influences in my life. The American mendicant, thief, and seafarer was a true connoisseur of our literary craft, and in *Martin Eden,* he verbalized the desire of every driven writer who struggles for fame and is nursing his own, unique voice. London's country house is now a museum that radiates the atmosphere of art and creativity. This is how America was coming of age along with its literature: still youthful but full of simple human wisdom.

On Sunday, Miłosz took me to mass at the student Jesuit ministry at Berkeley. The mass was celebrated at the tiny theater auditorium with an altar set up on the stage. For the oblation, we were treated to the "liturgical female student ballet." I watched the "ballet of angels," who were swathed in white flowing robes. There was no sermon. Instead, there was a brief skit on the harmfulness of TV, which steers people away from praying. This childish and supposedly innovative show was hard to imagine anywhere else in the church's realm. But it was the era of hippies, fights against domestic "Washington imperialism," and the Vietnam draft. Before long, those liturgical dances spread around the world. In later years, I happened to see them at the papal masses in Belgium and Australia. Miłosz was a conservative Catholic; he considered not using Latin in the liturgy a mistake. Generally, however, he was not a very devoted Roman Catholic. He was strongly anticlerical, and the priests who were involved in political life made him furious. Nevertheless, he had very close, friendly relations with Father Józef Sadzik, a Pole, who was living in Paris. Sadzik influenced Miłosz to translate books of the Bible into Polish; he published them with the Pallottine publishing house in France, during a time when publishing the Bible in Poland had been forbidden by the officially atheistic Communist government. Miłosz was also very fond of his friend the Trappist monk Thomas Merton. Before his death, Miłosz asked for confession and took the sacrament of the Eucharist.

I met Miłosz in the United States twice more in later years, when he could finally travel to Poland freely and started thinking about settling in Kraków. I was visiting my son, who had emigrated with his family and taught physics at Syracuse University in New York. I traveled from Syracuse to Manhattan to attend the ceremony when Zbigniew Herbert received the Bruno Schulz Award from the American PEN Club in September 1988. Herbert was ill and could not attend the ceremony, so Miłosz received the award on his behalf and recited Herbert's poetry. It was an especially important event because there was some antagonism between the two most important Polish poets of the twentieth century. After the ceremony, Miłosz and I had dinner together. He was excited by the evening's events. Miłosz often voiced grievances against Herbert, because he had translated Herbert and thus propelled him into the international literary arena, yet Zbyszek sometimes used to air his displeasure with Miłosz in rather unpleasant terms. The other time I met Miłosz in the United States was in 1990. I was visiting Boston when Jerzy Turowicz, editor in chief of *Tygodnik Powszechny*, received a *honoris causa* doctorate from Boston College and, likewise because of poor health, could not receive it in person. The editorial board of *Tygodnik Powszechny* sent me in his stead to accept this doctorate by proxy.

After the ceremony, I spent several days in Newton with Stanisław Barańczak, who taught Polish literature at Harvard. He invited Miłosz, who happened to be giving a lecture on poetry in Harvard at the time, to dinner. As far as I remember, our conversations were about Joseph Brodsky's poetry and about the situation in Poland, which had just gained its independence. Barańczak ended up in the United States because he had been a member of the Workers' Defense Committee and a prominent dissident. He was also a well-regarded poet; Miłosz held him in high esteem as a writer and a literature maven as well as a seminal translator of English-language poetry into Polish.

In 2000, I visited my son in Syracuse at the time of John Paul II's pilgrimage to Israel, where he made a memorable gesture by inserting a note into the Wailing Wall with a prayer to God, to Jahweh. The moment was broadcast on American TV. That evening Miłosz called me from Berkeley, his voice ringing with excitement; he shouted in the receiver that this pope would become a saint. Soon after, I received a poem from Miłosz, entitled "Ode to John Paul II," which soon after appeared in *Gazeta Wyborcza* in Warsaw.

At that moment, I discovered that my relationship with Miłosz had a definite pattern, and the persona of Pope John Paul II was a part of this pattern. From Jerzy Turowicz, I knew that the pope met with Czesław soon after the death of the poet's first wife, Janka. In her memory, Miłosz wrote a beautiful and fierce poem, which was also a reflection on the human condition and death. Turowicz and Miłosz were invited by the pope for dinner. During the meal, Miłosz asked the pope if he could read the poem written about the death of his wife and, having received permission, stood up and recited the verse.

During the pontificate of John Paul II, I went often to Rome. On at least two occasions, I met there with Miłosz, who, after vacationing in then-Yugoslavia, was on his way back to Berkeley via Italy. The meeting at a tiny pizzeria by the Spanish Steps stands out in my memory—Miłosz always stayed in a small hotel nearby. He favored it perhaps because a house where Keats used to live is not far from there, and so was the Caffè Greco, which was frequented by great poets and writers, such as Byron, Stendhal, Goethe, Keats, and D'Annunzio. Nowadays, Miłosz's name is also carved in a plaque in the café.

Rome and memories of John Paul II bring me back to Kraków, where Miłosz lived until the end of his days with his second wife, Carol, on Bogusławski Street, not far from the palace of Polish kings from the times when Kraków was the capital of the country. The poet was very fond of my wife, who was originally from Wilno, and we were invited many times either to their home or to some small local restaurant for a friendly dinner rather than for a literary discourse. It was around that time when Miłosz wrote his "Treatise on Theology" and published it in *Tygodnik Powszechny,* which the pope read regularly. I convinced Miłosz to send this poem to the Holy Father, which he did and later received a personal response from the pope. As a reporter who accompanied the pope on his pilgrimages to Mount Sinai and then to Athens, Damascus, and Malta, I flew to Rome often. Every time I was invited to a dinner with the pope, I would take Miłosz's letters to him and bring back the pope's replies. It happened four times. The last of Miłosz's letters to the pope contained a question: did the pope, who read everything that Miłosz had written, feel that in any of his poems Miłosz overstepped the boundaries of the Roman Catholic orthodoxy? This question moved me enormously, for it is well known that the chronicles of Miłosz's soul are very tumultuous. When Zbigniew Herbert died, Miłosz called that very day and asked me to meet him at the Noworolski Café, his favorite, on the Old Market Square. Very emotional, he gave me a poem, "Phone Calls after the Death of Herbert."

He told me, "Several days ago, I called him and we have forgiven each other everything."

"He was very ill," I replied to him then. "Poets suffer a lot, and he is in heaven now. In fact, lately he was writing religious poems."

"How is that possible?" protested Czesław. "He was always a Manichaean, just like myself."

"But what about his 'Breviary'?" I rejoined. Miłosz had not read it yet.

As Miłosz was getting more fragile and unwell with age, we were getting together more and more frequently at his home. Having obtained from the Beinecke Library my letters, which I had written to him over the course of several decades, I started writing a book based on this correspondence: *My Miłosz*, which was published soon after his death. It was the last text that was read to him (for he could no longer read himself) in his life. The book was read to him mostly by Joanna Miłosz and Joanna Zach.

From time to time, he would call me and ask, "Dear Pan Marek, have you already written what happened next?" The book was a history of our lives that reached back fifty years. In 2002, Carol was diagnosed with cancer, and so was I. Carol had returned to California for treatment.

On a Monday, Miłosz called me in the hospital, where I lay wondering whether I was going to make it or not, and he asked, "Dear Pan Marek, I just received news from San Francisco that Carol might go any minute now," but he had a plane ticket reserved for Thursday. Should he change it for an earlier flight against the advice of doctors who did not want him to fly? I told him then, "If you don't fly today, you will not be able to forgive yourself for the rest of your days." He flew and arrived just in time for a final conversation with her, before she died on Thursday, August 15.

Before he left Kraków, he had also asked my wife what divine intervention he might seek for Carol. My wife suggested Saint Faustina and a Divine Mercy novena. She took a taxi and delivered Miłosz the prayer with the Divine Mercy image. Pan Czesław prayed for Carol and gave the image to his wife in the hospital. When we asked him what had been her last words, he answered that she said, "Don't worry, Czesław, love will join us again."

After he returned to Kraków, he wrote a beautiful poem, "Orpheus and Eurydice." He called me and invited me and my wife for a visit and read the poem aloud for us. As for me, I had recovered from a difficult surgery. I remember also that at that meeting Miłosz said something that mystified me: "Dear God, how is it possible that I survived forty years in that country!" There, he buried two wives and lived as an exile. At the same time, he was a writer who belonged to the world. However, the motherland most dear to his heart was "City Without a Name." For Polish readers, it is clearly Wilno, today the capital of Lithuania. But it never was clear whether the motherland for Miłosz was Poland or Lithuania. In history, both countries composed one state: the kingdom of Poland and Lithuania. He had citizenship in both.

When Miłosz died, a rather conservative Kraków witnessed a scandal about his funeral and the burial site. A proper place for him was a crypt in

the cloister of the Pauline Fathers, which is traditionally known as "Skałka."
Many great Polish artists are entombed there. But even while Miłosz
was still alive, he was accused of a lack of faith and hostility toward the
Catholic Church. A dissertation could be written on the whole affair. The
discussion spilled over to the media. Finally, a letter from John Paul II to
Cardinal Franciszek Macharski, archbishop of Kraków, resolved the controversy of Miłosz's burial. The contents of the letter expressed some of
the same thoughts that had been included—as I know for sure—in the letter that unexpectedly arrived for me from the pope, replying to Czesław's
letter, in which he questioned the orthodoxy of his own writing. The pope
wrote to me from Castel Gandolfo on September 18, 2004: "I learned of
his death during my visit to Lourdes. The earthly period of the writer's life
has come to an end 'in a spirit of the Catholic orthodoxy,' as he put it in
his last letter to me; now he has met 'face to face' with our Lord and with
His great Mercy. Requiescat in Pace! We all grow old, but our lives are in
Lord's hands and only He knows when they will end."

We were lucky to have the former archbishop of Kraków for a pope.
Czesław Miłosz, like many intellectuals and other members of Polish intelligentsia, was decidedly an anticlericalist, which cannot be thought strange
by anyone who knows anything about the Polish clergy. A deeper under-
current of this entire affair was a particular brand of Polish patriotism that
bears the stain of nationalism, or even chauvinism and anti-Semitism. It
was exactly the dilemma of Polish patriotism that, to a certain degree, set
Miłosz and Herbert apart. But let's leave this to the literary historians.

Translated by Alla Makeeva-Roylance.

My Colleague from Dwinelle Hall

JADWIGA MAURER

When Czesław Miłosz came to Berkeley, Professor Francis J. Whitfield, chairman of the Department of Slavic Languages and Literatures, brought him to my office in Dwinelle Hall, on the campus of the University of California, where the department was housed. I was asked to describe our Polish literature program, describe the courses offered, and explain the general profile of the department. I was then a young lecturer in Polish, in the second year of my academic career. And I, of course, knew who Miłosz was. I knew his poetry and some of his prose, and I had read most of the attacks on him in the émigré press. I also knew that he had joined the postwar Communist government in Warsaw, had been in the diplomatic service, and then defected to the West. He had lived in France—in Paris, it was said.

Miłosz told me later that in France he really lived in the provinces and only went to Paris once in a while on business. But it was in Paris that he attached himself to the émigré periodical *Kultura;* he had published in its pages and joined the circle of Polish intellectuals around it. Many of these people he knew from before the war. Paris had a long and illustrious tradition of Polish emigration, particularly the "Great Emigration" of the first half of the nineteenth century, with the greatest romantic poets (Adam Mickiewicz, Juliusz Słowacki, and Cyprian Norwid) and the great composer Fryderyk Franciszek Szopen (known as "Chopin" in the West). And now, abandoning Paris and France, Miłosz was going to be a professor at Berkeley. The department reacted to his arrival with considerable, but short-lived, consternation. Miłosz did not have any academic credentials. He had graduated from Wilno University with a law degree. A law degree at that time transformed a person into an "official" member of the intelligentsia. Many aristocrats and people with private means in Europe had law degrees but never worked a day in their lives. Others went into government service or found positions with various institutions.

In his later (much later) prose, Miłosz time and again goes back to the circumstances of his speedy promotion to full professor with tenure at Berkeley. He repeatedly assures us, his readers, that he has absolutely no idea who supported him, a few months after his arrival, for the position of a full professor with tenure. Having spent several decades at three major research universities, I must confess that I don't believe him. Yes, I am aware of the custom of appointing famous writers to professorships, mostly in the English departments. But these appointments are for the most part temporary and therefore do not carry tenure. Apparently unwilling to the end of his long life to disclose the circumstances of his appointment at Berkeley, Miłosz writes in one of his essays that perhaps the time is coming when universities will consider a person's accomplishments before his credentials: deserving people will become academic teachers, regardless of diplomas. He made this statement forty years after his arrival at Berkeley.

Back to Miłosz's first visit in my office, in Dwinelle Hall. After some time passed, and I thought I had explained enough, Miłosz turned to Professor Whitfield. "I feel somewhat uncomfortable," he said. "My wife and children are waiting in the car." Much later, when I thought of this visit, it occurred to me that it probably took place on his first or second day at Berkeley. Academic year 1960/61 was about to start.

It was a very good time for Slavic studies in this country. There were government grants, the G.I. Bill (many of our male students were veterans), and scholarships from private foundations. However, Slavic departments were few (Harvard, Columbia, Berkeley, and the beginnings of some others, for example, at Indiana University). A large group of graduate students entered the Department of Slavic Languages and Literatures at Berkeley. They were older than traditional graduate students, enthusiastic and well prepared. They also liked to party. The faculty, with few exceptions, participated in this new year-round "Mardi Gras." In the permanent California spring, a euphoric atmosphere was clearly present. Miłosz liked to party. Decades later, he described many of these parties in his autobiographical prose. His laughter echoed through the house, and he seemed to be always in a party mood. His wife, Janka, usually accompanied him but didn't share her husband's exuberant party mood. She stood somewhere to the side and followed his movements with an ironic glance. She looked cool and collected—and critical.

Miłosz had a reputation for being aloof and somewhat distant, but a certain naïveté, real or pretended, softened his image. He seemed to believe everything that was told to him. He seemed to be full of goodwill toward people around him. One day Janka and I were walking down Telegraph Avenue, and as always, we talked about literature. A book of critical essays on Polish émigré literature had just been published in London. Janka and I did not think highly of it. "What does Czesław think of it?" I asked. Janka stopped abruptly in the middle of the sidewalk. "Czesław?" she exclaimed—"If it's printed!" From that moment on, I have been very kind to people who quote newspapers and magazines as a serious source of information. If the Nobel laureate . . .

As with so many members of the Polish intelligentsia, from the Borderlands and the old Grand Duchy of Lithuania, Miłosz was a Russophile, an admirer of Russian writers, Russian literature, and Russian culture from before the Revolution. He liked to converse with Russians in Russian. Berkeley provided him with the opportunity, with Russians on the faculty and students from nearby San Francisco, where there was a sizable Russian colony. But there was no Polish community to speak of—only some Polish professors in other departments, a few Polish students, and several Poles working for the university. In the Slavic Department, Miłosz and I were then the only two Poles on the faculty. Two other Poles, Professor Lednicki and a lecturer named Pawlikowski, were retired. A Polish academic club was moderately active.

One day when I was telling Czesław about some lecture in the Polish Club, and he listened with obvious interest, I asked him why he did not come to the Polish Club. His answer was that if he came to the club, he would have to frequent all the other clubs on campus. His answer puzzled me, but in my mind I connected it vaguely to constant attacks against him by various political groups, since he had been part of the Communist government and the whole émigré press constantly attacked him. Eventually, however, Miłosz abandoned this attitude, and I remember him participating in the club's activities.

My office was across the hallway from the departmental office; Czesław's office was in another corridor. On his way to the departmental office, Czesław stopped by my office almost every day. When I read his prose much later, I discovered that I was familiar with most of the material included in it.

At Berkeley, climate and landscape have an overwhelming influence on people's lives. The sun rises above the Berkeley Hills in the east in the morning and rolls into the bay in the west toward evening. From the balconies, terraces, and gardens of houses on streets climbing the hills, there is a fairy-tale view of the Bay. White sails dot it in the morning; at night, lights bob and move over the dark waters. This view is the subject of many of Miłosz's poems. Grizzly Peak is one of those climbing streets, and there Miłosz bought a house and lived in it with his family for over thirty years. In one of his late poems, he referred to the area as a "faded neighborhood." And rightly so. But the view is still the same. "I appreciate it [the view] when I see it through my window at dawn," he wrote in one of his last poems. And in another poem, he pays tribute to the Berkeley Hills: "I didn't know that the hills of Berkeley will be final." They weren't. Miłosz lived the last decade of his life in Poland and died there.

After I left Berkeley in 1965, I saw Miłosz briefly on summer visits to California and at Slavic conferences. At last, a memorable meeting occurred in the winter of 1990, at the University of Kansas, where he came to read his poetry and I introduced him, on a cold and nasty day, to a very large audience. It was at the reception afterwards that I overheard him confide to a Polish woman, a professor of mathematics, how lonely he had been at Berkeley and how lonely he, the Nobel laureate, still was.

Love at Last Sight

RICHARD LOURIE

First sight wasn't exactly auspicious. For him, especially. I entered
Czesław's classroom at UC Berkeley in the fall of 1960 looking "unkempt
and disheveled," a fair enough description of the twenty-year-old who
was ardently practicing the Beat code of dirtiness being next to godliness.

In contrast, Czesław—though at this stage of the game he was always
"Mr. Miłosz"—cut a very dashing figure on the campus and in the classroom. He wore his dark raincoat over his shoulders cape-like, his chestnut
hair with glints of red and blond was brushed straight back, his foxtail
eyebrows were always raised in amusement or amazement or alarm. And
the Slavic brogue was irresistible. He was not famous then or even well
known, which may have made his pride all the more fiery.

Czesław was a good teacher. He was grateful for the job, which paid
a human wage after the deprivations of his years in France following his
break with the Communist government of Poland, which had employed
him as a cultural attaché. He had a very strong dutiful and conscientious
side, which compelled him to do anything he undertook thoroughly and
well. The book that grew out of his lectures, *The History of Polish Literature,* is something of a marvel—a textbook that can be read for pleasure.

He liked the little theater of the classroom but was never tempted to ham it
up: a touch of underplaying it characterized both his teaching style and the way
he recited his poetry, to the slight detriment of the latter, I always thought.

One day, though, he did do something that was—for me at least—
rather dramatic and would have more than forty years of consequences. It
was right after midterms. Corrected in red, our blue books were stacked
on his desk. "Today," he said, "I am going to read aloud one of the blue

books without saying whose. It is rather well-written but betrays a typical American lack of any feel for history."

He read *my* blue book aloud. I burned with private shame.

To hell with him! I'll get one of those! I'll get a sense of history if it kills me! I vowed in the no-doubt-typical American belief that you can always get what you don't have. Later, I was much irritated to learn that for Miłosz, as for Joyce, history had always been a nightmare from which he was trying to awaken, but by then it was too late.

Czesław recalls the incident more matter-of-factly in his book *Miłosz's ABC's:* Richard "had written some nonsense on an exam and instead of simply giving him a bad grade, I invited him for a conversation in order to explain to him why he was mistaken. That was the beginning of our friendship."

Czesław was then more than twice as old as I, nearly fifty to my twenty. He had witnessed the Russian Revolution, lived through the Nazi occupation of Warsaw, and dramatically defected from Poland. How could I have been of any interest to him?

For one thing, he had a great appetite for my stories of the Boston underworld, my youthful rebellion having taken the form of crime before art. As he recalled them: "During his high school years he [Richard] had earned a lot of money as a chauffeur for a famous local gangster, which carried the risk of his being riddled with bullets by a rival gang, but also put him in the position of a little king of life."

Perhaps what interested Czesław most about me was that my father had been born in Lithuania when it was still part of the Russian Empire. By definition, my father had been born near Czesław's own birthplace of Szetejnie, because there are no great distances in Lithuania, though at the beginning of the twentieth century, a trip to Vilnius was fairly epic.

What baffled and infuriated Czesław was that I didn't know the name of the town where my own father had been born. I knew the province, Kovna Gubernia, and that was that. My father was still alive; there was time.

What fascinated Czesław, and what he taught me to appreciate, was the design made by chance, circumstance, and choice—a person's fate. The shape of an individual's story could be more interesting than his personality. He quizzed me on the path that had led from Lithuania to Boston to Berkeley.

Three people seemed to be key.

By choosing to leave the Russian Empire behind, my grandfather Nathan, the blacksmith, had made a decision before I was born that no doubt influenced my fate more than anything I myself would do. He had saved me from at least three deaths—by Cossacks, by Communists, and by Nazis.

I had studied poetry with Robert Lowell at Boston University. After awarding me the Sneath Poetry Award in the spring of 1960, he invited me to his office, where he foretold my future. In Lowell's version, I would major in English and creative writing, publish in little magazines, write a dissertation on some poet like John Dryden, then teach writing in a small liberal arts college. As much as I was in awe of Lowell, inwardly I screamed NO! I wouldn't study English, I'd study Russian and read Dostoevsky in the original. But where?

My cousin Jim Simons—whose mathematical genius was first expressed in the renowned Chern-Simons theory and later in the Medallion hedge fund, which creates wealth as in some fairy tale of wizards and gold—was doing postgraduate work in Berkeley. An only child, he'd always been like a brother to me, a good example to follow. In the best on-the-road style, I drove out. That wasn't yet the Berkeley of demonstrations and be-ins. People played bongos in Laundromats while their friends took rides in the dryer, but there was something stirring in the air.

Not that it was much felt in the Department of Slavic Languages and Literatures, which had a decidedly Old World ambiance. The teachers were an odd mix of Russian intelligentsia displaced by the upheavals of history, Hungarian poets in black leather jackets who had fled after the '56 Uprising (Hungarian was included among the "Slavic languages"), defectors like Czesław, and other flotsam and jetsam of history. Literary evenings were frequent and lively. The foreign poets read their own works in the original and painful translations and I read mine in English. The department decided I was worthy of support and gave me a job—running the mimeograph machine. I reported to work the first day, and the two Russian women who ran the office told me that there was only one thing I should know—poets must never touch the mimeograph machine. So what should I do? Sit down, have a cup of tea. It was there that I first really began to learn Russian.

Czesław also took note of my abilities at those readings and invited me to try my hand at some translations with him. He took translation seriously, even teaching himself Hebrew to be able to translate the Book of Psalms. His rendition is now part of the standard Bible in Polish. Translation was simply something that a writer did, part of the tradition in East Europe and Russia. It was admired and paid decently, and its practice, of course, made your own talent stronger. The custom practically does not exist in Western Europe or the United States. Saul Bellow translated one story by Isaac Singer—how much richer American literature would be had he translated a whole book of them! But in the United States, translation is, as Irving Howe once said to me, a "mug's game."

Czesław didn't want to translate only into Polish, however; he also wanted to translate Polish poets into English, to enhance the reputation of the many excellent poets of his native land—his own work, of course, not excluded. It was difficult to be from a country that was little known, to have a name that was hard to say. Great labor would be needed to change that.

We worked at Czesław's home at his desk in his book-lined study that had something of the Lithuanian manor about it. Smelling of leather, dust, and tobacco, it was cool and shadowy, unlike the vivid Technicolor California that waited outside. In fact, there was something folk-tale-like about the entrance to the house itself, which was located high in the Berkeley Hills on Grizzly Peak Boulevard. Invisible from the street because of a fence (I had to reach over it to undo the latch) and because of its location down a hillside, the house lay at the end of a winding, tree-shadowed path. The feeling was at once a bit dangerous and enchanted.

We worked, drank coffee, smoked like fiends. English and Polish words were examined in minute detail—their weight, flavor, associations. *Roundup (łapanka)* in Polish brought to mind mass street arrests of Jews during the Nazi occupation, whereas in English it summoned images of cattle drives to Laredo. A "communal apartment" in Moscow was a sort of hell with eight families sharing one bathroom, one kitchen, while in Berkeley the term tended to mean a bunch of hippies sharing the rent, each other's mates, and macrobiotic dinners.

It was a classic master-apprentice relationship; he taught me the tricks of the trade. One day he amazed me by saying, "This line is a little too smooth, we should make it rougher." The ability to make such a judgment, to know that rough was sometimes better than smooth, and to know how to roughen the too-smooth, was at the time simply dizzying.

Czesław's digressions on communism, the war, his fellow poets, the gossip of Warsaw cafés, the latest jokes from "over there" on God, evil, and metaphysics were as much a part of the experience as was his stubborn insistence that the perfect formulation already existed in some Platonic sense and all that was needed was the strength to persist until it was found.

Not all of the lessons were intellectual or literary. He taught certain virtues by example and by preaching. Though worldly-wise, he insisted on the value of sincerity and of not being embarrassed to express normal human emotions such as enthusiasm, admiration, or gratitude. It was part of his poetry:

> We were permitted to shriek in the tongue of dwarfs and demons
> But pure and generous words were forbidden
> Under so stiff a penalty that whoever dared pronounce one
> Considered himself as a lost man.

> ("A Task"[1])

And it was part of his daily struggle as well, and what he attempted to pass on to me.

Czesław took a somewhat fatherly interest in my future welfare. One day while we taking a break from translation, he startled me by saying, "You know, Richard, you could make a living from this." I had never thought about making a living; in fact, given the mores of 1960s Berkeley, I would have been ashamed to have done so. *Career, professional,* and *success* were all dirty words, and nothing more repulsive could be imagined than the three of them together—*professional career success.* In those days, we believed in the imminence of a new order.

Czesław influenced us, of course, but we influenced him as well. He was fascinated by my generation's millennial passions, its rebellions, visions, grotesqueries. The long lines of Whitman and Ginsburg made sense here, in Berkeley, as they never could when read in Europe. He became more American over time, with a passion for cheeseburgers and Levi corduroy jeans. He liked the new vocabulary but, for some reason, always pronounced *vibrations* as if it began with a "w."

As an academic, Czesław was adept at appearing inept when it came to administrative matters, but that was largely a ploy to keep valuable hours from being wasted in meetings and other such onerous duties. The principle of keeping poets away from the mimeograph machine apparently applied to faculty as well. Still, he was instrumental in scaring up funds to bring another Polish poet, Aleksander Wat, to Berkeley for a year.

Wat, a Futurist poet born in 1900 to a family of Warsaw Jews, had been the editor of the *Literary Monthly,* the leading communist magazine in Poland between the wars. Fleeing east to Soviet territory after the German invasion (as a "commie Jew," Wat would not have lasted long in Nazi-occupied Poland), Wat was separated from his wife and son, who ended up in the wilds of Kazakhstan. Wat meanwhile was caught up in an epic of prisons, including some time in Lubyanka, the secret police prison in the very heart of Stalin's Moscow. There, he was able to obtain books, including portions of Proust's *Remembrance of Things Past,* which did not at all repel him with its gossamer, gossipy, social side; in fact, he was "more charmed than ever by the power of its energy, its beauty of movement," as he told Miłosz.[2]

While in prison, Wat had a religious experience that converted him to Christianity without, however, causing him to reject his Jewishness.

The great physical suffering he had undergone, the illness that had come with age, and the alienation he felt in California made it impossible for Wat to do any real writing. But Wat was a brilliant raconteur, and Czesław hit on the idea of taping their conversations.

I was present at many of those sessions—Wat sitting by the window, the curtain open, the sunlight falling on his face, a blanket on his lap as if the prison cold was still in his bones.

At those sessions, I saw Czesław in a different light. He showed Wat deference. In part, it was because Wat was eleven years older, in part it was because of Wat's frail health, but really it had a deeper cause: Wat had a sort of spiritual seniority, a quality of presence that is instantly detected in prison cells.

Czesław himself was a great believer in hierarchy and glad to find himself in a position of deference and service. Wat called him an "ideal listener." The transcripts of those conversations between a perfect raconteur and an ideal listener were eventually published as two large volumes with the title *My Century,* appropriate for a life that began in 1900 and saw most of what the twentieth century offered. Apparently the title was Czesław's idea; in years to come, he would keenly regret giving it away, since he could have well used it himself.

In time, I would edit and translate *My Century,* reducing the two volumes to one, a labor of love which the love survived. The book fascinated such readers as Irving Howe, Saul Bellow, and Paul Auster.

Wat died in Paris in 1967 by his own hand. I wrote his obituary for the English journal *Survey.*

My father died the same year. Maybe some papers will turn up now, said Czesław; you've got to find out where he was born.

No papers turned up.

Czesław was on my Ph.D. orals committee in 1969. After a three-hour grilling, I was sent out into the corridor to await the verdict. After ten or fifteen agonizing minutes, Czesław popped his head out the door, paused for effect, and said with a grin, "Come back in, Dr. Lourie."

After a few years of teaching, I realized academia wasn't for me. School was school, no matter what side of the desk you were on. Entering a steam bath with two millionaires on a Jewish holiday, I came out in the film business, with a company of my own, bearing a name that Groucho Marx would have approved: Longshot Productions. (One of those millionaires was my cousin Jim Simons, who was beginning to use his math skills on numbers that added up.)

At first, I felt a little embarrassed to tell Czesław that I had even temporarily forsaken sacred lit for show biz, but he approved heartily. "Excellent! Excellent! Make a film about William Blake!"

I spent the second half of the seventies making jazz docudramas in New Orleans, a city where even the bankers partied so hard it was impossible to get any business done before eleven, when the hangovers started lifting. But then a trinity of events brought Poland back into the world's consciousness and my own: a Polish pope, John Paul II, was elected in 1978; in 1980, Lech Wałęsa and the Solidarity movement seized control of the Lenin Shipyards in Gdańsk; that same year, 1980, Czesław was awarded the Nobel Prize in Literature.

"Richard, you know the best thing about winning the Nobel," said Czesław, "is that you don't have to explain who you are anymore."

A gala reading was scheduled at the 92nd Street Y, and Czesław asked me to read the English versions, some of which were, of course, my translations or done in tandem with him at that desk in that cool, dark study on Grizzly Peak all those years ago.

We were in someone's apartment putting the final touches on our grooming.

"So," asked Czesław, both sly and serious, "do I look handsome?"

"Very," I replied. "And me?"

"Yes, very too."

We laughed. And then, a little more seriously, Czesław asked, "And so, Richard, do you have a copy of the poems in Polish?"

"No. Why would I? I'm doing the English."

Pandemonium. The great Nobel poet had prepared everything perfectly for the evening with one minor exception—he had no poems to read. In a nice touch for the always philo-Semitic (rarest of words) Czesław, the day was saved by a Polish Jew, Lucjan Dobroszycki, the great Holocaust scholar, who, unlike the poet, knew where his copy was.

Still, we were a bit flustered by the time we arrived, which the immensity of the overflow crowd did little to allay. But all it took was a shot of good whisky and a quick joke and we were ready to go on. It was a hit. And why shouldn't it be? Great poetry, excellent translations, two handsome guys.

In the fall of 1981, Czesław came to Harvard to deliver the Charles Eliot Norton Lectures. I was living in Boston at the time, beginning to weary of the film world. Czesław wanted help "Englishing" the lectures. We were back in business.

Our routine was unvarying. Czesław would cook dinner so we wouldn't waste time on the rigmarole of restaurants. Dinner was always what we began to call "Chicken Miłosz"—pan-fried chicken along with French bread, salad, and plenty of red wine. I remember being very impressed that Czesław washed the dishes immediately after dinner when there always was any number of good reasons for putting off that task.

As always, we worked hard. As always, we sought the perfect formulation. As always, there were long digressions sparked by a word, a look.

By then, Czesław was seventy, but his vigor was so extraordinary that he always just seemed an older contemporary. He devoured his food and quaffed his drink: there wasn't much savoring in his style. He had given up smoking years before, having received a diagnosis of nicotine poisoning, which always sounded suspiciously European and nineteenth century to me. Still, he would sometimes grab a cigarette from me and puff on it with a fury that seemed to justify the act. His habitual gestures were also quick and vigorous. He would rake a hand back through his hair, which kept glints of its fair reddish brown all his life. He would rub his mouth hard from time to time with bearish force.

The boy he'd been stayed alive in him. One year there was an Easter egg hunt and Czesław would come tearing through the bushes madly looking for every last egg with a fury that was both hilarious and scary.

He had his dull moments, too, of course, falling into some habitual attitude and story, relating incidents from Warsaw's literary cafés, or just becoming absent, empty for a time.

I only saw Czesław cry once, and it was during one of the digressions when we were working on the Harvard lectures that would become the book *The Witness of Poetry*. He was speaking of his first trip to Paris as a raw youth from the sticks of Lithuania, where he was well received by his uncle, Oscar Milosz, diplomat and French poet. "He said I was . . ."—here Czesław cried openly a bit before finishing the sentence—" . . . intelligent."

That benediction was essential to all that followed.

Meanwhile, things were heating up in Poland. In November 1981, I decided to fly over to see for myself what was happening in the shipyards, the streets, and the universities, which had been taken over by the students.

Czesław's name was magic in Poland. Restaurants that were full suddenly had a table for "Miłosz's translator." Busy running the Solidarity movement from within the Lenin Shipyards, Lech Wałęsa found time to confer with me. Outside the yards, a monument had been erected to the workers slaughtered during a previous demonstration. On its base were lines from Miłosz's poem "You Who Wronged," which begins, "You who wronged a simple man / bursting into laughter at the crime."[3] It ends with a prophecy of doom for tyrants.

Though the mood was tense inside the yards—Soviet tanks could come rolling in any day—there was also a sense of freedom and brotherhood. People weren't afraid of each other, anyone could talk with anyone. I asked one worker in cement-spattered blue overalls about the choice of

Miłosz's poem for the monument: "I thought Miłosz was totally banned in Poland." He smiled slyly and answered, "We always knew Miłosz."

I went right to see Czesław as soon as I returned from Poland. He opened the door of his Cambridge apartment and without wasting time on greetings just asked me, "So?" For a second, it felt like my Ph.D. orals all over again, except that this time it wasn't the written history being discussed but history live. I'd have to distill thousands of impressions into a single sentence. "There's no alienation there," I said. He smiled. I'd passed the test. Time for Chicken Miłosz, red wine, hard work, the best hours of life though they can't ever be recalled in detail.

I had returned from Poland in late November to spend Thanksgiving with my family. By December 13, martial law had been declared in Poland. Solidarity's leaders were in jail or in hiding. The beautiful dream of brotherhood and justice was dead again.

Somewhat later, Czesław was in Europe and paid a visit to the pope, who told him a rather startling bit of news. It turned out that a few shipyard workers had "liberated" some state-owned film equipment—35 mm cameras and black-and-white film, an odd combination. Solidarity filmmakers had documented life inside the shipyards but, more importantly, had also recorded the negotiating sessions between Solidarity and Communist Party officials, who had agreed to nearly all of Solidarity's demands—from the right to have independent trade unions to having Catholic mass broadcast on radio. Needless to say, all copies of this quite incriminating documentary had been rounded up—except for one copy that had made its way to the Vatican in the diplomatic pouch.

"I don't know what to do with the film," said John Paul.

"Don't worry," said Czesław, "I know the perfect person."

Not long thereafter, a large wooden crate from the Vatican arrived at the offices of Longshot Productions on Ninth Avenue in New York. I was now in the movie business with the pope.

My cousin Jim agreed to fund the production of an English-language version. I worked long hours with Czesław's son Toni to unravel the soundtrack, which often had several workers speaking, in slang and at once. Though raw and unprofessional, the film *Workers '80* did well. I showed part of it in Little Town Hall in New York during an evening of "Artists and Workers for Solidarity." Waiting for our turn to speak, Joseph Brodsky, Susan Sontag, and I sat onstage and smoked—another era entirely.

By then, I had done enough movies to know the film business wasn't for me, either. I couldn't return to teaching. Czesław's words came back to me: "Richard, you know you could make a living as a translator . . ." To my wife's intense dismay, I decided to do exactly that.

It wasn't an entirely idiotic decision. First of all, it gave me what I wanted most—independence. Because translators are the slowest readers, it also gave me deep immersion into the mind, culture, and language of writers like Czesław, whose book of essays, *Visions from San Francisco Bay*, I translated in 1982. It also gave me time, though not much, to do my own work. I was now a writer of prose, which in my days as a poet I had disparaged as "yard goods."

Czesław was very supportive both of my translations and of my own writing, watching my progress "with the greatest admiration" for the work and for my "truly iron discipline and efficiency." In those years, I did do a prodigious amount of work—fifteen books translated from Polish and another fifteen from Russian. At the same time, I began to produce enough of my own work to make phasing out translation altogether a realistic possibility. In any case, since 1973, I have been living entirely by my pen.

The progress that Czesław admired was also leading to a clash with him. Just as I was preparing to finally give up translation forever, after millions of words rendered into English, Czesław began pressuring me to translate one more book of his. But I had made up my mind, and I gave him a final no. It made me more sad than proud.

I've never seen anyone age as well as he. His hair stayed brown; his teeth stayed white. His appetites remained voracious, and his talent never faltered. The late work of some writers is very weak tea, indeed—but Czesław's, never.

When I spotted him from a distance at the wedding of his granddaughter, Erin, he looked a little like Jack Nicholson. He was wearing round sunglasses, and his face, still handsome, was just beginning to run to fat a little.

He was jolly at the wedding and also the next day, when he and his second wife, Carol, visited me at my loft. He was proud that his "unkempt and disheveled" protégé was now living in a five-thousand-square-foot loft overlooking the Hudson. Czesław loved the open space, the white columns, the windows blue with river. He pronounced the style "bohemian chic," and his only criticism was that it "lacked coziness."

We had all caroused quite a bit at Erin's wedding, and so I instituted one rule that day—no liquor before noon. With gracious reluctance, Czesław agreed. It was a close and easy time, like family. In fact, Czesław's granddaughter, Erin, would later ask me to be her godfather. The evolution of the relationship was complete—student, apprentice, colleague, friend, family.

I looked up from my hostly duties. Czesław was grinning mischievously and tapping his watch. Only minutes to go.

The fall of the Berlin Wall and of the USSR itself meant many things. One of them was that Czesław could go home again. For a period, he divided his time between Berkeley and Kraków, until he was in his late eighties and the long travel became too much. Then he settled in Kraków. The return to his "native realm" was probably a salutary shock to his system, reviving old memories that clashed with the new impressions stimulating the flow of creative energy.

We continued to see each other at one cultural jamboree or another and of course kept in touch by phone and e-mail. As always, we read each other's work. He continued to be generous in his admiration, especially when it came to my novel *The Autobiography of Joseph Stalin*, about which he said, "Magnificently written! I couldn't put it down even though it gave me nightmares."

He could be an ideal listener, with me as well as with Wat. He loved to hear of my adventures in Russia—getting arrested by the KGB in Stalin's hometown of Gori was an especial favorite. He was always pumping me for more anecdotes about my year spent working with the Russian police on the case of the serial killer Andrei Chikatilo. I told him that Russia's best homicide detectives were all Moslems from the Caucasus who justified their hard drinking by saying: "The Koran says we must not drink wine but says nothing about vodka." Czesław roared.

After my mother's death in 1999, I finally found the papers that told where my father was born—Raguva. The way the rest of the story played out was a perfect example of what Czesław, in his Nobel speech, called "life's God-given, marvelously complex, unpredictability."

In June 2002, my cousin Jim, by then wealthy enough to have his own private jet, decided to visit Poland and Lithuania with his wife and her father, who was of Polish descent and wished to see the land of his fathers. It only made sense to ask me along.

After a couple of days in Vilnius, we made a trip by van through fields bordered by dense evergreen forests to the hamlet of Raguva, which had a Catholic church, a Russian Orthodox church left over from the days of the empire, and a general store that sold cold beer in big glass mugs. I saw the creek where my father had to have played as a boy.

We then flew to Kraków, where Czesław loved the story, a Polish-Russian-Jewish fairy tale of people leaving by horse and wagon and their descendants returning a century later by private jet.

Czesław was about to turn ninety-one but was holding up fairly well. He had put on a little more weight and was sporting a sort of Amish-looking goatee. He was, however, having trouble reading, his hearing was not as crisp, and he needed a cane to walk any distance because of inner-ear balance problems. He had a touch of the shame of the aging about him, but he blasted through that soon enough. He was especially fond of my cousin Jim's father-in-law, Walter—his sky-blue eyes, his very Polish face and expression. A builder by trade, Walter did not see styles or periods when he looked at buildings but instead saw the work of others like him, done well or not done well. Czesław beamed at Walter's impressions of Kraków and called him "brother." The evening ended festively at Wierzynek, a restaurant that dates back to 1364. Czesław drank his whisky with gusto, and whatever he ordered for dinner, it wasn't on his plate long. Carol (blond, southern, much younger than he) complained of a "spring cold" but was otherwise in good spirits. She would be dead by the end of the summer.

We were leaving the next day. While my relatives toured Wawel Castle, I peeled off and grabbed a cab to say goodbye to Czesław. My Polish had gotten a little rusty over the years, and there was no question the cab driver could tell I was a foreigner. Worried that I might be cheated, and furious at the very idea, I kept a very sharp eye on the meter, which read 18 *złotys* as we pulled up in front of Czesław's house on Bogusławskiego.

"Fifteen złotys," said the driver.

I was completely flabbergasted. "But . . . but . . . the meter says eighteen."

"If you're visiting Miłosz, it's fifteen."

Fame has many measures.

It was late morning. We drank cappuccinos. Two young women assistants bustled about in the background dealing with Czesław's papers, correspondence. Time felt ample, not constricted by purpose or appointment. We talked about Russia, its glories and horrors, slipping into Russian, which always made Czesław laugh with pleasure, not derision. We liked to talk shop—our forthcoming books, royalties, the chanciness of the literary life. We took pleasure on appearing side by side on Polish best-seller lists, my *Autobiography of Stalin,* his *Road-side Dog.* We talked about wives, our children. By then there were no secrets, or very few.

But then suddenly time wasn't ample any more. I had to meet Jim back at the hotel, for the plane would soon be leaving for New York. Czesław and I hugged, kissed, and looked at each other, prolonging the moment, each of us sensing it was farewell.

At the door, I turned as I heard my name called out in that rich brogue. Czesław's face was so flushed with hilarity that he could barely speak. "Richard, I wish I was a gay!"

We roared with appreciation of the absurdity of the remark and the deep old love it expressed. Once again, he'd found the perfect formulation. One last time.

Notes

1. Trans. Czesław Miłosz, *The Collected Poems, 1931–1987* (New York: Ecco, 1988), 231.

2. Aleksander Wat, *My Century,* trans. Richard Lourie, foreword by Czesław Miłosz (Berkeley: University of California Press, 1988), 204.

3. Trans. Richard Lourie, Miłosz, *Collected Poems,* 106.

My Apprenticeship with Miłosz

REUEL K. WILSON

I graduated from Harvard in 1960. Although I majored in romance languages, I took Russian courses and a year of introductory Polish with Wiktor Weintraub, the distinguished scholar who had left Poland a couple of years before the German invasion in 1939.

After Harvard, I spent an academic year at the Jagiellonian University in Kraków. I was sponsored by a "student" organization in Philadelphia that had contacts with official student groups in the Soviet Union and other Eastern bloc countries. Supposedly affiliated with the Quakers, the Americans were, in 1967, exposed as a CIA front. During my time in hauntingly beautiful, though then very neglected, Kraków, I made many friends. The mixture of gray and repressive Soviet-style communism with free-spirited cultural ferment made life exciting. The contrast between the anti-Russian sentiments of the general populace and the governmental servility toward Big Brother to the east showed me that here politics had nothing to do with the predictable rituals of two or multiparty Western democracies. And in Poland, World War II was still a tangible presence—in the ruins still visible in Warsaw, in the press, in the movies, in the "Never Again!" slogans posted in public places along with pictures of the concentration camps. Everyone had a story to tell about wartime death and suffering. To be sure, the government suppressed any information concerning atrocities inflicted on Poles by the Soviets. That fall in Kraków, I decided to apply for graduate study in Slavic languages and literatures at the University of California, Berkeley. I knew that Czesław Miłosz had just taken a teaching job there, and I wanted to study with him. He would prove a valuable guide to the history of his unhappy nation, bound to the

West by cultural ties but physically dominated by its traditional enemies, Russia and Germany. Coming as he did from eastern "Lithuanian" Poland (Poland and Lithuania had once been a confederation), an ethnically very diverse region that Poland had reclaimed from Russia after World War I, Miłosz had a refreshingly open viewpoint, that is, he did not regard other groups—Jews, Lithuanians, Ukrainians, or Russians—with disdain. He had grown up speaking Russian, and he understood the Russian mentality, its tendency to cruelty and excess, as well as a capacity for deep spirituality and broadly sweeping philosophical thought. Miłosz's lack of prejudice and his omnivorous intellectual curiosity made him an ideal teacher. Having chosen to defect from his job as a diplomat representing his country's Communist regime, he made a total break from Europe when he moved from France to California. Isolated from old friends and his reading public at home, he successfully reinvented himself as an American university professor. Thanks to the law degree he had obtained many years earlier at the University of Wilno (he never practiced law), Berkeley could offer him a full professorship with tenure. While in Kraków, I hadn't read much of his work. It was banned in Poland, although some copies of his books, mostly published in Paris, were in circulation; his work was also available to those specialists and advanced students who had access to reserved library collections. He himself was convinced that he was not read in his own country; not so, I assured him.

The Berkeley Slavic Department accepted me as an M.A. candidate, and I arrived there around September 1, 1961. I would elect Polish as my major subject with Russian as a minor. The vast majority of my fellows chose a Russian major. I was lucky enough, then, to become one of Miłosz's two full-time students. For me, the move to California entailed a substantial culture shock. The differences, I found, between Poland and the East Coast were minimal, when compared to the drastic changes embodied in California's landscape, climate, laid-back mores, and the sense of geographic finality delineated by the Pacific Ocean.

I was delighted to find that my new professor was a born pedagogue— no dry-as-dust pedantry for him! Nonetheless, in his lectures he cited established literary and historical scholars. (Some of his lecture material resurfaced in his lively *History of Polish Literature,* 1968.) In the classroom, Miłosz dressed rather informally. He often wore a plaid work shirt under a well-worn brown sport coat. His looks were striking: of medium height, he exuded physical energy and wiry resilience. I think he worked regularly in the garden beside his Tudor-style house on Grizzly Peak Boulevard, where he lived with his first wife, Janka, and their two sons. His forward-leaning carriage and features reminded one of a lynx ready to pounce. He had bushy, jutting eyebrows; steely unblinking eyes; chiseled features; slicked-back, partly thinning brown hair; and a ruddy complexion. He could have stepped out of the primeval Lithuanian forest that his ancestors might have inhabited. Like them, he had a belief in the spirit world and a sense of intersecting time. He knew his Marx, too; possibly he had sympathized with Marxist ideas in his postwar avatar in the People's Republic of Poland. My impression was that he had little interest in current American politics. He was, to be sure, an astute chronicler of Soviet-style politics and an admirer of writers—such as Dostoevsky, Leo Shestov, and Simone Weil—who were obsessed by political and religious ideas.

Miłosz's courses were quite popular. I particularly remember his lectures on Polish theater and poetry. There was an extra incentive to take them, no or little required reading; the examinations merely tested the student's familiarity with the lectures' content. Since the vast majority of the students could not read Polish literature in the original, Miłosz probably thought it unnecessary to assign texts in the few and far between English translations, mostly of poor quality. Nietzsche's *Birth of Tragedy* was on the prospectus for a course in twentieth-century Polish poetry. No one who knew him could have doubted Miłosz's preference for the Dionysian over the Apollonian. His lectures were well prepared and highlighted the progress of ideas over the course of history. I was inspired to discover many writers, after hearing my teacher recreate them in the classroom. He had known or knew personally many of the contemporary writers on whom he lectured.

Always striving for objectivity, he gave a fair share of time and consideration, even to those whose work he found unappealing. In the course of his lectures, Miłosz would occasionally read a poem of his own, followed by an English translation. We listened, but for the most part uncomprehendingly. Reading our faces, the bard then patiently explained what the poem was about.

The first course I took with Miłosz (which may have been required of all entering graduate students) was a seminar on literary translation. He didn't waste much time on translation theory, which is now the dull domain of literary theorists. During one of our sessions, he read aloud Pasternak's touching poem about Poland and Georgia, two countries for which the latter had a special affinity. During my second year at Berkeley, I translated, on my own initiative, Miłosz's article on Apollo Korzeniowski, Joseph Conrad's father, a second-wave romantic poet and playwright. (The article can be found in *Mosaic* 6, no. 4 [1973]: 121–40.) Korzeniowski, his wife, Evelina, and their three sons were deported to northern Russia as a punishment for the father's subversive activities prior to the 1863 rebellion against Russia. The future Joseph Conrad emerged from this traumatic experience with a lasting distaste for Russia and Russians.

Although he maintained correct relations with his colleagues, Miłosz remained very much his own man. He didn't seem to have any defined circle of friends at the university. The other big Polish name at Berkeley was Wacław Lednicki, who was at the time retired, although he kept an office on campus. He was a haughty aristocrat who had left Poland in 1939 to settle permanently in the United States. He was rumored to have fought some duels before the war. When I stopped by his office one day, unannounced, I quickly learned that his language of choice was English; nor was he interested in a conversation. Miłosz, in contrast, always spoke Polish with me and was keenly interested in young people. He had met both of my parents, the writers Edmund Wilson and Mary McCarthy. During my first winter in Berkeley, he invited me and Włodzimierz Twierdochlebow, an odd, rather likeable, student originally from Poland, to visit him one evening at home. Because he had come down with a cold, Miłosz telephoned Twierdochlebow and cancelled the invitation, but he had been unable to reach me. I, in the meantime, had made the long ascent of the Berkeley Hills on foot and then had wandered over some open fields before reaching my professor's house at around 9 p.m. He answered the door and invited me in, explaining that he had disinvited the other guest. Despite feeling out of sorts, he ushered me into his study and produced a bottle of rum. One his first remarks was, "Knowing both your parents, I'm surprised you're still alive." We had a mostly one-sided conversation, during which I expressed my disenchantment with California, so lacking in deciduous trees and overall focus. I think I used the English word *vacuum*. All this bothered him, since he prided himself on having made a successful adjustment to the new land and its culture. And indeed he had, as shown by his book of essays *Widzenia nad zatoką San Francisco* (Visions from San Francisco Bay). Miłosz had a very special attitude toward the Californian poet Robinson Jeffers, some of whose work he translated into Polish. In "Carmel," an essay on his predecessor, who has seen a revival in the United States, he writes: "He played for the highest stakes, drew his own conclusions from his willingly chosen isolation, not trying to please others, faithful to himself." This formulation applies as well to the writer as to his subject, for whom he feels a deep spiritual affinity, while rejecting Jeffers's negative view of humanity. I might just add that Miłosz had no interest or stake in Polish communities abroad, and he advised me to avoid the local one.

The circle of graduate students to which I belonged loosely included people from other faculties as well as some of our teachers. Simon Karlinsky, a former musician who would become a scholar and an expert on Vladimir Nabokov, and Robert (Bob) Hughes, a personable young man of thirty who had been in air force intelligence, were the senior charter members. Hughes would later marry Olga Raevsky, another member of the group. The roomy Hughes apartment, on the ground floor of a large Berkeley house, became a venue for weekend parties. Miłosz, who seldom attended such events with his wife, was the standing guest of honor and center of attention. He much enjoyed these evenings, which gave him the chance to imbibe freely, flirt with young women, and preach his own special doctrine of a return to nature. On several occasions, he mentioned a childhood game that he had once played in Wilno. He and his peers would, on a given signal, throw themselves into a heap *(kupa)* on the ground. Should we, the assembled company, do the same, he suggested, the results might be liberating. One memorable evening, after the consumption of much inhibition-dissolving alcohol, some, although not all of us, decided to take up our mentor's challenge. Once at ground level, the latter made spirited attempts to grab the legs of those in his orbit who still remained on their feet. Alas, this half-hearted attempt at primitivism was only anticlimactic, and the now-sheepish participants realized that they had failed the test. After that evening, we noticed that Miłosz behaved with greater restraint at parties. Bob Hughes, we soon learned, had warned him that such behavior was indecorous for someone of his rank.

Of all the many teachers I had over my long zigzagging path through academe in the quest for a Ph.D., Miłosz was by far the most unique. He was generous in spirit but also ready to correct a student who had gotten his facts wrong. After I left Berkeley in the spring of 1963, I would never see Miłosz face to face again. My mother did see him from time to time in Paris, where she had an apartment at 141 rue de Rennes. One of Czesław's sons visited her there in 1963, just as student demonstrations were taking place in the streets not far away. Traits of the younger Miłosz would surface in the figure of Jan Makowski, a character in Mary McCarthy's novel *Birds of America* (1971). In the summer of 1988, Miłosz spent a week or so in my mother's apartment, while she and her husband were in their house in Maine. My wife and I were the next guests on the rue de Rennes. We deemed it an honor to sleep on the same sheets that the poet laureate had left behind.

A Difficult, Inspirational Giant

PETER DALE SCOTT

In my lifetime, I have encountered a few truly great people, thus learning the existence and importance of greatness. Each of these people was difficult. Czesław Miłosz, possibly the greatest of them all, was no exception.

In 1961, I was hired to teach at the University of California, Berkeley, while still completing my two-year term as a Canadian diplomat in Warsaw. All the Polish literary figures I knew told me that I must be sure to look up Miłosz when I arrived at my new job. (Miłosz had come from France in 1960, only one year earlier.) I had a special reason to do so: I had already translated some of Zbigniew Herbert's poetry, and Herbert, when I met him, spoke most enthusiastically of Miłosz. (There was no sign then that there might be future troubles between them.)

But when I arrived in Berkeley, I was surprised to find that many in the local Polish community advised fervently against meeting Miłosz, who had chosen to spend the first years after World War II as a diplomat for the Soviet-installed government. Many anti-Communist émigrés saw this as a treason that could never be exculpated. This was an ironic reversal of the isolation he had experienced in France, where the intellectual left denounced him as a traitorous sell-out to the CIA and its subsidized forum for anti-Communist writers, the Congress of Cultural Freedom.

When I met him in 1961 or 1962, he lived in a fine house just below Grizzly Peak Boulevard in Berkeley but with few friends outside the Slavic Department. His letters from that period reveal his alienation from the secular culture of America, when his friends included the Catholic monk-poets Thomas Merton and Brother Antoninus. For the next five years, I met regularly with him to translate Polish poetry—first contemporary poets, then the entire Polish canon, and finally focusing on Zbigniew Herbert (we published a book together)[1] and himself.

Those evening translation sessions were perhaps the most stimulating experiences of my life. I had never before met such critical acuity combined with such passionate erudition and such love of words. For example, he shared with me his fascination with Mandelstam, comparing different translations and explaining those qualities of Russian poetry that were almost impossible to render into English.

I felt him to be the representative on earth of a whole firmament of brilliant solitaries, to whose ranks he seemed already destined. Only once before had I experienced such excitement—the magical day a friend and I spent long ago with Auden in a Quebec apple orchard. (By contrast, the two times I met Eliot—once at his sister-in-law's near Harvard and once in his third-floor Faber office—were interesting but affectless.)

Through Miłosz, I learned to pay far more attention to translation than I ever had before. Versions (usually but not always beginning with him) would go back and forth and back between us, and our discussions of a single poem could sometimes take hours, with endless and priceless digressions. He taught me to avoid poeticisms and to focus on simple expression, in the style of his early and naïve, almost untranslatable sequence "The World."

On the critical level, I admired the breadth of his eclectic and sometimes surprising tastes, combined with his forceful aesthetic and moral discriminations among the greatest authors, not hesitating to put Tolstoy, on moral grounds, ahead of Dostoevsky, for example.[2]

Inevitably, we drank as well as worked; as the evening wore on, our discussions wandered further and further afield. To my expressed love for Poland's medieval landscapes with barefoot goatherd girls and armies of geese, he responded with the reminiscences of Lithuania that he had recorded in his memoir, *Native Realm*. He also opened my eyes to contemporary Polish poets such as Aleksander Wat, to Osip Mandelstam, to Jan Kochanowski, and to the remarkable enlightened culture of the Polish Renaissance. In the end, he even persuaded me to admire Robinson Jeffers, though never as much as he did.

Often I would not leave until well after midnight. On one memorable occasion, his head fell forward on the table; at that precise moment (2:30 a.m.), Janka, his wife, emerged from behind a curtain, to say that it was time for me to go home. I have no idea how long she had been waiting there, or if indeed it was her practice to watch over us every night.

Miłosz inspired me above all with his vivid awareness of the importance of poetry to language and therefore to society. I adopted as a personal mantra his memorable question in "Dedication": "What is poetry which does not save / Nations or people?" Little did I know that that poem, part of which I memorized in Polish, would some day contribute (as we shall see) to a rift between us.

Miłosz's awareness of the social function of poetry was not surprising in a man who came from a region where frontiers slipped periodically east and west and where both Poland and Lithuania had vanished at times from the map. As he wrote later,

> My faithful language,
> I have served you.
> Every night I have set before you little bowls with color. . . .
> You were my homeland because the other one had gone missing.[3]

As a Canadian, I too was attuned to the importance of poetry in confirming the cultural identity of an insecure nation. Thus, on my side, I felt somewhat estranged from the historical mindlessness of postwar American poets I had met, such as Richard Wilbur. I hoped for a poetry in English not numbed by ideological clichés such as "Poetry makes nothing happen" or "A poem should not mean, but be."

Miłosz encouraged me to think of a different tradition, in which poets, by default, became repositories and promoters of people's hopes. It was only much later that I learned of his major contributions in the 1950s and 1960s to preparing Poland for the intellectual culture of Solidarność, to which I have paid tribute elsewhere.[4]

My memories of our conversations are now so heavily overladen with later readings of his essays that I cannot accurately report them. But I remember my admiring impression of Miłosz as a figure of religious enlightenment, nudging the world toward a third and more spiritual way between the godless communism of the Iron Curtain countries and the godless capitalism of the United States. I saw in him a stubborn oppositional heroism in an enduring tradition, that of Blaise Pascal attacking the casuistry of the Jesuits, and of Simone Weil, never quite joining either the Communist Party or (until just before her death) the Catholic Church.

We shared a common interest in the poetry of Eliot, but for different reasons. Miłosz admired Eliot for his "oppositional stance" in an age of alienation and decay.[5] I, in contrast, admired Eliot for his use of the past in his search for a more integrated culture and community. Similarly, another common interest was Dante, whom I was teaching, though Miłosz seemed more interested in Dante's taxonomic analysis of sin, and I in his tears of atonement.[6]

Thus, our talk of poetry was often in the context of faith and spirituality. Interestingly, however, he never let me in on the secret of his regular attendance at Catholic mass; I first learned of it much later from a visiting Polish scholar who came to interview me. If I had known this, I might have revealed how I, a self-proclaimed agnostic, had made short retreats to three Catholic monasteries in France and one in Poland. Or how my self-taught medievalism, which had earned me a job in the UC English department, grew out of my investigations of Eliot's spirituality.

Our common interest in politics was fated to expose deep differences between us, differences that luckily took time to deepen. On the campus, I was caught up in the historical eddies after the Free Speech movement, and by early 1965 I was speaking out regularly against the Vietnam War. Obviously, Miłosz's hostility toward communism was irreconcilable with my desire then for peaceful coexistence with Moscow. But for two years at least, these differences did not trouble our relationship. We did not even discuss them.

I take partial responsibility for the rift that began to develop between us. As a North American who had greatly enjoyed working at United Nations Assemblies and Conferences, I did not yet fully appreciate, to the extent that he did, the "fragility of those things we call civilization or culture" and the "high cost" of our "growing consciousness of global interdependence."[7]

Furthermore, he was far more aware than I of disturbing developments in the so-called Polish People's Republic, which in the 1960s began to clamp down on its citizens more severely than when I had been there, between 1959 and 1961, toward the end of the so-called Polish thaw. On my part, I think I became more aware than he of disturbing developments in American foreign policy. This was particularly true after the U.S.-encouraged massacre of a million or more Indonesians in 1965, when Sukarno was overthrown. I became obsessed with the Indonesian massacre and less mindful of Stalin's massacres, such as the massacre of Poles at Katyń.

For a couple of years, the political differences between us did not seem to matter. Our long and sometimes drunken evenings above the fog in the Bay were still resulting in exciting new artifacts and new aporias, beyond the previous limits of either Polish or English. I think, for example, of our coined word *magpiety*, which has since become the title of both a poem by Philip Levine, and an English folk-song duo. I thought, wrongly, that these explorations transcended politics.

Then, in the fall of 1967, Miłosz attended a rally where I spoke on the same platform as Noam Chomsky. At our next meeting, he said stiffly that he could understand my remarks, but he could not forgive Chomsky's—meaning, I suppose, Chomsky's broad-brush denunciation of all American foreign policy. Chomsky, he said, was "the kind of intellectual who weakened Weimar." In those days, I still believed in the robustness of American democracy; thus, to compare America with Weimar seemed far-fetched to me, and I brashly said so. Since then, I have become more concerned by the divisions in American civil society to which left-wing intellectuals have contributed.[8]

By this time, there were other issues between us. Even though my feelings for Miłosz continued to be what I would call reverential, there were times when our failure to agree on specific translations revealed that my stubbornness was beginning to match his. (It is probable that what I learned from him about translation gradually made me more sure of my own opinions.)

To this day, I recall some of our differences clearly. Miłosz insisted on translating the last lines of Herbert's famous poem "Pebble" (Kamyk) as "to the end they will look at us / with a calm and very clear eye." I have always believed that we should have followed Herbert's carefully selected word order in Polish, which is "with an eye calm and very clear." In general, we agreed that it was important to respect Herbert's very precise choice of word order; but I think that here Miłosz followed his personal preference for a continuous vernacular style, over the heightened resonance of Herbert's final word, "clear."[9]

A more dramatic example was in one of Miłosz's own poems, "Dedication" (Przedmowa). The lines that answer his unforgettable question "What is poetry which does not save / Nations or people?" are, in Polish, "*To, że późno pojąłem jej wybawczy cel, / To jest i tylko to jest ocalenie.*" To me the obvious translation was "That I discovered, late, its [good poetry's] salutary aim, / This is, and only this is, salvation." Miłosz insisted on a toned-down, more subjective, and unmistakably altered second line: "In this and only this I find salvation."[10]

Something important was at stake here. I sensed at the time that in his isolated exile he was backing away from his earlier lofty hopes for poetry. Only later did I learn that even in his youth he had mistrusted the grandiloquence of all public poetry, including his own, and that for years he was ambivalent about the claims of this poem in particular.[11] It became clear that, for whatever reason, Miłosz wanted his poem to be not just translated but changed in English, and I resisted this.

I wish now that I had not naïvely assumed that I was on the same level, with respect to his poems, that I had been when we were both translating Herbert. As I wrote later, the sharp edges of our critical tools, "turned / on the sensitive flesh of your own poems / could only draw blood."[12]

The cultural tensions of the Vietnam War years in Berkeley expanded the gap between us. Like the young Wordsworth in revolutionary Orleans, I participated in the heady, euphoric aspirations of that short-lived era. Miłosz denounced them as delusional; he became more and more interested in what he later called the "inhumanism" of Jeffers, a poetry of withdrawal from, if not contempt for, history. Miłosz's distaste for left-wing utopias led him, by a kind of inverted Cartesian dialectic, to share Jeffers's rejection of hopes for collective humanity. As he wrote in his one published poem written in English, "To Raja Rao" (1969),

> I hear you saying that liberation is possible
> and that Socratic wisdom
> is identical with your guru's.
>
> No, Raja, I must start from what I am.
> I am those monsters which visit my dreams
> and reveal to me my hidden essence.
>
> If I am sick, there is no proof whatsoever
> that man is a healthy creature.[13]

How retrenched in tone this was from the lines in his earlier poem "Throughout Our Lands" (1961), which we had translated together: "The human mind is splendid; lips powerful, / and the summons so great it must open Paradise."[14]

About the same time, I discovered in Merton's published correspondence with Miłosz that Merton had developed the same reaction as I did to Miłosz's increasingly solipsistic alienation, albeit from a more Thomistic perspective. In an address to Miłosz, I let Merton's question speak for myself—"Should I really experience / nature as alien / and heartless?"[15]

Today my view of life is no longer so contrasted to his, but this is irrelevant. At the time, our meetings became more and more infrequent. The first public sign of trouble was a memorable faculty meeting in 1973 or 1974, in which he rose to warn that a proposal for a new experimental college program, which I was proposing with two colleagues, was a potential threat to Western civilization. As I remember it, the gist of his (in my opinion) misplaced criticism was that we were the type of pedagogical positivists whom he had once described as being "from the point of view of literature . . . Romantic arsonists."[16] He seemed to assume from the fact that we were proposing an avowedly innovative program that we would turn our backs on the traditions of European culture that were so important to him. But it was in this program that, for the first time, I began to teach Virgil, as I did for the remainder of my academic career.

It had become clear that there was a major rift between us. I was, frankly, broken-hearted.

Things went from bad to worse. In 1982, I was surprised to see my translation of Herbert's poem "Two Drops," which I had completed before ever meeting Miłosz, appear in an important poetic anthology, *The Rattle Bag*, ascribed to Miłosz and not to myself.[17] Then new editions of our Penguin edition of Herbert's *Selected Poems* appeared, both in England and America, without any communication with or permission from me.[18] Miłosz was very busy in these years, and I see no malice in these details. But they indicate how far I had receded from his attention.

The denouement was after I had been invited to a conference at Stanford, to participate in a panel with two other poets on translating Miłosz. A letter arrived telling me that my invitation had been withdrawn and Miłosz would be taking my place. I still have no idea who was responsible for this decision, but I was shattered by it.[19]

My despair resulted in a long letter-poem to him (it's in my book *Crossing Borders*):

> Now that I shall not see you at the weekend
> conference with your new translators,
> surprised, even hurt, to have been disinvited,
> I am also relieved: because we share no future,
> at last I am free to tell you, face
> to absent face, how much your gift,
> of loneliness inhabited, has meant.[20]

Someone (not myself) gave the poem to him, and to my delight he phoned me to set up a reconciliatory meeting. He scheduled it for 2:30 p.m., a half hour before the commencement ceremony for Slavic studies would begin. But we talked nonstop for three and a half hours, with a new and intense candor about our differences. I walked with him finally to the commencement, to find workmen folding away the chairs and tables. I recall that we were able to salvage half a plastic glass of wine each from the last remaining bottle.

Our reconciliation was fated not to be total. I tried to suggest to him on this occasion that we were both fundamentally striving for the same cause—nonviolence—and that the influence on our campus of people like me had served to help spare Berkeley the antiacademic violence one had seen at Columbia and Yale. His unforgettable response is printed indelibly in my memory, as in my trilogy *Speculum:* "My dear Peter, of course you gave the enemy comfort!"—the enemy being the forces of violence that had, for example, set fire to Wheeler Hall, where I maintained my office.[21] Equally memorable is the way he said it, with a fatalistic, almost despairing but also—dare I say this?—ultimately friendly chuckle.

If I cannot report that our old intimacy was restored after that meeting, at least after that, our occasional encounters were cordial and respectful. Whenever we met, he would discuss the dramatic political developments of the 1980s in Poland. I took his detailed analyses as a compliment, a recognition that, whatever our differences, there were still certain interests we two shared.

I last saw him in 1998 at a memorial dinner for our mutual friend Denise Levertov. He was at the time in his late eighties, and his second wife, Carol, sat me at the table next to his one good ear. For hours he proceeded to deconstruct the complexities of post-Solidarity Polish Catholicism with undiminished discrimination and ardor. It was clear that he was ambivalent about the forces that had uneasily replaced socialism in Poland.

And thankfully I was able to tell him how much I admired, loved, and had been changed by him. He responded in a low voice with some self-deprecating and almost indecipherable comment about his difficult misanthropy. But I deduced from his smile, and our subsequent long talk at dinner, that he was pleased.

Notes

A shorter version of this brief memoir was published in *California Monthly,* December 2004, http://www.peterdalescott.net/MiloszObit.htm.

1. Zbigniew Herbert, *Selected Poems,* trans. Czesław Miłosz and Peter Dale Scott (Harmondsworth, Middlesex, U.K.: Penguin Books, 1968).

2. These tendencies became evident as we worked on our first collaboration, *Postwar Polish Poetry.* Miłosz amply represented certain poets while privately deploring to me the adjustments they had made to the Soviet presence in Poland.

3. Cf. Czesław Miłosz, "My Faithful Mother Tongue," in Miłosz, *New and Collected Poems, 1931–2001* (New York: Ecco, 2001), 245. The translation cited here is by Agnieszka Tennant, in "The Poet Who Remembered," *Christianity Today* (Web site), September 1, 2004, http://www.christianitytoday.com/ct/2004/septemberweb-only/9-6-12.0.html.

4. Peter Dale Scott, "Czesław Miłosz and Solidarity; or, Poetry and the Liberation of a People," *Brick* 78 (Winter 2006): 67–74.

5. Czesław Miłosz, *To Begin Where I Am: Selected Essays* (New York: Farrar, Straus and Giroux, 2001), 391.

6. See Miłosz's intransigently antifashionable essay "Saligia," in ibid., 287–313.

7. Czesław Miłosz, *The Witness of Poetry* (Cambridge, Mass.: Harvard University Press, 1983), 97, 115.

8. Peter Dale Scott, *The Road to 9/11: Wealth, Empire, and the Future of America* (Berkeley: University of California Press, 2007), 253, 265, etc.

9. The issue is an open-ended and subtle one. What comes off in English as poetic inversion is in Polish a not unusual reversal of the adjective-noun word order at the end of the preceding stanza.

10. Miłosz, "Dedication," *New and Collected Poems*, 77.

11. Scott, "Czesław Miłosz and Solidarity," 72; Adam Michnik, "A Farewell to Czesław Miłosz," New School, Transregional Center for Democratic Studies, *Bulletin,* October 2003, http://www.newschool.edu/tcds/bulletinbackissues.htm.

12. Peter Dale Scott, *Crossing Borders: Selected Shorter Poems* (New York: New Directions, 1994), 35. It is significant to me that whereas at first his collaborators all spoke Polish to some extent, increasingly with the passage of time most of them did not.

13. Miłosz, "To Raja Rao," *New and Collected Poems*, 255.

14. Miłosz, "Throughout Our Lands," ibid., 184.

15. Peter Dale Scott, *Listening to the Candle: A Poem on Impulse* (New York: New Directions, 1992), 131 (quoting Thomas Merton, *Confessions of a Guilty Bystander* [New York: Doubleday/Image, 1968], 139).

16. Miłosz, *To Begin Where I Am*, 345.

17. Ted Hughes and Seamus Heaney, eds., *The Rattle Bag* (London: Faber and Faber, 1982), 441. In the 2007 Ecco edition of Herbert's *Collected Poems*, it says that the opening epigraph for "Two Drops" from Słowacki "was added by Miłosz and Scott." In fact, it was suggested to me by my language tutor in Poland, a friend of Herbert's.

18. Herbert, *Selected Poems*, trans. Czesław Miłosz and Peter Dale Scott (1968; reprint, Manchester: Carcanet Press, 1985; New York: Ecco Press, 1986).

19. I do not assume that Miłosz was responsible for my exclusion, which was of a piece with other minor harassments I suffered in this period. (For example, an invitation by mail to speak at a major antiwar conference in Europe arrived two months late, a day or so after a friend inquired, by telephone, why I had not replied to it.) When I phoned Stanford to ask for an explanation, I was told, "We understand that there is some kind of antagonism between the two of you." Rightly or wrongly, I deduced from this response that my interlocutor knew about the decision and that Miłosz had been at some distance from it.

20. Scott, *Crossing Borders*, 39.

21. Scott, *Listening to the Candle*, 131. Miłosz had brought up the torching of Wheeler Hall. What actually burned was a large assembly room used regularly for meetings by student protesters. At the time, the administration was systematically eliminating these potential meeting places, and in my view the responsibility for this act of arson remains unknown.

Remembering Czesław Miłosz

W. S. MERWIN

It is hard for me to believe now, in 2009, just how long Czesław and I knew each other. The memory of meeting him is as vivid as all our later reunions, though it took place more than forty years ago, in a time that I tend to date now by where I was living, or perching, for part of each year in New York. I think it must have been in 1966, when I was, for once, staying north of 14th Street, up near Lincoln Center. I was there to discuss the production I had done of a play by Federico García Lorca, and I believe it was Betty Kray, still directing the pioneer series of poetry readings at the 92nd Street YM-YWHA, who asked me to introduce Miłosz and Zbigniew Herbert there, together. The event was held partly to mark and celebrate the publication, in 1965, of the anthology that Miłosz had edited of *Postwar Polish Poetry,* a volume that was already very important—a kind of revelation, along with the sudden awareness of recent Latin American poetry—to many younger American poets. The event was to be their first appearance in New York.

Even before that book appeared, I had felt indebted to Czesław for the few poems of his that I had seen in translation, and above all for his prose work, *The Captive Mind,* which I had read soon after it was first published, actually, a year or so earlier. That was a book Miłosz had distilled from his own experience in the Polish resistance to the Russian and German occupations of Poland and from his years of exile in France and then Berkeley: an original, daring consideration of the perennial role of poetry, and the treasure of poetic imagination, in the history of the time when it was written. That book appeared at the height of the timely but noisy controversy over the differences, real and concocted, between "academic" and "Beat" poets. For me the New Criticism had once seemed a liberation from late Victorian literary and cultural assumptions, but I was trying to get past all that, and I had been drawn to the poetry of other languages and traditions. Miłosz's book had been a talisman and had made most of the literary bickering among the various ideological encampments, then most audible among the poetic doctrines in English, seem frivolous and silly.

The sound of both poets reading that night in Polish (of which I understand not a word) is still distinct in my ears, but I do not remember the sound of the translations or who read them, which leads me to suspect that I may have read them myself. Miłosz was fifty-four then, Herbert forty-one, and each read with an authority that was completely individual and as different from anything I was used to as Polish was different from English. I remained friends with them both, from that evening until their deaths, though our meetings were fewer and farther apart than I would have liked, and we seldom wrote letters. But it was probably during the summer after that first meeting in New York, when I was staying alone in the old farmhouse in southwestern France that had already been a part of my life for some fifteen years, that I heard from Czesław one way or another (I had no telephone) asking whether he might come and see me there.

He let me know that he had other engagements in the region, saying no more about them than that, but we had the whole of a long summer afternoon together, and when he arrived he told me at once that he was enchanted by what he had seen of the region, the uplands and valleys, towns and villages of the Lot, and that he was eager to see more of it. I led him through the village and up onto the *causse,* the limestone upland that began above the last farmhouse, with its garden of leeks and artichokes and peonies and old plum trees. In those years, I often walked up there in the afternoon, and I could walk for half a day along ancient overgrown lanes— some of them, and the walls on both sides of them, built by Roman legions. There were ruins of old farms and their stone barns, patches of oak woods, outcroppings of cliffs, ponds in hollows. Walking for hours there, I could be certain of meeting no one besides the occasional small flocks of sheep in walled, rough pastures closed with gates of brushwood, and sometimes wild boar—and birds, from wrens to merlins and black kites, and everywhere the resonant silence of the limestone causse in the last days before the coming of chainsaws. As we came back to the ridge above the village, Czesław turned to me with tears in his eyes and said, "Thank you for showing me that. I did not know that places like that still existed anywhere."

I realized, the more I read of his writings as they appeared in translation, that the upland, and the remains of the old life that he could glimpse there (where much of it had never recovered from the losses of the region's young men in World War I), had summoned up memories that were never far from the surface, of his own childhood, in Poland and Lithuania, about which he would write all his life. (I did not realize, then, that what I had shown him was also about to vanish, in turn, like a dream.)

As his later poems were translated (by Czesław, working with Robert Pinsky and Robert Hass) and I read them, I came to the opening sections of *With Trumpets and Zithers*, dated "Berkeley, 1965." References in that poem led me to think that either his visit had been in that year (which I think is unlikely) or that the year he came was not the first time that he had been to the region. In the poem, with its rhapsodic sections written in long fluid lines (New World influences from Whitman and Jeffers?), there are rich, tender evocations of the valley of the Dordogne upriver from Souillac, and just below the farmhouse where he had come to see me. As an example, "near Puybrun by the bridges my childhood was given back." One of those bridges was an iron railway truss dating back many decades (and now replaced). From the ridge across the valley, we could hear the trains crossing it, some ten miles away. From the sound the trains made, the peasants in the village taught me to divine what the weather would be like: a matter of greater importance in those days when the hay was cut in the morning, forked into rows in the midday sun, and brought in, at evening, piled on high carts drawn by the same cows that would be milked, after nightfall, in the barns.

Earlier in the poem, another line was a giveaway: "Water steamed at dawn by Calypso's island where an oriole flutters in the white crown of a poplar." The island he names lies just below the beautiful ancient village of Carennac. The entrance gate to its château opens to a small cobbled street and a church with a celebrated white marble tympanum above the door. At the time of Czesław's visit, and the year before, there was a small hotel in the château, and he may have been staying there, if he could look down to the side eddy of the river and the island in it. In the seventeenth century, the château had been the home of Bishop Fénelon, a learned man of letters with a distinguished literary reputation at the time. His novel, *Télémaque*, whose hero is the son of Ulysses, was well known then. Some of the landscapes in that prose epic are evocations of places along the river near Carennac, and Fénelon is the one who gave Calypso's island its present name. (The island was for sale a year ago, but it is subject to flooding and may escape improvement for a while.)

There are also lines in the poem about the valley of the Alzou, a few miles away, cutting deep into the causse and, on the cliff above it, the shrine of the most famous of the Black Virgins, at Rocamadour.

When he came to see me, he gave no indication of what he had already seen of the region, and my questions to him on the subject were answered only in a rather general way. Perhaps on the walk itself I showed him the ruins of the abbey-fortress of Taillefer, on its cliff over the river, which must have been one of the "castles on rocky spurs" at the beginning of the poem. Perhaps he had already seen that on an earlier visit. I do not, of course, remember everything we talked about. I know that I tried to express something of my gratitude for *The Captive Mind.* During his visit, I realized only a little of the depths of his reserve, and only in the years afterwards did I come to understand more about that walk on the upland and what he was seeing there.

He was always reserved but became less so with time, as we came to know each other better. I was surprised, every time we met again, by his warmth and grace and his evident regard for other poets. Some of his abiding reserve must have been simple shyness, and some must have been acquired and formed during the years of his underground activities during the German and Russian occupations of Poland. His subtle analytical descriptions of *ketman* in *The Captive Mind* reach deep into the subject of covert demeanor during periods of political and social oppression.

In Berkeley, where he was living when he came to see me that first time, his life had come to provide him with a benign haven and many friends, including the two principal translators of his poems into English. It was the setting, for some years, of his happy later marriage to Carol Thigpen, whom he met, I believe, on a reading tour. While he was living there, he came out to Maui to stay with my wife, Paula, and me, in the valley house among the trees, where we have lived since the early eighties. I had seen him, during the years between his first visit to me in France and that one, but not on Maui before or as a guest, and he was clearly thinking of the farmhouse above the Dordogne (and of his youth, I suppose) when he told Carol, as they followed the directions to find our house, that he was sure it would be somewhere far from the beaten path.

We had an affectionate visit, heads together over translations of recent poems of his and an anthology that he was putting together of poems that he called "luminous things"—capturing moments of great immediacy. But we live (by choice) on the rainy side of Maui, and it seemed to rain from the moment they arrived. Their room downstairs had an outdoor shower among the palms. After a few days, the lure of sun, beaches, and the comfort of resorts led them to a hotel on the other side of the island and a suite to which they invited us; we spent time with them over there. Czesław was over seventy by then, with an international reputation, and he had sailed into a peaceful, fulfilled phase of his life.

Yet Berkeley remained for him, in a sense, another Calypso's island, with something still missing, something provisional. And when the new Polish government welcomed him back home after years of exile and celebrated his return as a national hero, his odyssey was complete, and his rediscovery of the settings of his youth became a central theme of his late years. But he still spent part of the year in Berkeley, and in the spring of 1998 Robert Faggen arranged a conference in his honor, to last for several days, at Claremont College in southern California. American poets and critics associated with him in one way or another and old friends of his from the Polish underground were there and talked about him and his work and its influence. Czesław and Carol sat listening to everyone. On the last day, when it was time for Czesław himself to speak, I was sitting at a table with Edward Hirsch, and as Czesław talked about poetry in his life, including the Polish resistance, and the exile in Paris, Hirsch, clearly moved by his words, said to me, "He reminds us of the nobility of poetry."

I am indebted to Edward Hirsch for Paula's and my last visit with Czesław, in Kraków, 2003. For several years, when Mr. Hirsch was teaching in Houston, he had organized exchanges between the poets in the writing program there and poets, particularly young ones, and also critics and translators in Poland. The exchanges came to include summer visits to Kraków by American poets who had some connection with Miłosz and were invited. Young Polish poets—Adam Zagajewski, among others— who had established teaching schedules in Houston as a result of the program, were in Kraków, and there were seminars, joint readings, and interviews there every day for most of a week, including two big readings, one in the cathedral of Kraków and the other in the main synagogue, in which Czesław and others among us took part. The Polish audience's enthusiasm for poetry—and not just in Polish—was unmistakable at all the public gatherings and was clearly a basic element in the richness and originality of modern poetry in that country. Their awareness of American poetry was certainly far greater than it was among the general public in the United States. It was, for all of us who were visiting, an exciting moment.

But Czesław's wife, Carol, many years younger than he was, had died (quite suddenly, on a return visit to California, alone) scarcely a year before that, and I think all of us were being especially watchful of Czesław, then in his nineties, to see how he was bearing up after that shock. He had long had a complicated, rather ambiguous relation with the Catholicism of his upbringing and background. Carol and he had been very close. He seemed to have reached a moment of steady acceptance, whatever it may have been based on besides his own stoic courage and dignity. He had written a long elegiac poem, "Orpheus and Eurydice" (not included in the 2001 edition of his *Collected Poems*), and he gave us a copy of it. We visited him in his apartment a day after a larger-than-life bronze bust of Carol had been delivered, and it was standing in the middle of the living room floor. We all spoke of it politely. Our references to Carol and to the loss of her were cautious, touches around a fresh wound. He knew that we had been fond of her, and she and Paula had become friends before Miłosz and Carol moved to Kraków and the last years there. Several of our public conversations, including references to the Eurydice poem, took place after that private afternoon, and they seemed to offer an easier setting for personal references, and indeed a better, or at least a more comfortable, time and place to say goodbye to him, with affection and gratitude, quite aware that it was probably for the last time.

Nine Flashbacks

BOGDANA CARPENTER

1. September 1965, Dwinelle Hall, Berkeley Campus: "My First Encounter with Czesław Miłosz"

In September 1965, my American husband, John, and I moved from Paris to Berkeley, where I was about to start the doctoral program in comparative literature. When I arrived in Berkeley, I could hardly wait to meet Czesław Miłosz, the famous but somewhat mythical Polish poet: mythical since his books were not available in Poland and his name could only be whispered. I read Miłosz's poetry and essays for the first time in Paris, where I had lived since 1963. Now I wanted to match the name and the face, to make the myth become reality.

On the first day of classes, I went to Dwinelle Hall, where the Polish literature class was scheduled. Dwinelle Hall is a labyrinthine structure; I got lost and could not find the room. I was late for the class, the hallways were empty, and my Parisian high heels made a terrible noise. A man was walking in front of me. Because of the racket, he stopped and looked back. All I saw were the bushy eyebrows, sticking far out, and behind them sharp blue eyes, but I knew I was on the right track. I slowed down and followed the man to the classroom.

In the next three years, I took every class Miłosz taught. I have written elsewhere about Miłosz-the-teacher, but because our friendship was shaped by our first teacher-student relationship, I cannot leave it entirely aside. The courses I took with Miłosz proved formative in my own academic career. His lectures opened a whole new world; they were not only—as the official descriptions in the course catalogue claimed—about Polish literature but also about history, religion, philosophy, Freemasonry, and the Kabbalah. The digressions often surpassed, in terms of both time and interest, the subject itself. Miłosz's open and unconventional approach put Polish literature in a new and unexpected light, far from the stereotype image of my Polish professors. They were also a dialogue, in fact, a double dialogue: Miłosz conversed not only with us sitting around the table but also with the authors whom we were reading, regardless whether they were our contemporaries or had lived five centuries earlier. His lectures became for me an unattainable ideal in my own teaching, and I tried, however imperfectly, to imitate them.

2. December 26, 1979, San Francisco: "These Poets Do Not Deserve Such a Book"

In September 1974, we moved to Seattle, where I assumed the position of assistant professor in Polish in the Department of Slavic Languages and Literatures at the University of Washington. In the next ten years, I saw Czesław Miłosz only twice. Because of the prolonged illness of his first wife, Janka, this was a difficult period in his life. It also happened to be a difficult time in my life. In the fall of 1979, I sent Miłosz the manuscript of my book, *The Poetic Avant-garde in Poland, 1918–1939*, with a letter asking for his opinion of my work. I did it with trepidation, knowing well Miłosz's negative stance toward Polish avant-garde poetry. In fact, my last chapter, devoted to Miłosz's own prewar poetry, included a presentation of his virulent essay, written in 1938, directed against avant-garde poetics. His poetics diverged radically from those of the avant-garde poets, and the experience of the Second World War only deepened the difference. My decision to send Miłosz the book was an act of arrogance, but I was desperate: my tenure clock was ticking and I had no one to turn to for advice. Miłosz was an authority I trusted without reservation; if he proved critical of the book, it would have to be rewritten. Miłosz agreed to read the manuscript, and we arranged a meeting at the bar of San Francisco's Saint Francis Hotel during the annual Modern Language Association meeting. There is no need to describe my feelings; I was tense, apprehensive, fearful, panicky. I remember vividly the dark room with small tables; when I entered, Miłosz was already there holding my manuscript. He looked at me and said, "These poets do not deserve such a book." That's all, no other comments. The topic was closed. For another hour or so, we talked about our families and my job. No, Miłosz did not—could not—enjoy the task of reading a book about poets he wholeheartedly disliked, but he knew my situation and agreed to do it. This was generous. And he made a distinction between the subject matter and the writing itself, the poetry and my scholarship. His comment was honest; I have never heard flattery from Miłosz. Sometimes, to the contrary, he could be brutally frank.

3. 1980s and 1990s, Ann Arbor, Michigan: "Central European Dream"

"*And I, always* insatiable, just as in this moment when I come to the window, see a tower with a clock, snow underneath it on the lawns of the Ann Arbor campus, a girl walking on a pathway."[1] Miłosz's association with the Ann Arbor campus of the University of Michigan has a long history; it is an important, though little known, part of his poetic career in this country. In 1977, Michigan Slavic Publications under the editorship of Professor Ladislav Matejka published *Utwory poetyckie: Poems,* the first selection of Miłosz's poems in Polish spanning his entire career. The publication coincided with an honorary doctorate conferred upon Miłosz by the University of Michigan the same year. Ever since the mid-seventies, Miłosz had been a frequent guest of the Department of Slavic Languages and Literatures, the same department that for seven years hosted Joseph Brodsky as writer in residence. Brodsky was a close friend of Miłosz and, like him, a Nobel laureate. On his visits to the University of Michigan, Miłosz taught courses, gave lectures and poetry readings, and took part in various symposia. The visit he mentions in *Unattainable Earth* took place before we moved to Ann Arbor in the summer of 1983, but many more visits followed in the eighties and nineties, the last on October 29, 1993, when he gave a poetry reading to an audience of more than a thousand.

In January 1986, the Slavic Department organized a conference on Eastern Europe; the speakers included, among others, Czesław Miłosz, Josef Škvorecky, and György Konrád. Simultaneously, another conference, not open to the public, was quietly occurring behind the scenes in our house. Its topic was a center devoted to the culture of Central Europe that was to be an extension of *Cross Currents: A Yearbook of Central European Culture,* edited and published by Professor Matejka since 1983. Miłosz had been a contributor and an enthusiastic supporter of *Cross Currents,* and the idea of the center appealed to him greatly. The idea was also inspired by a dream of a political nature, to prepare the ground for a future Federation of Central European states. The memory of the Solidarity movement in Poland was still fresh, and the fall of communism seemed probable if not inevitable, though nobody foresaw that it would happen so soon. And with the fall of communism, a central European federation would be not only the ideal political solution for these small states belonging neither to the East nor to the West but also the best counterforce to an ever-hungry Russia. Needless to say, the idea behind the center was utopian, and the genocide in the Balkans a few years later showed how hopelessly unrealistic it was, but it was a great and beautiful idea, one that even Miłosz, despite the harsh lessons history had taught him, had embraced.

4. Spring 1991, El Cerrito: "Walks and Talks"

In 1991, I spent six months with my husband and daughter in Berkeley taking advantage of my sabbatical leave. We rented a small house on Colusa Avenue in the neighboring town of El Cerrito. It was a period of renewed friendship with Miłosz and the beginning of my long-lasting friendship with his second wife, Carol Thigpen Miłosz. The four of us saw each other frequently, in our respective houses, restaurants, and cafés and at the home of our mutual friends Professor Frank Whitfield and his Polish wife, Celina. When we visited the Miłoszes on Grizzly Peak, Czesław proudly showed us the spectacular garden planted by Carol. We took several walks together in the vast and beautiful Tilden Park. While these walks gave us great pleasure, for Miłosz they were bitter medicine, prescribed by his doctor because of circulation problems in his legs. These walks became, however, for Miłosz an occasion to speak Polish, something he missed since most of his Polish-speaking friends had passed away. He would skillfully let Carol and John walk together, speaking English, so that he could speak Polish with me. Sometimes he could be almost childishly cunning about it. Once, John and I took our walk alone, and as we were coming back to our car in the parking lot, Miłosz's car pulled up. He was alone, without Carol. Feeling that it would be impolite to speak Polish in front of John, he asked if I could accompany him while John—"for sure tired"—might enjoy a rest in the car. This little scheme seemed—to him at least—more polite and considerate. Needless to say, it was Czesław who spoke; my role was that of an understanding listener. But I was delighted and fascinated, for Miłosz was never boring, never trite. There was always a depth to what he was saying and a new angle from which he saw things. He was constitutionally unable to make small talk. He kept his listeners both entranced and on their toes. The "Tilden Park talks," almost always about various aspects of Polish literature, were a continuation of lectures I had listened to in Dwinelle Hall twenty-five years earlier.

5. June 1991, El Cerrito: "Eightieth Birthday"

On June 13, we celebrated Miłosz's eightieth birthday in our rented house on Colusa Avenue. It was a couple of weeks early because our departure date was set for June 22 (Miłosz's birthday was on June 30). The evening was delightful, with lots of wine and a delicious chocolate cake from the famed Cocolat bakery. Carol told us the story of their first encounter while Miłosz, sipping his favorite bourbon, purred on the couch like a happy cat. A dean at Emory University at the time, Carol was officially designated to meet the famous poet and Nobel laureate at the airport. They had barely had time to shake hands when Miłosz, visibly upset, asked (a request that sounded like a command) to be taken to a store where he could buy a battery for his watch, which had stopped running. It was late in the day, stores were about to close, and they had to hurry. Tense and annoyed by the commanding tone of her guest, Carol did not look at him with much sympathy. But the moment they left the airport in search of the store, Miłosz's mood and tone changed (such sudden changes of mood were not uncommon with him). Delighted to be with an attractive and intelligent woman more than three decades his junior, he displayed all his charm and seductiveness. Within minutes, Carol was won over. By the time Miłosz left Atlanta, the last big romance of his life had started.

6. March 2000, Berkeley–Ann Arbor: "The Ode to the Pope"

In the 1990s, the Miłoszes divided their time between California and Poland, spending the spring and summer months in Kraków and winters in Berkeley. During these winter months, Czesław frequently would call me from Berkeley to speak Polish but also to discuss his latest poem or essay. Often he would then send the new piece by mail, and as soon as I read it, I would call back to communicate my impressions. Once on a Sunday evening in March 2000, four of us—my husband, John; daughter, Magdalena; and her fiancé, Matthew—were addressing their wedding invitations when the telephone rang. It was Czesław. With great excitement he announced, "I wrote an ode to the pope!" Within five minutes the "Ode for the Eightieth Birthday of Pope John Paul II" was faxed to us, and ten minutes later we were talking again. I expressed my enthusiasm and mentioned some lines that struck me as particularly strong and moving. Miłosz seemed fidgety, not satisfied with my reaction. I had obviously missed something, a subtle hint in the poem's second stanza that John Paul II was an heir of Polish Romantic messianism:

> The prayers and prophecies
> Of poets, whom money and progress scorned,
> Even though they were the equals of kings, waited for you
> So that you, not they, could announce, *urbi et orbi*,
> That the centuries are not absurd but a vast order.

84

Miłosz was concerned that the readers of the poem, including the addressee, might find the allusion offensive. He wrote what he believed to be true, but as a staunch critic of messianic ideas himself, he was worried about a possible reaction. We discussed it further; a few weeks later I read the poem in a Polish newspaper. It was unchanged.

I was, of course, flattered by Miłosz's confidence and honored to be his first reader. I won't conceal that most of the time he heard praise from me, but never was the praise insincere, nor did it need to be. Anyone familiar with Miłosz's writings will understand why. Even though my enthusiasm was genuine, I was repeatedly surprised by Miłosz's need for an audience and his happiness when hearing praise. A Nobel Prize laureate, a celebrated poet, coveted and invited by every college and university in the country, giving poetry readings all over Europe and America, often to huge crowds of admirers, seeking praise for a poem from a former student? But the need was genuine, and the satisfaction after was well audible, even on the phone, as a characteristic clearing of the throat, a little happy grunt. The need for readers and praise is common to all writers, but the lack of inhibition on Miłosz's part was childishly disarming.

7. 2001–2002, Kraków: "Orpheus and Eurydice"

When the Miłoszes moved to Kraków permanently, we visited them regularly once a year, usually in the late spring, during our annual trips to Warsaw. It was always a pleasure to watch Czesław and Carol together, for their relationship was full of warmth, joy, and tenderness. I remember Czesław's delight when Carol would come back from her errands in town and report to him what she saw in the streets with all the prosaic, down-to-earth details. It was like a whiff of life in his seclusion. He roared with laughter when she reproduced her "conversations" with Kraków merchants in a mixture of English interspersed with Polish monosyllables and amply supplemented by a "body language" of gestures and facial expressions. He loved Carol's sense of humor and her pragmatic "American" approach to the world, her sober and unorthodox views of Polish politics and literary coteries. His love was reciprocated. It was not an easy decision for Carol to move to Kraków. She did not know the language, and she had no friends in Poland and hardly anyone to speak to. Poland is as different from America as it comes, and Carol was very American. I admired her—her courage, endurance, and devotion. A couple of times, during my brief visits to Kraków, we went together to a café and spent hours talking. Carol never complained. For several years, she did errands—including grocery shopping—by riding a bike in congested and heavily polluted Kraków. In 2001, Carol bought a secondhand red Toyota Corolla; when we visited them that summer, she showed us the car with great pride. Czesław could not walk anymore, and she bought the car to take him to parks and fields outside the city, to breathe fresh air and see the greenery.

In June 2002, I called the Miłoszes from Warsaw to arrange a visit. I spoke to Czesław. Carol was gravely ill; she was in a wheelchair, flying to Berkeley the next day to see her doctor. Czesław was not sure about the nature of her illness. A couple of months earlier, Carol had become very weak quite suddenly and spent several weeks in the hospital. Doctors suspected anemia, but the diagnosis was not decisive. I was not sure whether Polish doctors knew the diagnosis but did not want to tell Miłosz, or whether he knew but did not want to tell me, afraid to say it aloud. It was leukemia, and at such an advanced stage that there was little hope of recovery. Carol passed away a few weeks later, a day after Miłosz flew to California to see her. During the two weeks he stayed in Berkeley, Miłosz called me several times; he was unhappy and felt estranged. He described in detail his visit to the hospital, straight from the San Francisco airport. Uncertain whether she would live long enough to see him, Carol had written him a few days earlier a letter. It started: "Dear Czesław, my greatest love."

It was not easy for Miłosz—ninety-one years old at the time—to live without Carol. It was not so much a matter of everyday survival, for he had helpers who took care of him and performed household chores, but psychologically it was a blow from which he never recovered. Carol's passing away marked the beginning of his own final decline. When we visited Miłosz in February 2004, we sat in the lovely living room recently planned and furnished by Carol. Against a wall stood a sculpture of Carol; I was impressed by the way the artist had managed to capture his model despite having had to execute the sculpture, after Carol's death, from a picture. I was particularly moved by a small detail: the upright collar of a shirt-blouse Carol is wearing. This is how I have always remembered Carol: in a shirt-blouse, with the collar standing up. When I mentioned it to Czesław, he nodded and smiled; he liked it, too. Then he pointed to the sculpture and said, "Now I have her only in stone." I thought of the beautiful and moving poem "Orpheus and Eurydice" Miłosz wrote after Carol's death: "Only her love had warmed him, humanized him." And then his desperate cry: "Eurydice! How will I live without you, my consoling one!"

8. February 2004, Kraków: "Autographs"

In 2004, I saw Miłosz twice. The first time was in February. He was in high spirits; elegantly dressed, wearing a tie and a jacket, he greeted us at the door. We spent several hours together, while his daughter-in-law Joanna was taking pictures. She later sent me a few of these pictures, and I am grateful to her because they are, with a few exceptions, the only pictures I have with Czesław. During this visit, Czesław gave us his two recently published books: *Przygody młodego umysłu* (Adventures of a young mind), a collection of essays written between 1931 and 1939, and *Spiżarnia literacka* (Literary pantry). He wanted to sign them but could not see the page, and his daughter-in-law had to direct his hand, holding a pen to the spot on the front page where he could start writing his name. I have many books by Miłosz with his autographs and dedications, but no earlier dedication moves me as much as these last, almost unintelligible, scribbles. They are a graphic reminder of the many years we had known each other, as well as a testimony to the passage of time and the progress of age, both his and mine.

9. June 2004, Kraków: "Farewell"

When we saw Miłosz in June, he was bedridden. We were visiting our son in Slovenia, when Miłosz's health suddenly deteriorated and he was taken to the hospital. I called his Kraków number as soon as we came back to Warsaw. His son Tony answered the phone. Miłosz was back at home but weak. We decided that it might be better for us not to visit him at this time. I asked Tony to pass on my love to his father. Five minutes later our telephone rang. It was Joanna: Miłosz wanted us to come, and he had asked her to phone me. We took the train to Kraków the following day, Wednesday, June 9. Czesław was lying on his back on top of a high hospital bed in his bedroom, with his face to the window. He was happy to see us and shook our hands warmly. He was alert, joking and laughing. We talked about his poetry; his eyes shone happily when I mentioned that in his poetry I could hear Polish poets from the Renaissance all the way up to the twentieth century, like different instruments in an orchestra. He knew we were going back to the United States in a few days and asked me how I felt about it. Then he remembered and recited to us some rhymed couplets he had heard in his early childhood, when he was five years old. After about twenty minutes, he got tired and told us, "Now you can go." We hugged him and left. All three of us knew it was our last farewell.

I did not fly to Poland for Miłosz's funeral in August. I wanted to stay with the memory of Czesław as I had seen him in June and, in my ears, hear his living voice reciting children's rhymes.

Notes

1. Czesław Miłosz, *Unattainable Earth*, trans. by the author and Robert Hass (New York: Ecco, 1986), 40.

Miłosz the Refugee

HENRYK GRYNBERG

In February 1968, a new Jewish refugee from Communist Poland, I was a guest speaker at the meeting of the Bay Area Council for Soviet Jewry in San Francisco. I stayed overnight with the vice chairman, who in his private life was a manufacturer of club soda. The next morning my host drove me over "the shaky hills that rolled down to the sea" and among "the swaying houses that rolled down the hills," as I later wrote in a poem. It was drizzling and the rain-soaked islands were shrouded in fog. "What are we doing in this mist and this fog?" I wondered, looking at the vice chairman of the Jewish organization, who was wearing a Tyrolean hat with its small brim. I had the feeling that "the islands were scowling at us," and "the hills were trying to throw us into the sea."[1]

I got out of the car near the campus at an avenue of old plane trees paved with red clinker bricks like the old highway near Łowicz. I waited for Czesław Miłosz at the door to his classroom. When he came out, I introduced myself. He took me to his office. Jan Kott came in. A renowned specialist in Shakespeare, he had a contract at Berkeley until the end of this semester and after that was going back to Poland.

"Don't rush back, wait a little longer," I told Kott.

"Ah, we are of different generations, we look at things differently," he replied.

This was true, for I knew something he was not aware of, and I felt helpless.

Miłosz drove me to his picturesque home on Grizzly Peak above the foggy Bay. His first wife, Janina, baked us lasagna, which we washed down with red California wine. Kott was supposed to come, but he didn't. My gracious host drove me back across a very long, very high bridge, while I was continuing my inner monologue: "What are we doing on bridges that climb up to the sky, in the melancholy of swaying houses, of hills rolling down into the sea, and in the splash of islands that are unknown to the ships of our hope." It seemed as if we were "holding on to each other like to a life raft" or that "we were binding and gluing a raft out of our Polish words."[2]

Back in Los Angeles, I shaped that monologue into a poem, dedicated it to Miłosz, and mailed it to him and to the Paris *Kultura*. Suddenly, at eight in the morning, the phone rang.

"Please, remove that dedication."

"Don't you like the poem?"

"It's not that, just remove it, please."

"But why?"

"You don't yet understand the situation here. I'll explain it some other time."

I rededicated the poem: "To the Poles of San Francisco."

⌒⌒

Meanwhile, in Warsaw, Władysław Gomułka, the party chief, had ordered the stage production of *Forefathers' Eve,* the nineteenth-century national drama by Adam Mickiewicz, to close down because audiences ostentatiously applauded all the anti-Russian passages. Several hundred students marched to Mickiewicz's statue and laid flowers. Two students who had given an interview to the correspondent of *Le Monde* were dismissed from the university. Their friends collected three thousand signatures on a protest petition. The Writers' Union protested, too. On March 8 at noon, students assembled in front of the university library. At the same time, tourist buses with "Excursion" written on them pulled up at both university gates. But the "tourists"—wearing quilted workers' jackets—ran in through the side gate and pulled out batons from their sleeves, while uniformed riot police with helmets rushed through the main gate. The "tourists" in quilted jackets surrounded the demonstrators like hunters, while the uniformed police attacked anyone they could reach, beating and kicking, and they dragged into a truck anyone who fell. The news of students being beaten at Warsaw University was met with protests at universities throughout the country. Then Gomułka pulled his ace from his sleeve: stating that this was not a national matter but a conspiracy of the "Fifth Column." An open war had begun.

As usual, the preparatory artillery fire was entrusted to the press. "Whose interest does it serve?" asked the headlines. "Who profits from it?" "Whose influence is it?" "Who is behind it?" Was it accidental that people not just of Jewish descent but inimical to Polish state interests controlled foreign policy, foreign trade, the press, radio, television, our culture?

On March 19, three thousand party apparatchiks filled the Warsaw Congress Hall, and Gomułka himself took the podium.

"Be bold, Wiesław! Be bold!" the audience encouraged him as soon as he appeared beneath an enormous banner, which read, "Everyone has only one Fatherland."

"There were 3,145 signatures on the petition sent to Sejm[3] on February the 16th by student Irena Lasota-Hirszowicz," read Gomułka, inserting the Jewish surname Hirszowicz that twenty years earlier, at the request of the party, Irena's father had changed to Lasota. "On the 3rd of March, over a dozen people, mainly students of Jewish descent known for their revisionist views and pronouncements, gathered in the apartment of Jacek Kuroń. On the 8th of March, 1,500 students assembled in the courtyard of Warsaw University without the permission of the university authorities. . . . They uttered slogans of a hostile and demagogic content. The aforementioned Irena Lasota read a resolution. . . . This resolution was later read by two other students . . . (he hesitated for a moment) who were Polish . . . (he stuttered) that is, Poles."[4]

The press did not carry this sentence, but everyone listening to the radio or watching television heard it. Then a kind of dialogue ensued between the speaker and the audience.

> SPEAKER: Comrades, in the recent events an active role has been played by students of Jewish descent or origin . . .
>
> AUDIENCE: Out! Out! To Israel!
>
> SPEAKER: Comrades, please keep calm.
>
> AUDIENCE: Bolder! Bolder!
>
> SPEAKER: Are there Jewish nationalists in Poland, advocates of Zionist ideology?
>
> AUDIENCE: Yes! Yes! Yes!
>
> SPEAKER: Certainly yes, comrades . . .
>
> AUDIENCE: To Israel! To Israel! (A spontaneous, enthusiastic, vociferous shriek and roar.)
>
> SPEAKER: During last June's Israeli aggression against the Arab states a certain number of Jews showed their desire to go to Israel and take part in the war against the Arabs. (The

speaker never revealed the actual number or the source of his information.) There is no doubt that Jews of that category, though Polish citizens, are emotionally and mentally attached not to Poland but to the state of Israel. I suppose that sooner or later that category of Jews will leave our country . . .

AUDIENCE: Let-them-go! Let-them-go! Let-them-go! (A sincere, general enthusiasm, not heard at party meetings since the 1930s *Parteitagen* in Munich and Nuremberg.)

SPEAKER: To those who consider Israel their homeland, we are ready to issue emigration passports . . .

AUDIENCE: Right-a-way! Right-a-way! Right-a-way! (Again shrieks and enthusiasm in the Munich-Nuremberg style.)

SPEAKER (mumbling under his breath): No one has yet applied . . .

AUDIENCE: Let-them-go! Let-them-go! Let-them-go!

SPEAKER: Comrades, please stay calm and listen to what is being said from this podium . . .

AUDIENCE (impatiently): Bol-der! Bol-der! Bol-der!

SPEAKER (with understanding): No one can impose feelings of national belonging on someone who doesn't have them . . . Such people, however, should avoid working in places where the affirmation of national loyalty is indispensable . . .

Gomułka's "subtle" innuendos were immediately translated into un-ambiguous resolutions by organizations and work establishments. They demanded "the complete cleansing of Zionist elements from the apparatus of administration, education and culture," "the isolation of Zionist elements from honest-working Polish society," "the removal of not only the direct instigators of the late events, but also their hidden allies." "Our society condemns the Zionist provocateurs!" "Cleanse the party and the administration!" "Down with the Zionists!" "Down with the Fifth Column!" screamed the banners at mass rallies.

Blatant threats appeared as well. "Troublemakers have done the country too great a harm to be left unpunished," said the vice-premier. "Silesian water will crush their bones," threatened the party secretary of Upper Silesia. "No tolerance for the enemies of People's Poland," screamed banners and news-paper headlines. "We demand harsh punishment for the enemies of People's Poland." "Expose the culprits!" "Unmask the hidden enemies!" "Pack your suitcases, your end is nigh!" ran the headline for *Voice of the Young,* the weekly for "working youth." Anonymous phone calls woke people in the middle of the night: "The ovens are still in place" and "Remember Kielce?"[5] And phone calls from old-time friends: "The hiding place behind the cupboard is still there," "The cellar is still there," "The attic . . ."

Because the war waged by the People's Poland against the Jews had become obvious to everyone at that time, Kott had dropped his earlier plan to return to Poland and became a refugee like the rest of us. In April, I appeared in Berkeley at a public protest against the anti-Jewish hysteria in Poland. Miłosz spoke, too. A few days later, I got a letter:

> I'm writing to you because there was no time to talk at the meeting. First, let me congratulate you on your poems in *Kultura,* which are beautiful. Second, I promised you that I would explain why I didn't want the dedication. It had nothing to do with you or me personally. Simply, I am a professor in a department, which although not very favorably looked upon in Poland, still tried to maintain a certain exchange of instructors (Przybylska, Najder—both from Warsaw) and students. [Aleksander] Wat stayed in Berkeley for a year-and-a-half and that certainly was not well received by the [Polish] State Security. In any case, knowing the fantasies and gossip of Warsaw cafés, I tried to avoid supplying material for the legend that I am "the center" attracting all runaways. Your dedication would have added material to the legend, which of course, as you know, is absurd. That was the reason. Since then, the situation has changed. Nations probably have destinies and Poland's destiny is decades of émigré literature, which due to the new situation there, will now be reinforced by people like yourself, Jews and non-Jews alike. That whole evening [of the meeting] was surrealistically macabre. To incite anti-semitism in Poland, the country of Treblinka, it takes a band of bastards and idiots. The results could only be new poison and myth-making.

He always showed me understanding. Later he wrote, "I can imagine that this is an extremely difficult period for you, and all I can say by way of consolation is that it is subject to certain rules, and it takes the same course with everybody. But eventually it passes so that we can later smile at what had tormented us."

I would call it one of the paradoxes of the twentieth century that fate had brought us so close together—him, an aristocrat of the Polish landed gentry, and me, the son and grandson of Jewish dairy tenants. He admitted it himself in a letter (dated February 8, 1971):

> I am suffering very much, although it is something one could get used to over the decades. Therefore, "very much" is actually an exaggeration. I suffer because of both America and Poland. My situation is, by the way, as stupid as your situation, and I don't see much of a difference. The more so if you read a review by Gella of my book *Rodzinna Europa [Native Realm]* in the latest issue of the *Slavic Review*. I have read the second part of your "Ojczyzna" [Fatherland] in *Kultura.* It is very good writing, even better than the first part. It hasn't brought me relief, but *humanness [ludzkie;* emphasis in original] should not bring relief. I read the fragment about the tree to my son (who knows nothing about Jews and Poles but understands Polish). My elder son is married to a half-Jewish woman, but they couldn't care less about their parents' past: and we're here with our burdens.

The UCLA Slavic Department admitted everyone—the more students, the better—and everyone got good grades in the undergraduate classes. Yet only a few were allowed into the graduate school, and very few got an M.A. Out of eight candidates, only two passed, and only I got a high pass toward a Ph.D. I wanted to do my doctorate in Polish literature, particularly contemporary literature (for example, Marek Hłasko, the leader of our demoralized generation), but Slavic departments in the United States were dominated by Russian, and to choose Polish as one's area of study was risky. And so Professor Alexander Issatschenko took me for a walk.

"Look, who'll take care of you here? Who'll help you? Who'll need you?"

I wrote to Miłosz, but he could give me only a quarter of a slot. I would have flown there on wings and taken it, had I not had a wife and child, but as it was, I had no other choice but to stay under the "Russian occupation." Soon afterwards, he called to let me know that the University of Toronto needed a lecturer in Jewish literature in translation and that he had recommended me. I filled out the forms, but suddenly my wife rebelled: "I'm not emigrating anymore!"

ᴄ᷿

Working for the Polish Service of the Voice of America in Washington, D.C., during the 1970s and 1980s, I interviewed Miłosz on several occasions, and I was the first to get him on the phone when the news broke about his Nobel Prize. The media was confused about whether Miłosz was a Pole or a Lithuanian; I instantly became an expert, answering questions from all over the country. And, of course, I interviewed him each time he appeared in Washington as a Nobel laureate. He thought that American poetry is mostly incomprehensible because its "interiorization and subjectivization [*interioryzacja i subiektywizacja*] has caused a break in contact between the poet and the reader." He said that "Americans reading Polish poetry in translation are amazed by the amount of the objective, external world [depicted there], outside of the human being as the subject, not just a psychological state of mind and purely subjective perceptions." Off the record, he added, "You know, this is a very good country for poetry." I can guess what he meant, because I am from Poland and I have a degree in Russian literature, and so I know at least two other countries, in addition to America, where people feel the need for poetry.

Early in December 1993, in the fall/winter semester when I did a writer's workshop at Warsaw University, I attended a public conference on democracy at the Staszic Palace of the Polish Academy of Sciences. I was late, and so I sneaked in and took a seat in one of back rows. Suddenly, an umbrella poked my back. I turned around: it was Miłosz—very amused by my surprised face. For both of us, it was incredible to see each other in Poland. Just a few years earlier, neither of us could have even imagined such a scene. He took me to lunch to a nearby restaurant named Staropolska (Old Polish), quite appropriate for such occasion, and our vodka there tasted better than ever before.

I liked to amuse him, and I did so the last time I saw him, in his Kraków apartment, where I went to thank him in person for his generous support of the American publication of my collection *Drohobycz, Drohobycz and Other Stories* (Penguin Books, 2002). "An attempt to bring to life innumerable Jewish existences lost in the Shoah. The passion of the author deserves a large readership in many languages and countries," he wrote in a blurb for the book. He was wearing dark glasses after his eye surgery, and he walked with a cane. I told him he looked mysterious, like a character from a Hitchcock movie, which amused him. Photographs of his beautiful granddaughter and a baby great-granddaughter were on the coffee table. He told me that his granddaughter had married a Jew in New York.

"Congratulations!" I exclaimed, making him laugh again.

"And what about you, do you still work for that radio?" he asked, remembering my complaints that I had not enough time to read and write.

"Oh, no, I retired years ago, no more excuses," I said, which made him laugh once more.

He could not see well because of the surgery, but he clumsily signed for me his "Orpheus and Eurydice," the poem that moved me to tears because I had met both of his Eurydices and had lost one of my own in the same way. The San Francisco poem that was to be dedicated to him ended with melancholic lines: "And San Francisco will only spread his arms / when the Pacific inundates our breasts."

I knew he did not want to die there, and I am glad that my prophecy did not come to pass.

Notes

1. Henryk Grynberg, "Nasz Pacyfik," *Kultura*, April 4, 1968.

2. All the remaining citations for this chapter are taken from Henryk Grynberg, *Uchodźcy* (Warsaw: Świat Książki, 2004) and *Memorbuch* (Warsaw: W. A. B., 2000), both translated from the Polish by Theodosia Robertson and the author; and Henryk Grynberg, *Ciąg dalszy* (Warsaw: Świat Książki, 2008).

3. [The Sejm is the lower house of the Polish parliament.—Ed.]

4. [In Gomułka's mind (and in the minds of many others in Poland), Jews were not Poles.—Ed.]

5. [The remark refers to the 1946 Kielce pogrom.—Ed.]

Uneasy Exile

MORTON MARCUS

The gates of grammar closed behind him.

Search for him now in the groves and wild forests of the dictionary.

—Czesław Miłosz

In the fall of 1968, a few months after I had moved to Santa Cruz, I took part in a reading with Ronald Johnson, Dennis Schmitz, and Jack Marshall at the University of California, Berkeley. The occasion was the publication of *The Young American Poets,* the first all-inclusive anthology of new American poetry in ten years, and the publisher had given the book a big national publicity campaign, featuring poets in the anthology reading in the sections of the country where they lived.

For our reading, one of three in the Bay Area, the publisher hired Kenneth Rexroth to be master of ceremonies (and guide) and treated us to a dinner at a restaurant of Rexroth's choice. Rexroth chose a wonderful French bistro in Berkeley, fussed over the menu as if we were his children, and ordered several bottles of expensive wine while regaling the four of us with wonderful tales and some highly unorthodox opinions, such as his comment that the anthology was already passé, since the poetry of the future would be "off the page," or completely based on performance.

Slightly inebriated but in an elated mood, the five of us made our way by foot to the campus to find a crowd of three hundred to four hundred waiting for us in Wheeler Hall. I read second, after which there was an intermission and members of the audience, clucking their praises at what they had heard, crowded around us. One of their number, a middle-aged man with high cheekbones, pushed to the front of the others and stood quivering in front of me.

"You come home with me!" he demanded in a strong Slavic accent. Tears were coursing down his cheeks, and he had obviously been crying for some time.

I didn't know what to say and was as confused as the people around me.

"Come home with me!" he repeated.

"Well, thank you," I finally said, "but—"

"I open special wine for us," he interrupted me.

The crowd around us began to thin.

"I'd like to," I said, "but I have classes tomorrow and a long ride . . ."

The man straightened, regained his composure, and said, "Oh, you think I am weird"; he stalked away, heading for Rexroth, who was talking to several people. The man grabbed Rexroth by the arm and dragged him over to me. "Kenneth, introduce!" he commanded.

"Well, yes," said Rexroth in his most grandiose world-weary manner, as if bored by the man's feverish behavior. "Morton Marcus," he said, "this is Czesław Miłosz."

I was surprised but immediately understood the man's agitation. For my reading, I had selected a number of poems from my forthcoming book, citing the influence on it of post–World War II East European poetry, especially Polish poetry, and recommended Miłosz's anthology *Postwar Polish Poetry* to the audience. I was honored to meet him, and I grasped his hand warmly.

"Wonderful poetry," he said, obviously extremely moved. "Now you come home with me."

I refused again, once more citing my ride back to Santa Cruz that night and early classes the next day as my excuse, but we made an appointment for dinner at his house two weeks later.

In 1968, Miłosz was virtually unknown as a poet in the United States. His reputation here, if he had one, was based on a political volume in which he described the reasons for his defection from Communist Poland in 1951 and another volume, a novel, about the miseries of living under a Communist regime.

The first book, *The Captive Mind*, as well as the second, *Seizure of Power*, came out in the 1950s. Miłosz spent the remainder of the decade in Paris, where he had defected, struggling to support himself and his family, but since 1960 he had quietly taught in the Slavic Languages Department at Berkeley. Like many other artists living in the United States in political exile, he was renowned in his own country but unknown and ignored here.

Two weeks after the meeting in Wheeler, my wife and I and our two small daughters pulled up to Miłosz's house on Grizzly Peak Boulevard in Berkeley. It was a small house with a steep roof, set in a thicket of trees and foliage, and looked like a cottage out of a Grimm's fairy tale.

It was November, so darkness had already descended. Our knock on the thick wooden door was answered by Miłosz himself. He was excited to see us but dismayed at first by our arriving with our six- and one-year-olds in tow. I explained that we couldn't afford babysitters, and Miłosz, calling to his wife for assistance, good-humoredly found a place for the girls to amuse themselves, and the visit began in the way—I gathered from Miłosz's renewed enthusiasm—he imagined it should have started.

He formally introduced us to his wife, Janka, a striking woman with straight white hair and bangs, a sharp nose, and a kindly manner, who had taken the girls to play in the Miłoszes' youngest son's room. Then Miłosz opened one of the promised bottles of wine, and while Janka and Wilma talked in the kitchen, he hustled me to his study, where he told me, with a feverish emphasis I was beginning to suspect was his manner, about the new preface he was writing for the next edition of *Postwar Polish Poetry*, which Penguin was bringing out the following year.

It was written, he said, with me in mind. He had been impressed by my poetry, but he wanted to warn me—and other young poets—not to overuse mordant irony. Relying on such irony in one's poems, he said, was tantamount to accepting the horrors perpetrated by governments and individuals, since it implied in its tone and attitude an acceptance of them as the way the world worked. At times, irony is fine to warn the readers of impending political or social catastrophes, he said, but when the catastrophes occur, the poet has to sing songs of hope and redemption, for that, in the end, is the primal direction of the human spirit.

He spoke with an orator's vigor, and I was once more beside myself with humility and gratefulness that he would be so moved by my poems that he would write a warning to me and my generation concerning a dangerous path he was afraid we were following. I was so struck by his passionate words that the whole tenor of my work changed from then on. It was as if he had expunged sarcastic irony from my soul.

After he stopped talking, he calmed down, and all four of us spent a pleasant evening getting to know each other and talking about literature and the world. For the rest of the evening, Miłosz was not only composed and charming but also subdued, and I got the impression that his agitation at the reading and earlier in the evening had to do with the passionate warning he had delivered to me, like a wisdom figure out of some Slavic folk tale.

We visited the Miłoszes several times after that, and I remember on one occasion two months later how upset Czesław was about the strange death in Thailand of his friend Thomas Merton, the great Catholic contemplative. Miłosz was a Roman Catholic at heart, and his continued search for spiritual meaning in a world where moments of transcendent beauty implied a godhead amid the horrors of history and the dehumanization of science and technology can be understood in that context.

Certainly Miłosz's formidable intellect was fed and honed by a classic European Catholic education, as our conversations revealed early on, but it was his Slavic soul that drew me to him like a magnet. If he embodied the exile's isolation I had felt all my life, he also exemplified the Slavic personality in his passion as well as his intellect.

Nowhere are both attitudes more clearly voiced than in his poem "To Robinson Jeffers," where he delineates the difference between the Slavic and Anglo/Nordic temperaments. The poem is also an excellent example of Miłosz's methodology—a strong intellectual argument suffused with an intense concrete sensuousness. Or is it an intense concrete sensuousness suffused with a strong intellectual argument?

Although I thought I came to understand Czesław in our handful of meetings in 1968 and 1969, I was totally unprepared for the dramatic evening I was to spend with him in the spring of 1970.

_In 1970, I_ was the State Department's West Coast host for the great Yugoslav poet Vasko Popa. Through an enthusiastic Miłosz, I arranged the second of two readings in Northern California to take place at the Slavic Languages Department at UC Berkeley, and four nights after he arrived, Popa, his interpreter, and I found ourselves on the Berkeley campus.

Miłosz had primed his colleagues and students, and an audience of several hundred crowded into a small auditorium. Miłosz was very excited and, his face flushed, ran from one side of the room to the other, introducing Popa to one person here and another one there and making sure everything was in place for the reading. He had greeted Popa with a warm embrace and kept returning to him, saying several sentences in French before he would rush off again.

Vasko and I presented the same bilingual program we had at our first reading and, as before, received an enthusiastic response.

Afterward, Miłosz hurried us away from well-wishers and told me to drive to his house. When we arrived, we were greeted by what seemed like most of the audience that had been at the reading. Cars lined both sides of the narrow street; it seemed that more than a hundred people were jammed inside Miłosz's small fairytale-like cottage in the forested hills above Berkeley.

Miłosz had arrived before us and, with face still flushed, was moving with Janka from group to group, making sure everyone was taken care of. Several of the students came up to Popa, but most of them spoke neither Serbo-Croat nor French, and, his interpreter lost somewhere in the crowd, soon Vasko was ensconced alone on a sofa with a glass of red wine in either hand. Now that his responsibilities in California were over, he looked relaxed and pleased and stared in glassy-eyed exhaustion at the milling guests. His quiet contentment was disturbed only by Miłosz, who would break away from his duties as host to join Vasko and speak to him animatedly in French.

Miłosz was obviously keyed up by Popa's presence. I thought I understood his excitement. He and Vasko had been in the resistance against the Nazi invaders in their separate countries, neither one knowing about the other but both engaged in a common cause. Both of them had survived as well, while many of their friends had not, and each had gone on to be an important literary figure not only in his respective country but also throughout Europe. It made no difference to Miłosz, a staunch opponent of communism, what Popa's politics were. He and Popa shared a brotherly bond that was welded together by history—and blood.

For the most part, Popa listened to Miłosz, smiling and nodding. He seemed very comfortable talking to Miłosz, and his demeanor radiated affection. I watched the two of them with mounting emotions, pictures fluttering through my mind of haggard refugee faces and bombed-out cities.

The students strolled around the two men or sat in groups on the carpet, and it seemed that the world was going on around Popa and Miłosz, who were encapsulated in a bubble of time that none of the guests could understand or were willing to allow themselves to imagine, even though they certainly knew that both men had experienced some of the most traumatic historical events of the century.

The guests, in fact, seemed totally absorbed in their own concerns. Many of them wore white handkerchiefs as armbands, which identified them as demonstrators against the U.S. government's sending troops into Cambodia. This group was going straight from the party to the staging area of a huge protest march that was to take place the following morning.

Miłosz talked to Vasko more vehemently as the evening wore on, darting away to refill his glass or say goodnight to a departing guest. Soon he was more flushed than ever and slightly drunk. The party began to thin. Those who stayed were the students wearing white armbands. They stood talking in groups or chatted while seated on the floor. At one point, Miłosz, returning from refilling his glass, almost fell over one of the seated figures.

"What do you think you are doing?" he asked the person, a young man in a white shirt, who looked at him uncomprehendingly.

"What do you think you are doing with that armband?" Miłosz explained, swaying and pointing at the white handkerchief on the young man's arm. The young man looked down at his arm, then up at Miłosz.

"We are demonstrating against U.S. involvement in Cambodia."

"And what are you demonstrating *for?*" Miłosz retorted.

"For peace and love," replied a young girl seated in the group. Miłosz swayed, saliva flecking his lips, clearly belligerent.

"Love? Love for what?" he asked in a challenging voice.

The party had grown silent and everyone in the room was staring at Miłosz and the girl.

"Love for everything and everyone," the girl replied.

"I taught you better than that," Miłosz growled. "If you love everything and everyone, you love nothing. Love is selective."

The young man Miłosz had first interrogated came to the girl's rescue. "We demonstrate to stop the injustice going on in Vietnam and now Cambodia," he said.

Miłosz's face was crimson.

"Children!" he spat out. "You are children! You know nothing! If you marched in Poland or the Soviet Union, they would shoot you down."

The girl was now incensed and said, "What's wrong with love? It's the only way to stop what is going on. We have to love each other."

"Love, love, love!" mocked Miłosz, his voice rising to a shout. "Talk to me about love when they come into your cell one morning, line you all up, and say 'You and you, step forward. It's your time to die—unless any of your friends loves you so much he wants to take your place.'"

Shocked silence washed over the room. Miłosz blinked and swayed, his feet planted angrily. Then he hoisted himself erect and made his way over to Vasko, where, in agitated French, he translated what had just taken place. Vasko listened, nodding and smiling, his eyes half closed, balancing the two half-filled wine glasses on his knees.

The young man in the group Miłosz had just harangued snickered and murmured some words to the others, who laughed and turned toward Miłosz. Other chortles and snickers sprouted around the room. Miłosz almost certainly heard them but chose to ignore them and continued talking to Popa.

Once more I visualized the two of them encapsulated in a time bubble. In no way could the students fathom the agony as well as the anger that prompted Miłosz's words. It was an anger at the memory of millions of dead bodies, an agony felt for all those who had lost their lives in another time and place. At the same time, Miłosz seemed incapable of understanding the young people's commitment to their history and the lives they were seeing destroyed around *them*. It was one of those moments filled with tragic irony, the kind of irony Miłosz never abandoned in his work and which is all too poignantly a part of the human condition.

I continued to see Miłosz on and off, although my trips to the Bay Area became more infrequent as the years went on. After he won the Nobel Prize in 1980, Miłosz was extraordinarily busy, in demand everywhere, and I felt uncomfortable bothering him. When he came to read at the University of California, Santa Cruz, Miłosz asked specifically to see me, and at the party after his reading he asked the host to allow us to talk alone in an unused room.

He asked after me and was sorry to hear about my divorce; he told me that Janka was ill. It was a quiet meeting, a father asking after his long-absent son. A few years later, Bob Hass, who had become his reader as well as translator, plucked me out of an audience waiting for Miłosz to read in San Jose and told me Czesław wanted to see me backstage. There was a brief but warm meeting, and I congratulated him on the many honors that had been bestowed on him since I had last seen him.

Our last meeting was at the reception following another reading he gave, again in San Jose. It was 1989, and Miłosz was to fly to Poland several days later, his first visit to his homeland, I think, since his defection in Paris in 1951. Janka had died three years before, and Czesław had a new female partner who acted as organizer and go-between.

When I told her I was an old friend and wanted to say hello, she led me to him. His eyes were rheumy, and he had aged greatly. I said hello and realized he didn't know me. I tried to spark his memory by briefly recalling our first meeting in Wheeler Hall and Popa's reading, but he didn't remember what I was referring to. I smiled warmly, shook his hand, and took my leave.

Oh, yes, I was embarrassed—and feeling the stares of the people around him. A few moments later, his new companion, who later became his wife, came up to me and said Czesław wanted to see me. When I went up to him, he had tears in his eyes and held his arms out to embrace me. "Morton, Morton, of course I remember you," he said. We talked for several minutes, and he asked me to write and send my new book to him. I did, and he wrote back the day before he left for Poland. It was good to see me, he said in the letter, and he liked the book, a sequence of poems about my ancestors in Poland and Russia, but he remembered nothing about Popa's reading or my visit to his house.

In Miłosz's last comment, the irony he had warned me about twenty years before is painfully evident—although it is of a different order than sarcasm. As an exile in a foreign land and an alien culture, he returned again and again in his poetry and essays to memories of the Poland in which he had grown to manhood—a Poland that had vanished first with the Nazi invasion and then the Communist takeover.

In fact, memory is one of the major subjects of Miłosz's poetry, along with spiritual decay and the search for a moral foothold in the ruins of twentieth-century history. That he would not remember meeting such an important fellow poet as Popa, who represented a connection with that vanished world, a meeting that must have been one of the more memorable events of his first decade in an America that ignored him and his country's history, is disarmingly ironic, and I can't help thinking that my rescuing that memory with this remembrance may be the kindest act I could perform for him—and, of course, that is an irony, too.

Note

From Morton Marcus, *Striking through the Masks: A Literary Memoir* (Capitola, CA: Capitola Book Company, 2008).

Wanderer

ALEXANDER SCHENKER

I was invited for the 1969/70 academic year to the Slavic Department of the University of California at Berkeley. In all honesty, there was no good reason for me to accept this invitation. I was busy preparing an anthology of Polish short stories; all necessary materials were within easy reach, either at home or in the library of Yale University, where I taught Slavic linguistics. Therefore, I was not at all surprised when the dean, after hearing my request for a year-long leave of absence, smiled and asked, "Wanderlust?" Embarrassed, I nodded, unwilling to acknowledge that no scholarly considerations attracted me there; the sole magnet that drew me to Berkeley was Czesław Miłosz.

I had met him two years earlier in New York, at a poetry reading that featured several prominent New York poets, with Denise Levertov among them. Miłosz had translated her poems and dedicated to her a sizeable entry in his *Inne abecadło* (Further ABC's).[1] The spacious Young Men's Hebrew Association on Lexington Avenue, which rented out its very large auditorium for various cultural events, was packed to the rafters. Miłosz read in Polish and English, from time to time turning to one of his American colleagues for help in reading translations. It was my first time listening to Miłosz. His voice was loud and unaffected, and he read with obvious relish and wit. Some may think that this reading style, so different from the solemn declamation that was taught to us in school, is not befitting for poems of such density and depth. Yet today it is impossible for me to think of them and not hear Miłosz's unique intonation, with his feet stomping and his stentorian laughter booming.

At that time, I was barely familiar with Miłosz's writing. As if answering my childish prayers, World War II interrupted my general education in the ninth grade of a Polish high school. As a result, I had to spend my formative years outside Poland, and I did not have a chance to fill the gaps in my knowledge of Polish literature beyond what I had learned as a fourteen-year-old youth. Miłosz entered my universe only in the 1950s after his *Captive Mind* gained international renown. I became fascinated by his *Treatise on Poetry* not only because of its unusual idea—the analysis of origins and state of contemporary Polish poetry set in verse—but also because of the conciseness and clarity of the exposition. Miłosz's poem became my first introduction to Polish literature of the interwar period.

All the offices of the Slavic Department in Berkeley were on the same floor. So Miłosz and I became neighbors at the university, and at the first opportunity, I reminded him of our New York encounter. In the course of the conversation, it turned out that we had many common acquaintances, especially in Paris, in the circle of my childhood friend Olga Scherer— among them, the painter Jan Lebenstein, literary critic Konstanty Jeleński, Father Józef Sadzik from the Center of the Pallottine Fathers, Zygmunt Hertz from *Kultura,* and Zbigniew Herbert. Herbert and I had become friends in 1968 when he stopped at Yale on his way to City University of Los Angeles for a yearlong appointment. I also met a lot of Miłosz's friends and colleagues during my visits to Poland in 1965 and 1967 when I was collecting material for my anthology. So we had a lot to talk about when we met at the university, usually in the swimming pool, where Miłosz swam almost daily.

These meetings brought us closer together, and before long I became a frequent guest at the Miłoszes' home. They often invited me for modest dinners and conversations at their home, situated in the scenic hills of Berkeley with a postcard-perfect view of the Golden Gate Bridge, which seemed suspended from the sky when morning mist seeped under it toward the Bay. Even Janka Miłosz, who had a reputation as a person rather aloof and discriminating in her choice of friends, was always warm and open toward me. Our friendship was a result of a confluence of circumstances. It was partly due to my independent position in a different university, which ensured that my admiration for Miłosz's writing was unbiased and without any self-interest. It was also helpful that I had no relationships within the Polish literary circles of Warsaw and London, that our political convictions were relatively close, and that the Miłoszes led a rather solitary life.

America is not an easy country for foreigners to settle in. At first blush, Americans appear easygoing, even friendly, but closer encounters reveal that it is a country of social alienation. Interpersonal contacts outside the family are generally superficial and tend to be limited to a workplace or to a group of people who have similar interests but lack emotional ties. Polite *how are you*'s, *nice to meet you*'s and assurances of desire to meet again for lunch are often no more than a simple courtesy.

It is true that Miłosz valued solitude, but he was not a hermit by nature. Always sensual in his desires, he longed for personal contacts based on common interests and mutual affinity. He couldn't deal with the invisible boundaries that the locals drew around themselves. Cocktail parties, particularly numerous at the beginning and the end of an academic year and during the holiday season, were insufferable for the poet. With every fiber of his being, he detested the small talk—in other words, idle blather—that was the prevailing atmosphere at such parties, and out of boredom, he sought a respite at the bar. He equally disliked formal dinners where he felt obliged to stay till the end in the assigned seat, often bored by his neighbors.

He got on with students the best. He attended their meetings and gatherings; during lectures, he never disparaged their comments and questions, never mind how naïve they were. He never brought himself to reprimand them, even when they hurt him. That happened during the famous student revolution at the end of the 1960s. With great distress, he watched well-dressed kids toss library books out the windows—but perhaps remembering his own youth, the only criticism that he allowed himself to utter was a bitter Russian saying: "What makes them rage is that they have too much."

He must have been born for the stage. In Polish, there are no good matches for the English terms *performer* or *entertainer*, but it seems to me that these words would reflect precisely Miłosz's public image. He gladly accepted invitations to speak at colleges and universities, even though they cost him a lot of time, which he valued above all. But reading his poetry aloud and contact with the audience thrilled him. He felt the need for success, and he needed to know that he was successful. This knack for acting would come in handy during his lectures at the university, where, by his own admission, he liked to clown around. He was the first one to laugh at his own puns and asides, keeping the atmosphere in the classroom easygoing and relaxed. The popularity of his lectures testifies to the success of his method.

However, even a good relationship with students could not satisfy his needs. He longed for contact with a Polish readership and with the writing confraternity, or as he used to put it, he longed for "intellectual ping-pong." He was tormented by fears that his writing was nothing more than spelling exercises, that no one read his poems, and that, instead of sending them to *Kultura* magazine, he just as well could throw them into the ocean, which shimmered below with immutable indifference. He undoubtedly was aware that his writing reached Poland, but it was little consolation for him, for he craved fast, immediate feedback. As an example, allow me to cite an episode that occurred barely two months after my arrival. One day, Miłosz came to my home with a freshly published volume of poetry, *Miasto bez imienia* (City without a name), titled after an eponymous poem in the collection. In the inscription, he asked for my "linguistic evaluation." I put this skinny volume on my desk, but the next morning I left for a few days without having a chance to take a look at the poems. After I came back, I spent some time trying to figure out what he meant by his request (today I am surprised at myself that I did not realize right away that he was primarily interested in my opinion on the poem "My Faithful Mother Tongue"). Evidently, the lack of prompt feedback exasperated Miłosz. He came to me again and asked me with bitterness how I would feel if I gave someone my work for criticism and was met with indifference. I was devastated by these accusations; I had not yet realized that more than literary analysis, Miłosz craved the knowledge that his poems found a reader and met with due approval. I understood a few years later how little he was in need of my remarks when I received from him typescripts of his poems accompanied by a request for comments. Still smarting from our Berkeley misunderstanding, I promptly replied, yet just a couple of weeks later, I found the poems on the pages of *Kultura* in their original versions. Still, memories of my only conflict with Miłosz haunt me to this day, for I know that unawares I opened his most painful wound, his "somber . . . self-love."[2]

I knew that Miłosz was superstitious; therefore, I never dared mention a possibility of his being nominated for the Nobel, although such a speculation circulated quite openly by then. Still, I was confident (and for good reason, as it turned out ten years later) that a simple comment on the "nobelization" process did not warrant a jinx from whatever dark forces were at play. Therefore, I allowed myself to remind him how important it was to have good English and Swedish translations of his work. As an example, I cited the case of a Bosnian writer, Ivo Andrić, who received a Nobel just a few years after his *Bridge on the Drina* appeared in a Swedish translation. I did it deliberately because I was satisfied neither with the quantity nor with the quality of existing English renditions of Miłosz's poetry, which, unlike Herbert's or Tadeusz Różewicz's, does not lend itself easily to translation. Although clear as crystal in his prose, in his poetry Miłosz makes his exposition denser and emphasizes the phonetic aspect of the verse, especially in his frequent references to the language of bygone centuries and to dialects. The fact that, even in the loosely fitting garment of the English tongue, Miłosz achieved such an enthusiastic following among international readers and literary critics is yet another measure of his greatness.

Miłosz's 1967 poetry collection *Wiersze*, published in London, by then had sold out; therefore, I suggested publication of a new volume to our common Czech friend, Ladislav Matejka, who was the director of the University of Michigan Slavic Publications. Matejka liked the idea, but he insisted on an English-language introduction, without which he would have a hard time securing a grant for the publication. The consideration that such an introduction could influence the Nobel committee was also a factor. I assumed this responsibility, and in 1976, to the great satisfaction of all three of us, *Utwory poetyckie: Poems*, selected by the poet himself, appeared in print.

After I returned to Yale, we kept in touch through correspondence, but because we were so far apart geographically, our personal contacts were rare. Therefore, I was overjoyed when Miłosz moved to Kraków, where my wife and I had an apartment and where we used to go at least once a year. I would always pay him a visit, and we would stroll to one of the cafés on the Market Square, passing on our way by old-fashioned horse cabs whose coachmen dozed under St. Mary's tower.[3] On our way, we met scores of people he knew, but also complete strangers who would bow to the poet. When I saw the smiling face of the wanderer who had happily reached his safe harbor, I could not help harking back to Miłosz at the time when he was still halfway on his journey and, with his head hanging low during his solitary walks under the eucalyptus trees on Grizzly Peak Boulevard, pondered the source of Evil. At such times, I had no doubt that God exists.

Translated by Alla Makeeva-Roylance.

Notes

Slightly adapted from a piece included in *Czesław Miłosz: In Memoriam* (Kraków: Znak, 2004).

1. Miłosz's *Abecadło Miłosza* (1997) and *Inne abecadło* (1998) were abridged and published in a single volume in English as *Miłosz's ABC's*, trans. Madeline G. Levine (New York: Farrar, Straus and Giroux, 2001). The Levertov entry is included in the English edition, on pages 180–83.

2. This phrase comes from the last stanza of the "Lenten Song," inserted into a very long poem titled "From the Rising of the Sun." It's a lament over the transience of things and a poet's futile attempt to counteract, or slow down, their evanescence.

Mirrors, shadows on the screen,
Are all that can be sensed and seen.
My face, kind by the light of day,
Will all too soon fade away.
Light flashes and goes out above
The somber hues of my self-love.

This stanza, translated by Czesław Miłosz, Leonard Nathan, and Robert Hass, appears in Czesław Miłosz, *The Collected Poems, 1931–1987* (New York: Ecco, 1988), 278. The translation cited here is by A. M. Schenker.

3. This phrase is taken from the first line of the *Treatise on Poetry*. Translation by Czesław Miłosz and Robert Hass in Miłosz, *Collected Poems*, 112.

Seeing the Bear

LILLIAN VALLEE

For me, Czesław Miłosz was never the gentle Berkeley professor emeritus described as a "silver-haired charmer with great bushy eyebrows and bright blue eyes," whose drawing power at poetry readings was compared to that of a rock star in one *San Francisco Chronicle* write-up.[1] I am grateful to have known him before all the big prizes began coming his way: before the Neustadt International Prize for Literature in 1978, before the Nobel Prize in Literature in 1980, and before he became lionized and idealized and mythologized out of a more problematic existence. I write this not because I begrudge him the hard-earned peace and joy and recognition that came after the prizes but because the most important things I learned from him and his work, I learned as a student, at a moment in which he thought he was utterly defeated, heartsick with what he thought were personal and professional failings, and because he talked about all this openly, with regret and tenderness, exposing a vulnerability and the price he had paid for his vocation. "I would give it all up in a second," he said to me once in reference to his work, "for happiness in my personal life."

U.S. poet laureate Robert Hass, his friend and translator, once told me that Miłosz was like an old growth forest. He didn't elaborate, but I knew what he meant: you could wander in Miłosz's presence, in his mind, in his work and find the harsh abiding truths, the wild and uncontrollable primal urges, the bewildering and devastating beauty. He could be volatile, full of ferocious anger at a perceived slight, or just as suddenly playful, exploding into laughter at his own (usually dark) jokes. He could be the wizened, hypersensitive, generous paterfamilias or an alcoholic making cutting remarks. For me, the relationship had what Thomas Merton called a "terrifying ambiguity" that characterizes all profoundly transforming experiences.[2]

Merton once gave a lecture on William Faulkner's short story "The Bear," in which Merton traced the various stages of the protagonist's development and spiritual growth in relation to an old and mutilated bear. The boy (a prototype for Miłosz's Thomas in *The Issa Valley*?) learns how to sense, track, and finally see the wild creature that becomes for him the vehicle for contact with some transcendent truth that is, simultaneously, a key to his own identity. The lecture on cassette, which was sent to me by some kind person who remained anonymous, reminded me of the seven years I spent as a graduate student under Miłosz's tutelage.[3] To *see* the bear and to *be seen by* the bear, the boy must gradually divest himself of everything he has learned from experienced hunters in preparing for the bear's capture. In the final stage, he gives up the gun, the watch, the compass, the stick. The boy must lose himself in the woods to have the encounter—only to have the bear return the boy to where he began, no longer the child he was. My years of grappling with Miłosz have the flavor of a similar kind of initiation.

By the time I had decided to undertake graduate study in Slavic languages and literatures at the University of California, Berkeley, Czesław Miłosz had already been there a decade. My parents were Poles who had spent the war years as teenaged forced laborers in Germany, and my oldest brother and I were both born in displaced persons camps in that country. These were camps set up for people who had found themselves in various zones occupied by Allied forces. Those who could not return to their homelands were sponsored by charitable organizations in various countries and shipped to their new countries of residence after a battery of screenings.

I grew up in Detroit, a city with a large Polish population, and my first language had been Polish, but when my parents moved the family from Michigan to California, we lost the community of native speakers that kept the language alive, and it was not until I was a student at UC Berkeley that I spent years reclaiming my mother tongue.

My interest in Poland was rekindled when, as an undergraduate in English, I was taking an honors course in James Joyce as well as classes in German literature. The stories in *The Dubliners* were intimately familiar; I began to think about parallels between Poland and Ireland—the role of the Roman Catholic Church, my own upbringing, and the deforming weight of martyrdom and nationalism. I wrote a quirky honors thesis that consisted of fishing out the Polish from Joyce's *Finnegan's Wake*. Reading novels by Günther Grass and Eduard Von Keyserling also returned me to Poland and the Baltic states because Grass wrote about his memories of Danzig (the Polish Gdańsk) and Von Keyserling about German aristocracy in what had been ethnic Lithuania.

I remember two other events that kept the idea of studying Polish and Polish literature before me. The first were the Polish bread riots of shipyard workers protesting price increases in Gdańsk in December 1970 (many were murdered); the other was a tiny blurb in a San Francisco newspaper announcing the publication of Miłosz's *History of Polish Literature*. I cut the announcement out of the paper. A trip to Poland after graduation in the summer of 1971 resulted in the decision to enter "limited status" in the Department of Slavic Languages and Literatures at UC Berkeley. Limited status allowed graduates to make up undergraduate requirements in a subject other than their major to enter graduate school in the new field. I was beginning to hear the rustling in the woods.

I first met Czesław Miłosz during the fall semester in 1971. His appearance and accent struck me as exotic, Eastern. During our first meeting, he was reserved, perhaps even wary. I was twenty-one; he was sixty. I knew nothing about him as a writer or poet. I had nothing but an inchoate love for a country and a language I knew little about and a hunger for older people who somehow embodied the history I was interested in. My three siblings and I grew up without any extended family. We never met our grandparents, and they, in turn, never saw their children after parting with them during the Second World War; my mother refused to take her children back to a Poland she was convinced would forever be war-torn. For many reasons, Miłosz did not really lend himself to being a grandfather surrogate, and it amuses me now to think I had that expectation.

I found out quickly that Miłosz did not have a high regard for Polish Americans in general and for Polish American students in particular. He saw Polish Americans as unformed, as primitive, or as straw fires, passionate for the short haul but without the resilience of Lithuanians, whose doggedness was legendary. Polish American students were notoriously unreliable, to his way of thinking—flawed, undisciplined. He had had his share of bad experiences: incomplete work, theses left unfinished. He did not seem to take much personal interest in his students. Despite our collaboration on various projects, never in those seven years did he ask me about my parents or our family history. Maybe he had heard all the stories he needed to hear of immigrant sorrows, but eventually I realized that all the assumptions he was making about my family were simply untrue.

Yet in examining my life, I had to agree that he was right about something— I was not a whole person. He told me once that I was a "maverick," and when I answered that remark with a puzzled look, he corrected himself and said "a dark horse." There was pride without healthy ambition, a profound distrust of normalcy, and an inability to project myself into the future that seemed linked obliquely to my parents' wartime experiences. My mother refused to plan anything in advance, because her girlhood had been organized down to the last detail yet, in a few weeks, her well-ordered and meaningful life was undone by uniformed men smashing through a semaphore.

My mother remembered the summer of 1939 as a time of unusual bounty in orchards and fields. The fruit trees had to be propped up to keep the branches from breaking. Lurking beneath my childhood was the conviction that a normal life was an aberration, a momentary respite. For years, my mother stockpiled soap and staples in the expectation that war or some calamity would return at any moment. Anything—the Cuban missile crisis or a tornado warning or just sirens wailing amid tall buildings in San Francisco—triggered panic. She had been a teenager fleeing the fiery destruction of Hamburg, and nothing could eject that hard pit of fear. I think now that my turning to Polish literature was an attempt to free myself from the hidden baggage of a war experienced secondhand.

Miłosz's classes and seminars were very small by university standards—a handful of graduate students and auditors. He delivered his lectures to an invisible point in the back of the room from handwritten notes in small composition notebooks. The lectures followed the material in his *History of Polish Literature*, with slight variations, and were not the breathtaking forays into intellectual history that I would come to know in lectures by Martin Malia or William Bouwsma—or even in Miłosz's Dostoevsky lectures much later. What distinguished Miłosz's lectures on Polish literature, however, was a sense of commitment, of loyalty to something I couldn't grasp in its entirety, a specific ethos that he called "private obligations" that had to do with the same "old verities and truths of the heart" that Merton found in Faulkner: "Love and honor and pity and pride and compassion and sacrifice . . . the capacity to endure well grief and misfortune and injustice and then endure again."[4]

Privately Miłosz complained about the poor sales of his *History of Polish Literature* and his first volume of translated poetry. He showed me the royalty slip for the *History;* if I remember correctly, barely a dozen volumes had been ordered by libraries. Sometimes he blamed the Polish community for its lack of interest in his work and in its own literature. I was beginning to see the mutilated paw prints.

In the small seminars, I was getting the interdisciplinary education I had sought, because there was no way to study Polish literature without also studying Poland's history, including politics and its religious and ethnic history. I received a Stanford-Warsaw Exchange Fellowship to study in Poland for the academic year 1972/73. After the year I spent in Poland, Miłosz warmed considerably; he was eager for news, and he liked reliving Poland and Polish literature through fresh eyes. Miłosz's contact with Poland was mainly through his visits to Paris and the émigré publishing house Instytut Literacki. Miłosz's defection in a political firestorm in the early fifties made it impossible for him to return to Poland until after he had received the Nobel Prize.

From this period, I remember an incident that struck me as particularly silly. Once, when he took to wearing a youthful jean outfit (snug pants, jean jacket, red bandana)—I think he simply wanted to look more "with it"—he complained of being followed around by a gay guy who thought Miłosz needed a partner. I was recruited to "rescue" him by calling him out of class early and by walking back with him to his office to demonstrate his heterosexuality!

With students, Miłosz did not engage in self-promotion, and it was during some independent work in the library that I came across his books and those of his cousin Oscar Milosz. *Native Realm (Rodzinna Europa)* was available in English, and I must have read it at least a dozen times; *Dolina Issy* (Issa Valley) was still untranslated, and reading it required constant and grueling vocabulary work. In the process, I acquired some rudimentary nature literacy, so studded were the first pages with the names of Polish birds and plants I knew nothing about. As I learned more about his essays and poetry and asked questions, I began to tinker with translating from Polish into English.

For Miłosz's sixty-third birthday, I toiled over a translation of another favorite work, "The World: (Naïve Poems)." He was mortified because the translations were so bad. "Where did you get that *sage* grouse?" he asked with genuine exasperation about a bird known as the western capercaillie or wood grouse. Nonetheless, he began entrusting me with editorial and translation tasks, something he did with many students and colleagues. Many outstanding translators—among them Catherine Leach, Louis Iribarne, and Richard Lourie—served an apprenticeship with Miłosz.

I began to edit some of the essays that were compiled in *Emperor of the Earth,* for which I also translated a piece called "Brognart." My first version of this translation elicited another irritated response: "Why, this reads like the work of a *beginning* translator!" That sounded logical to me; that's exactly what I was. Whatever loyalty to the text held me back the first time vanished in the retranslation. I finally understood that I had to make the text come alive in English, even if I had to re-contour the original.

I worked very hard to polish one essay in the collection, changing most of the language and even rewriting the text for clarity, and when Miłosz got it back, he said, "Hmm, my English was pretty good when I wrote this." He was completely oblivious to the changes, which made me think even he had his brief moments of self-delusion.

During this time, he began to open up and to confide in me. Life at home was difficult. His affairs had made relations with his wife thorny;

his children, he said, showed no interest in his work. He felt belittled and berated at home because he had violated too much trust and too many expectations to satisfy his pansexuality, which seemed to require no specific object. He lamented being an absentee father. "If I were any other kind of worker, I would add texture to the family when I returned from my job," he told me. "But I am there, and I am inaccessible and that adds very little to family life." He also thought of himself as an indecisive person: "All my troubles come from my not being able to make up my mind," he would say. His honesty was powerful, disarming.

We were not lovers, but he talked a lot about his love affairs, especially about a woman he had loved in Wilno (now Vilnius) when he was a young man. They had conceived a child out of wedlock, and he had left her out of overweening ambition. He could not forgive himself for rejecting her at such a vulnerable time. He had wanted to leave his mark on the world and Wilno was simply a small, provincial town, inadequate to his high aspirations. When the Second World War broke out, he had returned to Wilno to find her, but it was too late. She was already pregnant with another man's child, and Miłosz returned to Warsaw. When I was awarded a Fulbright Fellowship and was about to return to Poland in 1976, he told me to tell people that I was his illegitimate daughter. I bristled at the suggestion at the time, but I think that on a symbolic level he wanted to compensate for a lost child (maybe a daughter?) and also to make it easier for me to have access to people in Poland who understood him and his work. He also saw that my interest in his work, his past, was passionate and genuine, and perhaps this is the way he wanted to honor it.

While I was in Poland on the Fulbright, Miłosz wrote me many frank letters about his daily life, encounters with various other writers, and so forth, and I would write to him about readings I had gone to and about life in Warsaw. I treasured the letters because they were full of affection and curiosity. I remember one, in particular, on which he drew a heart with a red crayon under his signature.

In June 1977, after my Fulbright year was over, I traveled by train through the Polish countryside and over the eastern border toward the Lithuanian capital of Vilnius. I spent the few days that were allowed to foreigners in Soviet Lithuania and learned a great deal about what had befallen the city of Miłosz's youth. It was still virtually an occupied city (on the days I visited, Soviet troops were engaged in maneuvers) in which residents were fighting valiantly, some openly and others through the underground press, to sustain their cultural heritage. When I returned and told him about my trip, he was upset, saying he would have advised against it if I had asked him. And that's probably why I didn't. I needed to confront the Wilno of Miłosz's poetry with postwar Vilnius to understand what had survived and what had been lost and what poetry could sustain in those conditions. I had elaborated an earlier notion of the city, from its compelling presence in his poetry, as a point of contact with the divine. He saw the trip as tacit recognition of an illegitimate regime.

In 1978, Miłosz was awarded the Neustadt International Prize for Literature, the "little Nobel," and I was hired to teach at the University of Wisconsin that fall. The last big project we worked on together, in addition to a small volume of poems entitled *Bells in Winter,* was the special issue of *World Literature Today* (1978) devoted to Miłosz and his work. I put together a chronology of his life, translated essays by Polish literary critics, wrote one of my own about *The Issa Valley,* and earned high marks from both Miłosz and the Estonian editor of *World Literature Today,* Ivar Ivask. It was a moment of being apprehended; the bear was watching, but I had yet to see him. I was beginning to use the tools I had acquired, and I could now see how I could be of use at the intersection of two cultures, two languages. I was also beginning to understand the scale of the work and the sacrifice it had required, but I was far from possessing the knowledge it would take to assess the richness of Miłosz's multidimensional oeuvre.

The day Miłosz won the Nobel Prize, he called me to say that two people had given him wholehearted support during the most difficult time—me and Renata Gorczyńska. Afterwards, however, he asked me to return the letters he had written to me, saying he was worried that his family members might be offended by his offhand remarks. The letters harbored complaints that are pretty standard fare in family life, but he had written the letters in absolute trust, and so I told him I would return them. I read them one last time and sent them off. I had my own children and understood how painful it might be to read something a parent had written in a dark moment that did not represent in any way a parent's devotion. Shortly thereafter, I ran into someone organizing Miłosz's letters for sale to Yale's Beinecke Library. She told me she had been reading my postcards and letters and how much she enjoyed them. I wrote to Miłosz about this, disturbed that he hadn't reciprocated the respect shown for his privacy. He took my observation to heart and asked the library to put the letters out of public access until a later date.

What followed was a series of glories and defeats, disappointments and estrangements. To Miłosz's chagrin, I lost the job at the University of Wisconsin because I could not finish my dissertation within the contractual time. I am sure he saw it as surrendering a valuable and authoritative position from which to influence Polish letters. I made up for it somewhat with a stint as a freelance translator; during that time, I translated over a dozen volumes from Polish literature, and I know that he especially valued the three volumes of my imperfect but spirited translation of Witold Gombrowicz's literary *Diary.* Yet translating Polish into English was not as satisfying as translating experience into language, into English, my second and, for better or worse, the only language that could offer me both distance and precision. And I finally understood the poet's vocation as the cobbling together of all the disparate pieces of a life into a meaningful whole that would have value wherever he or she was.

I did finally finish the dissertation, not on Polish anti-utopian literature but on the works I loved for their primordial power and resonance: Miłosz's *Issa Valley;* his cycle of naïve, wartime poems, "The World"; and much of his later poetry. In 1984, I settled in Modesto, in the Great Central Valley of California, and thus began a bioregional adventure that still has me in its thrall.

The last long letter Czesław wrote to me was dated April 10, 1999. It reads as follows:

Dear Lillian,

[. . .] The large font is for my eyes because my vision is failing. To be eighty-eight years old is to be, alas, constantly aware of it. Actually I am writing to you because of your Modesto and the Central Valley, whose discovery and assimilation by you may, in fact, be the highest contribution of my books.

I think that I should write to you about how *The Issa Valley* bore fruit because only you will be able to appreciate this. A foundation called the Ceslavo Miloso Gimtines Fondas, that is, The Foundation for [the Preservation of] Miłosz Family Places, is no longer just an entity on paper because, after overcoming numerous bureaucratic obstacles, the only surviving building (in addition to the park), an enormous old granary or silo, will be restored in my place of birth, that is, in Szetejnie. In it will be a lecture hall, and upstairs, guest rooms. The academic meetings arranged there will take up topics touched on in my books, that is, quite a broad spectrum of issues for Lithuanian and Polish scholars. Perhaps some day you will take part in one of them. The most important thing, however, is that the area, its history, will draw historians and also that this stretch of the Nevezis River valley will have some ecological opportunities, such as preserving the old oaks in Sventybrastis, where I was baptized. Not everyone is allowed to live to an age when honors are realized in practical ways. It's an odd feeling.

A few years ago in Szetejnie I became the heir to whom ownership of the manor was solemnly returned, though, in reality, it was only ten hectares of the very heart of the property and the park. For twenty-four hours I was a member of the landed gentry, after which I transferred ownership to the foundation. Now a renovation is underway according to the plans drawn up by a Kaunas architect and by mid-June the building should have a roof; then there will be an official ceremony in which the president of Lithuania and I will take part.

The valley itself is beautiful but the fields alongside are empty because all the neighboring villages were deported to Siberia.

Of course, while thrashing around in life I never expected that what befell my beloved writer Selma Lagerlöf, author of [*The Wonderful Adventures of*] *Nils Holgersson*—whose country house was preserved as a museum that I visited during one of my trips to Sweden—would also happen to me.

Greetings and thanks for everything you have done.

Czesław Miłosz

P.S. In Sventybrastis, I recently visited Magdalena's grave.

Magdalena was the mistress of a popular priest in *The Issa Valley*. When she was exiled for flaunting the relationship and creating a scandal, she killed herself with rat poison and then proceeded to haunt the parish. Her body was exhumed by the parishioners, and a stake was put through her heart, after which the haunting ceased. Miłosz told me he had based the literary account of Magdalena on a real event.

Perhaps it was in visiting Sventybrastis that the illegitimate daughter could finally accept her irregular status and *see* the bear, which she learned was nothing more than understanding the fidelity a poet has to a bend in the river, to a staircase leading to a small wooden church, or to a gravestone marking an imperfect love.

Notes

This contribution is a segment of a longer essay entitled "Meditations on Lithuania."

1. Jesse Hamlin, "A Poet Gives Witness, A Crowd Falls Silent," *San Francisco Chronicle*, February 4, 2000, C-1.

2. Thomas Merton, *The Bear: The Voice of Thomas Merton Recorded Live at Gethsemani*, cassette recording (Kansas City, Mo.: Credence Communications, 1987).

3. Ibid.

4. Ibid.

The Exile Who Rejected Pathos

IRENA GRUDZIŃSKA GROSS

Reading Czesław Miłosz and meeting Czesław Miłosz were for me two radically different things.

When I was a high school student in Warsaw in the 1960s, Miłosz was a forbidden poet. I still managed to read his poems. I owed this to my future husband's mother, Hanna Szumańska-Grossowa, herself a poet, who knew Miłosz and loved his poetry. She used to tell stories about him—how, in war-torn Warsaw, he resisted the pompous, pseudo-patriotic posturing that was such a temptation for young men humiliated by the occupation of their country. The well-used volume she lent me contained his wartime poems. It was named *Ocalenie* (Rescue). Miłosz became for me a war poet.

In 1975, soon after I came to the United States, I traveled with my future husband, Jan Gross, to California, to see Berkeley and pay homage to Miłosz. I expected a venerable old man, a solemn exiled poet. Instead, we were greeted on the Berkeley campus by a sun-tanned, handsome, jeans-clad professor, happy to see young visitors and ready for beer and gossip. In his antique-looking, brown, shiny leather briefcase, he had some student papers and the latest issue of the Warsaw literary monthly *Twórczość.* We immediately began to quarrel about a short story from that issue. The story, written by a youngish author, was a bitter mockery of an earlier text by an older respected writer. Knowing that fresh immigrants had a horror of censorship, Miłosz declared categorically that literature has to console and give pleasure, not criticize. He was quite amused when we erupted in protests. It was then that I encountered for the first time his deep, unique laughter that later made me laugh with him as a matter of course. He was a war poet no more. He looked a happy man, a happy man from California.

Miłosz's life in Berkeley was not easy. He took care of his incapaci-tated wife, had lasting disagreements with one of his sons, and felt isolated from his Polish readers and misunderstood by American ones. Yet he told us nothing about it. He laughed; he joked; he walked with a long stride showing us around campus and bragged about swimming for an hour every single day. He was sixty-five years old and had some thirty years of verse-writing ahead of him.

What Miłosz demonstrated with his every gesture during that first meeting was a rejection of pathos. Neither in his behavior nor in his writ-ings did he ever slide into a romantic model of an unhappy poet. Such was his demeanor over the years, in the many meetings I had with him. This is why I was always so startled at my Polish friends, especially those from Kraków, who repeated that only his return to Poland, to their warmth and friendship, made Miłosz happy.

Miłosz was a suffering man, a man visited sometimes by depression, sometimes by discouragement. But he was also joyous, vital, disciplined in his work, appreciative of the pleasures of life, grateful for the gift of talent. His almost forty years of exile were a lesson in dignity. For us, then in Berkeley, he made any feeling of self-pity ridiculous. By his matter-of-factness, energy, and springy walk he showed me that it was work that saved him every day, and work was what he seemed to be recommending to us. This is why, in the nights of doubt, I would remember the lines from one of his California poems, written a few years before our visit:

> Day draws near,
> another one
> do what you can.

("On Angels")

I Can't Write a Memoir
of Czesław Miłosz

ADAM ZAGAJEWSKI

I can't write a memoir of Czesław Miłosz. For some reason, it seems
impossible to me, although I had almost no trouble when I wrote about the
late Zbigniew Herbert, for example (but I wouldn't envisage writing this
kind of essay about Joseph Brodsky either, someone I knew well). Why
is it so? Was Herbert more of a "unified person"? Not really. All three of
them—Miłosz, Herbert, Brodsky, so different as poets and human beings—
enjoyed, or suffered, the complexity of a life divided between the utmost seriousness of their work and the relative jocularity of what the other people
perceived as their socially visible personalities. All three enjoyed joking,
being with other people, dominating the conversation, laughing (Miłosz's
laugh was the loudest, the most majestic), as if needing a respite from the
gravity of their vocation.

Yet sometime ago I was able to write a few pages about Herbert's life.
Was it because I met him briefly when I was almost a child, when he visited my high school in Silesia? Or because his personal predicament, his
illness, stamped him with a drama that was so gripping in its ferocity that
it made him differ even more from the music of his noble poetry than was
the case with other poets and artists (none of them is ever identical with
their work)? Or because I had the feeling that—as we were born in the
same city of Lvov, some twenty years apart and only two hundred yards
away from each other—I had a special claim on his fate, the way veterans
from two different wars but from the same regiment may feel close, almost
like members of the same tribe, the same family?

I had read Miłosz for many years before I met him in person. In the late sixties and in the seventies I didn't believe I would ever meet him. He was then for me a legend, a unicorn, somebody living on a different planet; California was but a beautiful name for me. He belonged to a chapter of the history of Polish literature that seemed to be, seen from the landscape of my youth, as remote as the Middle Ages: he was a part of the last generation that had been born into the world of the impoverished gentry (impoverished but still very much defining themselves as gentry). He grew up in a small manor house in the Lithuanian countryside where woods, streams, and water snakes were as evident as streetcars and apartment houses in the modest, industrial city of my childhood. His Poland was totally different from mine: it had its wings spread to the East. When he was born in 1911, he was a subject of the Russian tsar; everything Russian, including the language that he knew so well, was familiar to him (although, as his readers well know, he was also very critical of many things Russian). I was born into a Poland that had changed its shape; like a sleeper who turns from one side to another, my country spread its arms toward the West—of course, only physically, because politically it was incorporated into the Eastern bloc.

I grew up in a post-German city; almost everything in the world of my childhood looked and smelled German. Cabbage seemed to be German, trees and walls recalled Bismarck, blackbirds sang with a Teutonic accent. My primary school could have belonged in any of Berlin's middle-class suburbs—its Prussian bricks were dark red like the lips of Wagnerian singers. The first radio in our apartment (a radio I worshipped—it received signals from an invisible realm, it had music, it brought strange sounds from different continents) was German and probably still nostalgic about Adolph Hitler's endless speeches. The first foreign language I had begun to learn (unwillingly), because of my grandfather, himself a Germanist, was German, too. For Miłosz, who was a polyglot, learning German never existed as a possibility—especially after World War II—and German poetry never played a major role in the vast universe of his reading.

There were no manor houses and water snakes in my childhood. Coal mines and chimneys played the part of woods and meadows. Aristocratic families were squatting in the smallest apartments, surviving on minimal wages; my family, I hasten to make clear, was not aristocratic at all. I was supposed to be a lucky inhabitant of a classless society in which falcons and sparrows were condemned to mandatory friendship. Classless society: practically, it meant that everybody was very poor, with the exception of party dignitaries and a few cunning merchants who were able to outwit the party but whose sleep was rather nervous; the wealth they accumulated could have been taken away from them in one day, for no solid law protected them. The language we spoke was a plebeian Polish, hard, ugly, filled with typical Communist acronyms, abbreviations, and clichés, punctuated with giggles, swearwords, and ironies—a language of slaves, good only for basic communication in a kind of a Boolean algebra of resentment. In the mid-seventies, I venerated a performance of Adam Mickiewicz's *Dziady* (Forefathers) staged at the Teatr Stary in Kraków; it was directed by Konrad Swinarski, who would die tragically soon after in an airplane accident in Syria. Sometime later, I was told that Miłosz, when offered a recording of the performance, commented sourly, "I can't stand the way these actors speak the Polish language." He found their pronunciation barbaric. These barbarians were my peers, my contemporaries; I knew many of them from rather benign military training sessions at the university. When they portrayed the rebels from the Mickiewicz generation, they sounded to me like my friends; I was transported back to early nineteenth-century Wilno, and I was one of them. They spoke my language, a language that didn't have the sweet music of Russian or the elegance of French.

Also in the seventies, one of my friends, a painter, Leszek Sobocki, traveled regularly to the United States (his mother lived in Los Angeles at the time). He was a part of a vague constellation of young artists and poets who were critical of the Communist system (although they hadn't known any other from personal experience) and tried, being faithful to a more or less realistic aesthetic, to create art that would matter socially and politically. I belonged to the same archipelago. Sobocki, once in L.A., mailed a package to Berkeley that contained excerpts from poetry and fiction produced by us, as well as reproductions of the paintings and prints made by him and his friends. After a while, a long letter of reply arrived from Miłosz; it couldn't have been more devastating. Miłosz basically dismissed the whole business of socially critical art, reducing our efforts to the well-meaning but aesthetically uninteresting and totally predictable reactions of inexperienced youngsters. He extolled "metaphysical distance," quoting Aleksander Wat's sentence on the necessity of fighting against communism on a metaphysical ground, which meant going to the very foundations of somebody's convictions. The letter was a cold shower for us, for me. Was Miłosz right? I was of two minds even then. He gave me pause. Now I think he was mostly right, although there must have been also a bit of jealousy in his judgment, jealousy of the directness of our action. An intellectual in exile is often "metaphysical" by necessity—for exiles, it's not a matter of free choice, because they have lost access to the unmediated spectacle of life in their own country. A much younger Miłosz, the Miłosz of the great poems written under the Nazi occupation or right after it, was, after all, somebody who didn't disdain directness at all.

And yet, against all odds, I fell in love with Miłosz's poetry. Its melodies seemed at times ancient, but its intellectual content couldn't be more modern, more attractive, more complex, more intoxicating. I say I fell in love with it, which is true—still, first I had to find Miłosz's poems, which was very difficult indeed. My parents had a significant library (where, however, fiction dwarfed poetry), but there was nothing by Miłosz on the shelves. His name had been erased from all the textbooks. My high school literature teacher never mentioned the name of Czesław Miłosz. In an encyclopedia, there was an entry "Miłosz," but it was devoted to "Miłosz Obrenovic," a brave Serbian prince, not to the author of *Native Realm*. Beginning in 1951, the year of his defection, Miłosz had become an outcast, a nonperson. If his name did appear somewhere in print, it was frequently accompanied by an official Byzantine formula: "an enemy of the People's Republic of Poland." Poor republic, having such a potent enemy!

To read his poems and his prose, I needed a special permit from the dean of my college. Once I even got it. It wasn't easy. I was not allowed to check these books out; I could only study them in one of the reading rooms in the Jagiellonian Library, my Kraków alma mater's crown jewel. Each day, I had to say "goodnight" to a pile of books—they had to stay on the shelf while I walked home. I was assigned to the Professors' Reading Room, which in my eyes, the eyes of a young graduate student, added to the importance of the occasion. I sat there for hours discovering the writings of the enemy of our republic. Sweet hours! Made even sweeter by the conspiratorial conditions under which I approached Miłosz's poetry. The richness of this work was overwhelming. I wasn't able right away to grasp the whole extent of the poet's achievement. I was swallowing lines of his poems like somebody given only a short moment in a magical orchard, as a trespasser avidly reaching out for cherries, pears, peaches. I didn't have enough time and leisure—or maturity, I'm afraid—to discern the different layers within his work, to understand the meandering of his thought, to define the stages of Miłosz's complicated poetic evolution. I read for enchantment, not for any critical insights. I remember walking home after these sessions in the library and repeating lines from his poems—I was inebriated with them. Had I been a driver then, police could have arrested me for driving in a state of drunkenness. But I was only a chaotic walker, and nobody could stop me; even a totalitarian state was not able to control my daydreams, my poetic fascinations, the pattern of my walking.

What was it that attracted me to Miłosz's poetry? Precisely everything that was different from my own experience, my own situation, my "people's republic" language. I fell in love with the freedom with which Miłosz both respected and defied the rules of poetic modernism. He was saying more than the poets I had known before; I mean he didn't keep a strict diet of puristic metaphors but instead was willing to tell the reader more than was accepted among contemporary poets. The reader knew that Miłosz believed in something and hated something else, knew what Miłosz's weltanschauung was—yet many of his poems were violent quarrels of the poet with himself, not at all easy to decipher. He was never doctrinaire; he never quite agreed with himself. I was also struck by a constant, energetic quest for the invisible in his poetry, a quest that arose amidst the most concrete, sensual images, not in an ascetic monastery chapel. In his oeuvre, ecstatic tones mixed with sober reflection; there was no easy way to classify this poetry. It burst taxonomies, it was not "nature poetry," it was not a "poetic meditation on History," neither was it "autobiographical lyric"—it was all of those. The ambition of this poet knew no limits; he tried to drink in the cosmos.

After so much intimacy gained from the contact with his oeuvre, I nevertheless felt a considerable shock at meeting him in person. And the contrast between the immense, complicated territory of his powerful work and the gentleman (a seventy-year-old "smiling public man") I finally met was sizeable too. How can a single person embody all the nuances and contradictions of a vast opus? I don't want to say that I was disappointed with Miłosz's human incarnation. Not at all: I admired him, I loved him, every moment spent with him was fascinating. He was a kind friend; he wrote a most generous preface to *Tremor*, my first collection of poems in the United States; he showed interest in my life and work; and much later, in Kraków, when we became almost-neighbors, I saw him often. Yet I know that for him I always remained a younger friend, not somebody he would confide in the way, I imagine, some from his generation might have enjoyed—or endured.

I met him for the first time in June 1983 in Paris in the spacious apartment of Leonor Fini and Konstanty Jeleński (near Place des Victoires). I was then somebody who had recently left Poland and had no idea how long his Parisian emigration would last. Konstanty Jeleński was an exile like Miłosz, a brilliant critic, and a great admirer of Miłosz's poetry. The Miłosz I met then was an elder statesman: old and yet strangely young and handsome, serene, witty, radiating an energy that made him the center of every social event; wild and tame at the same time, rescued by the renown of the Stockholm accolade from the trials of his Berkeley solitude. In January 1986, I read with him and some other famous poets during the PEN conference in New York City's Cooper Union Hall, where a huge and enthusiastic audience that consisted mostly, I thought, of very young poets greeted the readers (what a wonderful audience it was!). I saw him now and then in Paris, in California, in New York, in Indianapolis. In Houston, where I taught creative writing, I introduced a reading he gave, and later I would visit him many times in Kraków in his Bogusławski Street apartment, where he eventually settled down with Carol. I saw him walking—more and more slowly—in the Kraków old town, where almost everybody recognized him and looked at him with awe. Given the slow pace of his walks, the awe had enough time to be richly deployed. He was like Goethe in Weimar, though his apartment was much more modest than the house in Frauenplan—but the centrality of his position in the small world of Kraków and Poland was never questioned. This in itself was an enormous achievement for an exile who had returned to his country after so many decades of absence. His intellectual authority was overwhelming. In the restaurants, he spoke very loudly because he was hard of hearing, so loudly that it was a bit embarrassing for his friends—not much privacy in these conversations. Yet he was never diminished by his great old age. His memory was invincible, his laughter irresistible, his mind alert.

In 2002 and 2003, he was enthusiastically received by American poets, very young ones and also the well-known ones, during summer conferences I organized then with Edward Hirsch in Kraków; Miłosz refused to participate in panels because he couldn't hear what the others said but agreed to meet students from Houston. He gave several Q&As, answering endless questions and embarking on long, unforgettable soliloquies (someone would always help him by repeating the question near his better ear). And he read with the other poets; I'll always remember him at a reading in the beautifully restored Kraków reformed synagogue, wearing a yarmulke on his regal head, old David speaking to his nation, feeble yet strong, solemn but also visibly savoring—with a courteous, content smile—the din of the ovation that went on and on . . .

There was something absolutely splendid in the way he stood up to the challenges of his last years. He never withdrew into the comfort of a well-deserved retirement. With those he loved or liked, he was tender, magnanimous, charming. He received many friends and many strangers, young or old admirers of his work, poets and critics—but when he spoke in public, he retained the tone of an angry prophet. He had always attacked the pettiness of his compatriots. He defended the visionary homeland of his dreams, pluralistic and tolerant, while castigating the vices of the existing society: he hated anti-Semitism, narrow-mindedness, nationalism, stupidity. He had a religious mind, but he also believed in liberal, democratic principles and tried to teach his contemporaries the implications of this complex creed.

I witnessed his deep sadness after Carol died. He realized he would face the end of his life in an empty apartment whose every corner bore traces of Carol's tender hand and imagination. Even then, after he returned from his last trip to California where he bade her good-bye, he was able to write the beautiful elegy for Carol, "Orpheus and Eurydice." His gift of transforming life's sorrows into poetry was intact, but he was tired and, it seems to me, maybe even a bit ashamed of always succeeding as a magician against all odds, all catastrophes, all deaths. "What is poetry which does not save / Nations or people?" he asked in the mid-forties. What's the use of magic that doesn't assuage despair? His religious hope, his faith, and sometimes dreams brought him signals of divine presence, but—we know from the poems—despair was also one of his frequent visitors. Although his laughter still triumphed over the baseness of biology, the last years made him frail. This great life had its secrets: how many times had Miłosz told us in his poems that he was an "evil person"? His friends never believed it, although I think he wanted us perhaps not to accept it as true but at least to consider it more seriously. Friends are usually too well meaning, too polite, too well bred. They always tell you "You'll be fine," "You exaggerate." They want to cheer you up; that's their business—which is probably the last thing someone coping with the grave images at life's end wants to hear. The poet who decided early on that poetry was about communicating with other people, not about lofty hermeticism and language games, was dying in the silence of his solitary days and nights. One of the last humans who spoke to him in his hours of agony was an uneducated woman who took care of his small household, a wonderful person with a great heart. I like to think of it: in the vast polyphony of the almost hundred years of his dramatic existence, the ultimate sound he heard was an unschooled voice of goodness. Perhaps in this soothing voice he found something like an arch between his early idyllic childhood in the Lithuanian countryside and his closing moments; in between there remained, bracketed out for once, the rage of modern history, the loneliness of his long exile, the violence of his struggles, of his thought, his imagination, his rebellions.

I can't write a memoir of Miłosz: so much was hidden in his life. Besides, he was an ecstatic poet and an ecstatic person. We'll never really know people like that. They hide their great moments of elation; they never share with others the short joys of their sudden discoveries—and the sadness when the vision fades. They thrive in solitude. With their friends, they are usually correct, measured, just like everybody else. They are like a ship we sometimes see in a peaceful port: a huge immobile mass of metal covered by spots of rust, a few sailors lazily sunbathing on the deck, a blue shirt drying on a rope. One wouldn't guess that this ship was once struggling with the hurricane, barely surviving the onslaught of big waves, singing an iron song . . . No, I didn't know him enough. I have to return to his poems, to his essays.

Spring in Berkeley

TOMAS VENCLOVA

In late March 1977, I came to California. I had never seen America or any Western country before, but it was rather clear for me and for the Soviet authorities that I would stay here forever. As a dissident, I was surely not expected back in the USSR, even if I still had my Soviet passport.

My journey from Moscow to Berkeley, where I was invited to give a course of lectures, took almost two months—by planes and by trains, via Paris, Washington, D.C., New York, and Chicago. A Lithuanian acquaintance of mine, a professor at UCLA, offered me a stay in his summer house in Berkeley, so I had two half-empty rooms for myself in the heart of a garden leading to Ridge Road. This small street went down the hill, then up again, from where the vast expanse of San Francisco Bay, enclosed by the contour of the Golden Gate Bridge, opened up. On the left, another incredible bridge could be seen, and at its far end, the city's skyscrapers. From the bottom of the street, a small path led to the left into an almost paradisiacal park with university buildings showing white here and there. Still farther, there was Telegraph Avenue, with tiny bookstores that sold Aleister Crowley and G. I. Gurdjieff, with aging hippies, barefoot girls, and various peculiar characters hanging around. *Beelzebub's Tales* were sold in cellophane packaging, preventing the reader from learning the secret teachings unless the book was purchased. Although the distance between the house where I stayed and the university was almost negligible, dozens of bars and restaurants loomed in the shady courtyards along the way. It was all so unlike the world I was used to, so different even from Paris and Chicago, that it took me a week to acclimatize myself. Two days had scarcely passed before Czesław Miłosz, to whom I owed the invitation to Berkeley, stopped by to see me.

In Soviet Lithuania, where I spent the first half of my life, the ban on Miłosz's name was even stricter than in Communist Poland. But I knew at least something about him. My father wasn't reluctant to talk about Miłosz; they even had a common friend—the Lithuanian Socialist-Democrat Pranas Ancevičius, or Franciszek Ancewicz, whom Miłosz often mentioned both in his conversations and in print. In my father's library, there was a prewar Lithuanian magazine with some translations of Miłosz's early poetry—the translations, to tell the truth, were awful. Later, when I learned Polish, I came across a copy of *Rodzinna Europa* (*Native Realm*). I have already written about it more than once, but I should probably recap once again the incredible story of how this book made it to Vilnius: its separate pages were sent to a friend of mine in letters, so the process of transporting the entire book took about a year and a half.

When I finally visited Poland in 1970 (the Soviet authorities wouldn't allow me to travel to other countries, and soon not even to Poland), I read all of Miłosz's poetry: I borrowed his émigré editions from Professor Jan Błoński, though more than one person in Warsaw and Kraków possessed them as well.

By that time, I had already switched to reading banned literature almost exclusively; predictably, my own writing also somewhat departed from socialist realism. It was easy to foresee the consequences. My works stopped being published, and I entered an irreversible conflict with the authorities. Miłosz, who always kept an eye on what was going on in Lithuania, especially in Vilnius, found out about my problems; he even translated one of my poems and published it in the famous émigré journal *Kultura*. When things became unbearable for me in my home country, he arranged to invite me to teach at the American university where he worked. At first, the Soviet authorities didn't want to let me go. Miłosz called me and wrote me a letter: there were reasons to believe that when the West showed interest in dissidents, it gave them, as Pasternak put it, a sort of "safe conduct" (though not fully reliable and usually only for a while). In any case, in January 1977, when it became clear that I should be either imprisoned or exiled abroad, the authorities, to my great surprise, opted for the latter. They issued me a Soviet foreign passport (which they took away only in August, when I was already in the United States) and stamped an exit visa in it. That was how I found myself in Berkeley, leaving my family behind in Vilnius.

Although I had never seen Miłosz before, except in the photographs, I recognized him as he was walking along the brick-paved garden path. Although he was sixty-five years old, he still looked quite young: slender and sturdy, sportive and elegant, slightly taller than average, with stern eyes under shaggy brows and a charming smile that compensated for his rigorous glance. To this day, I have met only one man who looked as youthful as Miłosz in his late sixties: Boris Pasternak. Incidentally, there was something imperceptibly similar between them, which had to do with their spirited behavior rather than their outward appearance.

I knew I was dealing with a great poet and, as always in such situations, grew apprehensive. But soon Miłosz broke the ice between us and even suggested that I call him by his first name, which I promptly did, though not without fear—I was a good quarter century younger than he was, after all. In his car, we drove across the bridge from Oakland to San Francisco, where we boarded the city tram that rolled up and down the hills, at times almost vertically. It was the first time I saw the city so near—the skyscrapers, villas, squares that looked slightly Latin American to me, Coit Tower (which Miłosz, like all the locals, called "coitus tower"). We reached Fisherman's Wharf, ate shrimp, drank wine, and talked about Lithuanian and Polish affairs, about Vilnius. During that conversation, a sort of "diplomatic" etiquette was established between us: talking to me, Miłosz would always use the Lithuanian, not the Polish, name of the city, "Vilnius," while I always went for "Wilno," the Polish form—as if we both were making allowances for each other's patriotism. On the way back to the car, Miłosz boyishly leaped into a tram, and I joined him. As it rolled through the seedy quarters of the city, he allowed himself a remark, which wasn't exactly politically correct: "Here, and only here, do I almost agree with the communists: all these unsavory characters should be forced to commit to some decent labor."

During the three months of my stay at Berkeley, we saw each other almost daily. Miłosz even attended my lectures: I was giving a course on Yuri Lotman's semiotics, and the problems of signs and symbols, clearly, interested Miłosz a lot, though mainly in relation to Gnosticism and European mysticism rather than to poetics as such (still, Miłosz and Lotman had one common interest: Freemasonry). Through Miłosz, I got to know the entire Slavic Department, where many remarkable scholars, mostly his friends, taught: Joan Grossman; Robert Hughes and his wife, Olga Raevsky-Hughes; Simon Karlinsky. One of Miłosz's colleagues, Gleb Struve, had already retired but was a legendary figure for me: the son of the famous prerevolutionary Russian politician Petr Struve, he was a friend of Marina Tsvetaeva and Vladimir Nabokov and a publisher of Nikolai Gumilev, Anna Akhmatova, and Osip Mandelstam, whose works, smuggled into the Soviet Union, we read from cover to cover. At Berkeley, one could meet another living legend: the Polish logician Alfred Tarski, the founder of the theory of models, which at the time, in Lotman's vein, I was studying. In addition, I also established a contact with the Lithuanian émigré community, which was relatively small in San Francisco and Berkeley. Strange though it may seem, the name of one of its leaders was Adomas Mickevičius, that is (in the Polish variant), Adam Mickiewicz. Miłosz knew many members of the community and more than once said that he got along better with Lithuanian émigrés than with Polish émigrés, who, according to him, frequently seemed lost in anachronistic internecine quarrels.

Of course, Lithuanian is nearly as different from Polish as Gaelic from English, but it was by no means foreign to Miłosz (in almost the same way, Gaelic wasn't foreign to the English poet William Butler Yeats). Miłosz avoided speaking Lithuanian (probably out of shyness), though he certainly could, and he perfectly understood written text: I became sure of it when I lent him a Lithuanian émigré newspaper, *Draugas,* with an anonymous article about Czereia, an estate where the French poet Oscar Milosz (Czesław's elder relative, friend, and mentor) was born. Incidentally, the Gospel served as Miłosz's "textbook" of the Lithuanian language: knowing many of its chapters by heart, he could read it without a dictionary. I have heard that later, when he was in his eighties, he started to study Lithuanian in a more formal way.

Once, in early September 1978, Miłosz and I happened to be at Tabor Farm, not far from Chicago. The place was the property of Valdas Adamkus, a figure of the Lithuanian émigré community, whose confederates gathered here to listen to each other's lectures in a large village shed and, in the evening, to chat by the fireplace or at a bar counter. The enlightened views of this group's members were similar to the views of the Poles, who associated themselves with *Kultura,* including Miłosz (he had been to Tabor Farm before and already knew many of its people). At the poetry reading, we presented "Mittelbergheim," my favorite work by Miłosz: the author read the original; I read the translation. Then we drank beer, which the host of the farm, Adamkus, poured straight out of a barrel, collecting one dollar for a glass. Back then, none of us—least of all, Adamkus himself—could tell that, in nineteen years, he would become the president of independent Lithuania.

The hills of Berkeley resemble those of Vilnius, though they offer a splendid view of the sea, while the Lithuanian capital is a continental city. Miłosz's house stood on a high slope, above the university campus. There was no better place to enjoy the panorama. I grew more and more accustomed to visiting Miłosz in his house and would even stay overnight in the attic of a little hut next to it. It was in this attic that Miłosz once read his poem "A Magic Mountain" to me:

> I don't remember exactly when Budberg died, it was either two
>   years ago or three.
> The same with Chen. Whether last year or the one before. . . .
>
> Sultry Octobers, cool Julys, trees blossom in February.
> Here the nuptial flight of hummingbirds does not forecast spring.
> Only the faithful maple sheds its leaves every year.
> For no reason, its ancestors simply learned it that way.[1]

This poem seemed somehow related to one he wrote back in 1950, "On a Bird's Song, Above the Banks of the Potomac," which was also about the difficulties of taking root in a new world, about the change of generations and inner transformations of a man. "I am not sure, it's been a while," Miłosz said in a slightly vexed tone. He stressed the ending: "Wrong Honorable Professor Milosz / Who wrote poems in some unheard-of tongue." That year, not yet knowing what awaited him in the near future, he had to reckon with the possibility of being forgotten, of becoming just a part of the "magic mountain," dissolving in its landscape like Budberg and Chen. It is not so important, after all, as long as there are poems, but he did suffer from the lack of an audience. Once he took me to San Francisco, where he had to read for the English-speaking public. The reading took place in a small room; the audience consisted of twelve people. It was consoling that they were enraptured with the reading.

The customs at Miłosz's house, especially food and simple but distinguished hospitality, reminded one of the old-gentry Lithuania, with which Miłosz always tried to maintain a connection, no matter how hard it could be. I remember an American lady who paid Miłosz a visit two weeks after her return from Vilnius (alas, her impressions of it were most gloomy). She even met with an old acquaintance of Miłosz's, the hero of his poem "Father Ch., Many Years Later"—the priest Chomski, who under Soviet power remained in the village Voke (in Polish, Waka), close to Vilnius, and who had already turned ninety-two. Miłosz would often ask me about the city, the university (formerly Stefan Batory University but without the name of that king in my time) we both graduated from, the people and their attitudes. I could tell him about the poet Kazys Boruta, whom Miłosz had translated back in his youth (these were his very first translations), and about the journalist and editor Juozas Keliuotis, whom Miłosz met after the fall of Poland in 1939 and who published Miłosz's poetry in his magazine. Lithuania is a small world; therefore, I have met these people in person (as for Boruta, I knew him quite well). Keliuotis's and Boruta's fates were similar (both were imprisoned under Stalin) but different at the same time: Boruta, being a leftist and a former socialist revolutionary, endured the pressure, while Keliuotis, a Catholic in the style of Jacques Maritain, succumbed to a psychosis. But most of all, Miłosz was interested in his native village Szetejnie (Šateiniai, in Lithuanian), where the action of his novel *The Issa Valley* is set. I had been to that place, though not to the village itself, and told him that there was nothing left (I was wrong: there remained a neglected park and one random building). In a day or two, Miłosz told me that he saw the village in a dream ("Probably, under your influence, because you were also there," he added); it was a dream in colors, which, as Miłosz confessed, he rarely experienced. A bit later, the dream turned into a startling poem—"The Wormwood Star"—about trees that continued to grow even though they were no more.

Trees were a permanent motif of Miłosz's poetry and conversations. He had an instinct of a botanist, naturalist, or hunter—no doubt, also inherited from traditional Lithuania. Once, he asked me as we were walking across the university campus, overgrown with subtropical verdure, "Do you know about plants?" From his intonation, it was clear that he couldn't imagine a poet who did not. As for my poem "Winter Dialogue," which Miłosz translated into Polish, he was mostly interested in the motif of tree rings: according to the Samogitian tradition of lowland Lithuania, especially cold winters happen before insurrections, and so one can tell the year of the uprising by the narrow ring on the stump. I remember he kept asking me about this for a long time, looking for the right adjective modifying "ring."

It is not easy to remember exactly what we talked about, sometimes for many hours in a row. Fortunately, I can restore some things from my diary. Talking to a man whose individuality, talent, and experience by far exceed your own is not only a blessing but also an obstacle. We rather rarely discussed poetry, perhaps both being embarrassed to touch on the subject. I felt uncomfortable praising Miłosz's poetry but didn't dare criticize it either—not that I could find a serious reason to do so, even though he might have expected me to. As for my own verse, he told me right away, "I am too vaguely familiar with the Lithuanian poetic tradition to understand how you fit into it, or how you stand out against it. I can say only one thing: I am against Russian classical meters. In any case, they don't do any good to the Poles." (In Lithuanian nineteenth- and twentieth-century tradition, the metrical structure of poems usually approaches Russian classical patterns; in Polish tradition, it never does.) He seemed to like only one of my poems, "A Museum in Hobart," which is about Tasmania and its peoples exterminated by the colonists (probably, by association, with the fate of Lithuania). It was Miłosz who instigated my interest in Aleksander Wat and gave me books of his poetry and memoirs. We talked a lot about Norwid and Pasternak and even agreed that Pasternak's verses about Chopin from his *Second Birth* stem from Norwid's "Chopin's Fortepiano": later, I came across a similar argument in Krystyna Pomorska's scholarly book. As a joke, Miłosz used the Lithuanian version of the poet's name, Ciprijonas Norvydas, and even invented a leader of a *kolkhoz* in Lithuania with the same name in our conversation (I remember vaguely that he referred to Norvydas in his writing on at least one occasion). Much more often, though, he would expand on the general issues of philosophy, especially on his favorite topic, Manichaeanism. "My main ambition is to introduce a Manichaean perspective into Christianity," he once said, filling a glass with wine. After a short while, our conversation switched gears to the discussion of the devil: his being capable of many things, at one time representing the spirit of chaos, at another representing the spirit of the mechanistic order. We also talked about painting. Neither of us liked the lecture by an invited art historian from France, who was trying to prove that Jan Vermeer was an abstractionist because, supposedly, he wasn't interested in the plot and only cared about painting as such. Trying to follow in Yuri Lotman's steps, I said, "A kind of tension accumulates between the plot and pure painting. The same happens in Malevich, although his plot is mystical." "Yes," Miłosz concluded, "and when only one of these polarities remains, art evaporates."

I knew Miłosz's life was far from unclouded: his first wife, Janina, or Pani Janka, was seriously ill, and he often had to play the role of a nurse. It explained, at least in part, his depression and occasional harsh nervousness. Once, nearly a year after my arrival in California, I also complained to him about suffering from depression. "Well, that's quite natural," Miłosz remarked. "What is *not* natural is that until now you were suffering from euphoria. I envy you, though. Nowadays, the world pays attention to dissidents, but in my times I had to exist in sheer vacuum, at the very bottom." In my diary, I have another entry about one of our conversations: "In the forties, there was a communist power in Poland, as well as the so-called patriotic society which sang *Red Poppies on Monte Cassino*. True, I was equally alienated from both. But here, abroad, there was nothing at all. They let me out of Poland, figuring I wouldn't be able to stand it and would come back. Adam Michnik told me many years later: well, looks like you won."

The years 1976 and 1977 gave rise to a particularly daring dissent in Poland, Lithuania, and Russia. It was nearly the first time the opposition-ists of the three countries—previously isolated, hounded, and immersed into their own problems—established connections with each other. The Poles founded the Workers' Defense Committee (KOR) and a noncen-sored magazine, *Zapis;* Andrei Sakharov, who had just received the Nobel Peace Prize, was working in Russia. In Lithuania, an underground press was emerging and the Helsinki Group was formed. The Polish Helsinki Group was, incidentally, founded after the Lithuanian one, apropos of which Miłosz joked, "Ex Lithuaniae lux." Wiktor Woroszylski (or Andrzej Drawicz) commissioned us to write a dialogue about Vilnius, which was to be published in *Zapis.* But the text was intercepted by Miłosz's close friend, Jerzy Giedroyć, who printed it in *Kultura,* the journal he edited. This caused a conflict among dissidents in Poland and émigrés, albeit nei-ther a serious nor a prolonged one. The name of Adam Michnik, the most active Polish dissident, who would be released at one moment and impris-oned again at another, had great resonance. We were celebrating one of his releases from prison, and I compared him to the Polish interwar leader and hero Józef Piłsudski; Miłosz did not mind the parallel. He kept an avid eye not only on the Polish but also on Russian underground publishing. I remember he liked Valery Chalidze's ironical phrase from *Criminal Rus-sia:* "Cannibalism, as such, is not forbidden by Soviet law." Chalidze had in mind the fact that there was no special paragraph in the code of laws of the USSR qualifying cannibalism as a crime, but his phrase had obvious overtones, reminding one of Stalin's truly "cannibalistic" atrocities. The memory of the Soviet cannibalism was actually stronger in Miłosz than in us, who were relatively young. In my diary, I wrote down the words he said later, when the Soviet Union had invaded Afghanistan, yet before the introduction of martial law in Poland by General Wojciech Jaruzelski: "All that is happening is a part of a global catastrophe. The monster is stretch-ing out its tentacles. I've never been, nor will I ever be, an optimist."

During that strange era, people from the Soviet Union—even those who wouldn't normally be granted a visa to Western countries—frequently visited the United States. We never avoided meeting them, and they also seemed eager to meet with us, but sometimes we failed to find a common language. Once, a famous bard, Bulat Okudzhava, came to Berkeley to give a concert. Miłosz liked him, but they exchanged only a few words—as Miłosz said, some dubious pro-Soviet characters tried to keep Okudzhava away from the émigrés. Without any unwanted witnesses, we managed to talk till morning with the well-known poet Bella Akhmadulina and her husband in the Cheshire Cat pub, not far from my house. She arrived in the United States via France with an American visa but without official permission from the Soviets; at the Soviet consulate, she had to listen to a long reprimand on how a decent Soviet citizen must behave in a foreign country. Incidentally, to intimidate her, the consul told her, "Do not follow the bad example of Tomas Venclova." Miłosz was struck by the number of poems she remembered by heart, both her own and others'—a habit hardly known outside Russia. The specifically Russian genre—verses dedicated to great poetic predecessors—was also perceived by Miłosz as unusual: "Hymns to Akhmatova or Tsvetaeva are sheer mythology, much like Homer's hymns to Athena or Aphrodite," he said. Alas, our conversation with Akhmadulina involved a light conflict, for which I was the one to blame: we talked about Miłosz's *Captive Mind*, and I started expanding on the concept of *ketman*, or servility. Akhmadulina took it personally (which by no means was my intention—like Okudzhava, she never demeaned herself before the authorities and, in this regard, was one of the most dignified representatives of the entire "generation of the sixties"). The misunderstanding was settled when Miłosz asked our guest what she thought of Aleksandr Solzhenitsyn. "I ado-o-re him!" Bella replied.

Of course, the only Russian poet truly close to Miłosz was Joseph Brodsky, who had already lived in the States for five years (beginning in 1972). I remember how delighted Miłosz was about most of Brodsky's poems, though not all of them; he highly praised, for example, "1972" ("Birds don't fly through my skylight nowadays"). Brodsky, in turn, once said, "Miłosz is the most accomplished man I know" (the word *accomplished* was said in English). But much has already been written about this friendship, and even more will probably be.

Three months after my arrival at Berkeley, in June 1977, my lectureship ended, and I was out of a job. Miłosz must have worried about my situation more than I did—I was still going through euphoria, while he knew perfectly well how difficult things could turn out for an immigrant in America. In August, I received a letter from the Soviet consul that informed me that I had been deprived of citizenship "for activities that defile the title of a Soviet citizen." However, earlier still, I had been invited to UCLA, and again I owed this invitation to Miłosz: he was friends with Marija Gimbutas—a famous archaeologist, a UCLA professor, and a Lithuanian from Vilnius—who had had to leave her country in 1944.

Perhaps I should finish here. I kept seeing Miłosz quite often, first under similar circumstances, then in a totally different era, sometimes in America, sometimes in Poland or even in Vilnius. From time to time, I feel

I see him even now. The very fact that I met him gives me the right to say that my life was a happy one. But in the beginning there was Berkeley, the house on the hill with the view of the bridge and hundreds of sails—the house that, like no other place in the world, suited Miłosz's words: it was filled with "order in which whatever exists must exist forever."[2]

Translated by Yasha Klots.

Notes

1. Czesław Miłosz, *New and Collected Poems, 1931–2001* (New York: Ecco, 2003), 335.
2. "Powers," *New and Collected Poems,* 471–72.

He Also Knew How to Be Gracious

ANNA FRAJLICH

While trying to recall my first encounter with Czesław Miłosz, I realized that the best way would be to go to my library at home to find all the books he had inscribed to me. The earliest ones are two Polish books published in France by Instytut Literacki, Miłosz's most dedicated—and for many decades only—émigré publisher. It is with these editions of *Miasto bez imienia* (City without a name) and *Człowiek wśród skorpionów* (Man among scorpions) that I approached the poet in the Guggenheim Museum on October 17, 1978, where his reading in New York was held. This was, coincidentally, just the day after the first Polish pope had been elected in Rome. After the reading, I caught up with Miłosz on his way out of the auditorium and thanked him for writing *Man among Scorpions,* the philosophical biography of Stanisław Brzozowski (1878–1911), whom Miłosz in his book *The History of Polish Literature* calls "one of the most original Polish thinkers of the twentieth century,"[1] also writing, "The complexity of his brilliant mind was such and his evolution so rapid that it is extremely difficult to follow all the transformations of that man." Probably Brzozowski's brilliant mind and equally tragic life lay at the core of Miłosz's attraction to the writer.

Miłosz, a bit taken aback at first by my approaching him with this particular book of 1962, suddenly stopped and asked, "Who are you?" I introduced myself, and when I handed him his books to sign, he wrote in Polish, "Annie Frajlich-Zając *na wieczorze* 17.X.78 *w* New Yorku *b. przyjaźnie* Czesław Miłosz" (To Anna Frajlich-Zając [my full hyphenated name] on the poetry evening 10.17.78 in New York with very friendly regards); on the second book, he repeated my full name and "very friendly." To me, these words indicated that he recognized my name from publications and was predisposed in a friendly way to what I have written. At that time, I already had one book of poetry to my name, and even though I was associated with a different émigré magazine, he had probably heard of me.

The book that I had thanked him for writing was the first book of Miłosz's that I had ever held in my hands. This was when I was still in Poland, writing my M.A. thesis on Brzozowski at Warsaw University. Miłosz's name was on the index of censorship. To read this book, I had to travel halfway across the city to the National Library (where the book was held in the restricted collection), clutching my professor's letter stating that this book was necessary for my research. No wonder it was one of the first books I purchased in New York.

At the Guggenheim reading, I saw Renata Gorczyńska, a friend from my Warsaw University class, an editor at the *Polish Daily News* at the time. As I learned later, this was her first meeting with Miłosz as well; she had approached him a few hours earlier with the idea of a book-length interview, published under the pen name Ewa Czarnecka in 1983 as "Podróżny świata." Although Aleksander Fiut's conversation with Miłosz was the first book to break the silence on the poet in Poland, Gorczyńska's book fulfilled such a role in the world of Polish exiles. Controversy surrounding Miłosz's name played on both sides of the Iron Curtain: on the one hand, in Poland, until 1980, he was on the index of censorship; on the other hand, the Polish political émigré community could not forgive him his initial postwar role with the Communist regime, which he represented as a diplomat in the United States and France. Both Renata Gorczyńska and Aleksander Fiut started to work on their conversations much earlier, but it was a Nobel Prize that eased these books into existence.[2]

From 1976 to 1980, I was a part-time graduate student in New York University's Slavic Department and a freelance cultural correspondent for Radio Free Europe (RFE) in New York. One of my articles, published in the émigré *Polish Daily News,* in Polish and in English translation, concerned Miłosz's Neustadt award, the so-called little Nobel Prize. I knew that the *Polish Daily News* made sure that Miłosz received a copy, and when I met him personally for the second time, on October 12, 1979, at the national convention of the American Association for the Advancement of Slavic Studies, held in New Haven, Connecticut, Miłosz signed his *Land of Ulro* (the Polish edition) for me, again with the "very friendly regards" inscription, using only the first part of my last name (Frajlich), my pen name, again indicating thusly that he was familiar with my publications. The 1979 convention was truly exceptional as far as the participation of

Polish American intellectuals—as well as American Slavists specializing in the Polish culture—was concerned. In one little room, you could see Czesław Miłosz chatting with Jan Kott, the author of the renowned *Shakespeare Our Contemporary* and a professor at Stony Brook University; Harvard University professor Wiktor Weintraub; Ohio State University professor Jerzy Krzyżanowski; New York Graduate Center professor and expert on the Polish avant-garde Daniel Gerould; and, of the younger generation, Julia Przyboś, a French literature professor of Hunter College and the daughter of avant-garde Polish poet Julian Przyboś. Lively intellectual exchanges concerning Polish poetry, theater, and cultural politics took place at several sessions, especially two sessions on the theater of Witold Gombrowicz and Sławomir Mrożek. We, the audience, were happy to hear from people who personally knew them both. Kott said at a certain point, "Forty-four years ago I used to spend hours with Gombrowicz in the Warsaw cafés and now comes the moment of reflection." On the session dedicated to Mrożek, whose plays were staged at the time by many experimental and professional American theaters, Miłosz pointed to the functioning of certain stereotypes, among them the typical accepted wisdom about the decline of the West, going back to the once-famous book by Oswald Spengler, *The Decline of the West.* Along with scholars and writers known in the American Slavic world, there were many young American and Polish scholars affected by the bug of the Polish literature.

Miłosz had organized a conference session dedicated to the four-hundredth anniversary of Stefan Batory University in Wilno, of which he was an alumnus. He approached this topic in a truly original way by inviting alumni of different ethnic backgrounds: Professor Irena Sławińska of Poland, a noted theorist of theater who represented the largest student population (that is, Polish), discussed the rich theoretical and critical tradition of that university; Professor Arcadius Kahan, of the University of Chicago, a noted twentieth-century economic historian, represented the Jewish students of Wilno; and Vitaut Tumash of the Byelorussian Institute of Arts and Sciences in the United States represented the Byelorussian students. Kahan and Tumash underlined that, for Jewish and Byelorussian youths, the university was a center of intellectual and cultural life. They both agreed, however, that the polonizing policy of the university did not admit the parity of different cultures, and for Jews or Byelorussians, enrollment meant acceptance of the gentile model of culture. The university was founded in 1579 and named after its founder, King Stefan Batory. Being an alumnus of Wilno University (the alma mater of the greatest Polish poet, Adam Mickiewicz) remained forever in Miłosz's writings a matter of great sentiment and pride. After World War II, when, based on the Roosevelt-Stalin agreement, Lithuania became a Soviet republic, the university became a Soviet institution with Russian compulsory language and Communist rule.

Lithuanian poet and scholar Tomas Venclova, a Yale University professor, who had then only recently arrived in the United States, spoke about the situation of the university under the Soviet regime. It is necessary to add here that twentieth-century Polish literature is determined by history; hence, the terms *war, interwar,* and *before the war* always relate to those two global conflicts affecting Poland's fate. The history of the university, said Venclova, reflected conflicts of many nationalities; after 1944, university politics was directed toward sovietization and the total leveling of differences and individualities. The discussion at the seminar was very vivid and full of controversies. Some expressed disappointment that instead of talking about the university's scholarly achievements, the talk was about mutual animosities. I expected that, Miłosz told the group, but we wanted the regrets and bitterness to find their expression at the moment when neither Wilno nor the university existed in its former shape or character.

I was impressed by Miłosz's creative and courageous approach. While I listened, I reflected on how a poet of such stature took time away from his writing to fulfill his professorial obligations. His peers in Poland did not have to attend to such duties. In the evening, Miłosz's reading gathered his devoted admirers.

Almost exactly a year later, Czesław Miłosz was awarded the Nobel Prize. The news electrified the worldwide Polish community, including Poland, of course, where his name was still on the index of censorship. I still keep the copy of the congratulatory mailgram I sent to him on October 9, 1980.

In the aftermath of the Nobel, I conducted a telephone RFE interview with Jan Kott, who had known Miłosz since before World War II. Kott reminisced about Miłosz's visit to Warsaw University in the 1930s; all his peers considered Miłosz the leading poet of their generation. Kott ended his very emotional interview, in which he compared Miłosz's Nobel to the election of the Polish pope, by quoting a poem by Miłosz, written in 1934. The poem, permeated by dark symbolism that is untranslatable into English, expresses the grim catastrophic anxiety of that generation with a passage: "Fame will pass you by." The message of Kott's interview was that Miłosz in his life overcame that dark self-prophecy. Miłosz was very touched by Kott's interview, which was subsequently printed in a literary supplement to the *Polish Daily News.*[3]

On October 24, 1980, I met Miłosz in Toronto, Canada, at an international scholarly conference on Polishness. The conference was dedicated to the topic of national identity in such fields as literature, sociology, and political science. The conference was scheduled long before he was awarded the prize, but his entrance was greeted with a standing ovation, as if a celebration of his victory, which indeed it was. He seemed very gracious. One of the participants was his former student Louis Iribarne, a professor of Slavic literature and translator of several Polish masterpieces by Gombrowicz, Stanisław Ignacy Witkiewicz, Bruno Schulz, and, of course, Miłosz. Also, two Polish scholars and poets, Bogdan Czaykowski and Florian Śmieja, were on the same panel with Miłosz, discussing how the drama of the Polish diaspora finds its reflection in the literature of exile. They were poets of the group Kontynenty, who as young children were forcibly removed from Poland during the war by either the Russians or the Germans. After the war, they all studied in England and, rather than join the older generation of émigré writers, established their own group and practiced their own modern poetics. In 1950, only this little group of Poles in London welcomed him when Miłosz defected to the West.

Like every other society, the Polish community may look like a monolithic whole, but this is only to an outsider. Actually, its composition was always quite complex. The core of the Polish American community goes back to the nineteenth century and was mainly rural in origin—an immigration in search of "bread," very much like the Irish immigration of that time. Quite oblivious to high culture, they retained their ethnic identity based mainly on folk culture. Another wave of Polish immigration was represented by postwar émigrés, largely educated people and World War II veterans who were deported or imprisoned after the Soviet attack on Poland in September 1939, many with experience of the gulag in their backgrounds. Their experience determined their strong anti-Communist stand and their great animosity toward Miłosz, who in the late forties had represented the Polish government as a cultural attaché in the Polish consulate in New York and in the Polish embassy in Washington, D.C. To a large degree, RFE represented that portion of the Polish political émigré community.

When Miłosz defected to the West, he was in quite a desperate situation for many years. During this period, he received an offer from RFE to address his colleagues behind the Iron Curtain—which he found humiliating. He therefore did not want to hear about giving an interview to that organization. Trying to entice him to forget the past, they had asked me to convey their congratulations in Toronto during the conference on Polishness. Their dealings toward me were also quite offensive; even though I had been their cultural correspondent for many years, they had offered the interview to a newly arrived intern from Poland, who apparently had written his M.A. thesis on Miłosz.

In the meantime, overwhelmed with his status as Nobel Prize laureate, Miłosz asked Renata Gorczyńska, who was already working on *Conversations with Miłosz* in New York, to come to his home in Berkeley as an assistant. Renata finally persuaded Miłosz to give an interview to RFE, arguing that because he had given an interview to *Trybuna Ludu,* the Communist Party daily in Poland, he should give one to the independent Polish radio, RFE. Miłosz consented under the condition that I would conduct the interview, which took place on November 8 in Miłosz's home on Grizzly Peak in Berkeley. It was an honor for me, a certain vindication as far as RFE's treatment of my services, and again the indication that he valued my published work, both poetic and journalistic.[4]

It was my first trip to California. This was an America totally different from the one I knew. The marina, numerous cafes with cappuccino, and even the abundance of flowers reminded me of Italy.[5] I arrived in Berkeley a day early, to be best prepared. I rewrote my questions a few times in longhand (there were no laptops at that time, so in my hotel room I used pad and pen)—the result of a couple of weeks of intensive reading. I went to the flower shop to buy a bouquet of red roses and blue cornflowers, and I got into a taxi at the appointed hour with a big, old-fashioned standing microphone, which I had brought from RFE. Seeing the magical view of the San Francisco Bay from Miłosz's house, I could not believe my eyes. The view from Grizzly Peak Boulevard was breathtaking, and I was happy to see for myself the landscape that inspired the great poet. Miłosz met me by the fence gate and led me to a small room situated over his garage. Even now when I listen to the interview, I hear the heavy microphone rubbing against the desk blotter as we shoved it back and forth. The interview lasted almost an hour and went quite smoothly, despite my nervousness. At the very beginning, Miłosz strongly emphasized that he had never cooperated with RFE and that listeners in Poland should distinguish between various émigré institutions. He was wise to stress that he supported RFE as an American taxpayer but that this was all. At that point, I had to assure him that even though he was not an RFE author, we informed people overseas about his successes. Later, Miłosz invited me to his house proper to meet his sick wife, to whom he presented the bouquet.

Miłosz's first wife, Janina, mostly bedridden at that time, was very unhappy about the fact that he had agreed to do the interview. She could not forget and forgive the RFE's attitude toward Miłosz in the fifties. Neither could Miłosz, who at the beginning of the interview took a stand distancing himself from this medium. Miłosz's wife said that the Nobel Prize was the worst thing that had ever happened to them. She resented all the demands and commotion related to the Nobel Prize honors and obligation.

As I mentioned, their life had been a nightmare in the fifties. She was still in the United States, pregnant with a second child, when Miłosz, then in Paris and under the pressure of being sent back to Poland, asked for political asylum. At a certain point, someone informed on Miłosz to the U.S. State Department, saying he was a Communist spy, which prevented him from getting an entry visa to the United States. Miłosz's wife totally depended on the help of Miłosz's true supporters, mainly admirers of his poetry. In such a scenario, getting a political offer from RFE instead of the literary one was adding insult to injury. That was a background for Janina's irritation and Miłosz's reluctance to deal with Radio Free Europe.

We were both exhausted by the interview, and Miłosz offered me a glass of Scotch, which I readily accepted even though I had never had Scotch before. Later, after arriving by taxi at the hotel, I went straight to the bar, for the first time in my life alone, and had another glass of the same to relieve the tension and to celebrate the completion of the task. The following day I had dinner with Renata and her husband, Andrzej, visiting from New York. The interview, some fifty minutes long, was broadcast to Poland four times. RFE was so pleased that they interviewed me about my trip to Berkeley and my conversation with Miłosz. Soon after that interview, I quit my freelance relationship with RFE. Seeing that their attitude toward me was mainly exploitative, I decided to concentrate on my doctoral dissertation.

The experience of the interview, of course, placed my social contact with Miłosz on a different level, and whenever we met he always found a few minutes to greet me and to talk. I remember in particular another conference at Yale University, organized by Professor Alexander Schenker, which proved to be an interesting gathering in the early eighties, the years of martial law in Poland. Kott invited me to join him at a lunch with Jan Nowak Jeziorański, the very first and famous director of RFE in Munich, the same person who had extended the offensive offer to Miłosz some thirty years earlier.

After the sessions, I invited Kott and Czesław Miłosz for ice cream. Miłosz actually liked the idea of talking over ice cream; he made sure that it was okay that I wanted to pay for it. He was both chivalric and concerned about my having enough money for my return ticket to New York. During our talk, I mentioned an article by a prominent poet and scholar, hostile in its tone toward the interwar cult Polish poet Julian Tuwim. "Why did he do it?" I asked, in reference to the article's author.

"He is from Poznań."

"No sense of humor."

While I remember this exchange, I don't remember who said what. Years later, at the end of his life, already in Poland, Miłosz wrote a preface to the new edition of Tuwim's *Ball at the Opera*, perhaps knowing that his text would establish the standard interpretation. This act casts a very important light on his character. Like everybody else, Miłosz had his idiosyncrasies, but he would rather control the damage than cause an injury by defaming the memory of the older poets with whom he might have differed in poetics or politics.

Although in his American years he lived and worked in **Berkeley, California, Czesław Miłosz visited New York on many occasions.** His first address in New York, in April 1946, was 342 West 71st Street; he and his wife resided in a small room and were looking for something better. In his letter to a friend, Miłosz complained of racketeering in the apartment market in New York. Later he often stayed in hotels there—his favorite, it seems, was the Wales Hotel on Madison Avenue. He even had an apartment in New York City for a short period of time in the eighties, so he did not have to stay in the hotel while coming for readings or meetings. Miłosz read his poems in many prominent New York institutions, including repeated appearances at the Guggenheim Museum in the seventies and eighties, and also at the Poetry Center at the 92nd Street Y, University Hall, Center for the Arts, Barnes and Noble bookstores, and many other venues.

I attended all of his many New York readings. At each of these events, he was received enthusiastically, the halls were filled, and sometimes people were seated in the adjacent rooms with video screens provided. There were two readings organized by the Polish Institute of Arts and Sciences of America, one of which was a fundraising event for the institute with a one-hundred-dollar donation. I see on the invitation from April 23, 1988, that my name was also included in the honorary committee. It was an emotional meeting for us all—obviously, Miłosz's Polish readers and admirers were excited about another Pole being a Nobel laureate. I see myself in two photos talking to Miłosz, laughing. I don't remember what the conversation was about, but I remember him saying to me in amazement, "Not long ago I was known only as Herbert's translator."[6] Indeed, Miłosz did a lot to introduce and popularize Herbert's and other poets' work in the United States by publishing anthologies and translating them. He seemed to enjoy his status of a renowned poet—not merely a scholar, not merely an interpreter of someone else's poems, to be recognized not as a middle-man of letters but as a man of letters himself. Even though many knew Miłosz by his *Captive Mind*, he wanted to be seen as a poet first, not a political writer.

I was and am aware that there are people who resent many sides of Miłosz. Some resented even his writings. In Poland, his erstwhile friends attacked him cruelly after he defected to the West; in the West, most Poles attacked him equally cruelly for his former associations. With the passing of time, he forgave most if not all of them.

I am among those who see that in very trying circumstances (and sometimes very hostile scrutiny on both sides of Polish border), he did an incredible amount of work for himself, for Polish culture, and for other people simultaneously. There are many Polish writers who would never have come into existence in the English-speaking world—among them Aleksander Wat and Anna Swir—were it not for Miłosz casting his light on them. He hoped so much for Swir to catch the reading public's attention that he persuaded her to shorten her last name from Świrszczyńska to Swir. There are many works that he wrote or edited, not because they would bring him financial rewards or public recognition but because he knew that nobody else would or could bear witness to this or that particular problem. As a poet and intellectual in exile, in France and the United States, he strove to represent the best of Polish high culture. He made an enormous effort to show what is significant about the Polish contribution to universal values and culture. He did this by teaching, by translating his fellow writers—even when his former friends back in Poland denounced him—and by publishing Polish literature in the original and in translation and writing about it.

He chose exile with a very heavy heart. He even said once that it is better to be locked up with a smart and enlightened person than to be free among simpletons. He believed at the beginning that by choosing exile he was committing spiritual suicide as a poet.

The simpleminded communism of American and Western European intellectuals in the fifties held no appeal for him, and the simpleminded anticommunism of the Polish diaspora was equally unacceptable. He was also repelled by the anti-intellectual attitudes of Polonia of that time. "Polonia" was then a term defining the Polish economical immigrants who came to the United States in the mid-nineteenth century, preserving their ethnic identity but totally alienated from Polish high culture. He did more to promote Polish culture in America than most of the institutions did. He understood the importance of cultural interaction, and he translated both into Polish and from Polish. He is praised for introducing English and American poets and thinkers into the Polish intellectual canon. He educated a generation of translators and scholars, for example, Richard Lourie, Louis Iribarne, Lillian Vallee, and many others. For years, the only institution to support him was the Paris-based monthly *Kultura,* whose founder, Jerzy Giedroyć, was for decades his only publisher. It was the home of *Kultura,* near Paris, where Miłosz actually found refuge immediately after asking for asylum in France, and for some time his *Kultura* friends would not let him walk alone in Paris, for Communist security forces were known to kidnap political refugees.

One has to remember that in Poland, his books were on the index of censorship until his Nobel Prize—that is, thirty years, at least two generations.

In his novels, books of essays, and anthologies of various texts, he always made every effort to present the reality, or his view of reality, in its complexity. Reading his books is never easy, never soothing, but always fascinating.

In May 1984, the Committee for International Poetry and the Writer's Voice organized a bilingual reading and discussion with Czesław Miłosz, Stanisław Barańczak, Tymoteusz Karpowicz, Henryk Grynberg, Richard Lourie, Renata Gorczyńska, and me at YMCA West in New York City. Renata did not attend the event. I heard rumors that Miłosz was not happy about participating with this pack of lesser-known poets, but he nevertheless attended. I stood near the entrance, and he greeted me more cordially than ever. Perhaps it was then that he inscribed for me the Polish edition of his *Unattainable Earth,* which was published that same year. This is the inscription I cherish the most, because it contains only our two names: "[To] Anna Frajlich—Czesław Miłosz" (in Polish there is not even a preposition, only the two names).

Some people resented his record of nonappearances: the fact that he would commit himself but at the last minute fail to come. Sometimes this was for acceptable reasons—his first wife was very sick for many years—and sometimes it was simply because he changed his mind.

I remember two such events that affected me personally. On October 6, 1993, the Kościuszko Foundation opened an exhibit of a series of paintings by Chet Kalm, inspired by Miłosz's poetry. It was a two-part event: first an elegant lunch for a smaller group and later a public reading. During lunch, the news came that Miłosz had become very sick upon his arrival in New York and could not attend the lunch. His appearance at the reading was uncertain. Joseph Gore, the president of the Kościuszko Foundation, alerted me that if Miłosz didn't come they would ask me to do the reading in Polish, with Chet Kalm reading the translations. And that is what happened. Little did I know that I had the same doctor as Miłosz. At my next visit to the doctor's office, he, knowing that I teach Polish at Columbia, said, "Do you know that a few days ago Czesław Miłosz sat on that very chair?"

"I know, he had a urinary tract infection," I replied.

"And how do you know that?" the doctor asked in stunned disbelief.

In early 1995, I started planning a big international conference dedicated to the work of Józef Wittlin (1896–1976), a formidable Polish writer who spent his postwar years as an émigré in New York City. I knew that Miłosz respected Wittlin enormously for his novel *The Salt of the Earth* and for his poetry. In his *Treatise on Poetry*, Miłosz wrote, "There Wittlin still puts a spoonful of soup / into a crusted mouth of human hunger."[7] I also knew that in the late forties, when Miłosz was working in the New York Polish consulate (and while some other political refugees in New York would smear Miłosz with the dirtiest of words), Wittlin's apartment at 5400 Fieldstone Road was one of the very few émigré homes that welcomed Miłosz. Wittlin's widow explained to me once that Józef Wittlin never rejected friends for political reasons. I asked Miłosz to participate and to give a talk about their mutual friend, Manfred Kridl, who was also Miłosz's professor from the University of Wilno and an important person in Miłosz's early American endeavors. Miłosz wrote about him in several of his books. The conference was supposed to commemorate Wittlin's contribution and at the same time to enliven the Polish studies at Columbia. Miłosz agreed to participate, perhaps without ever really intending to come. Perhaps he saw it as a way to support my efforts. A few days before the September 1996 conference, Miłosz came up with his favored excuse that his wife didn't want him to go (but that was a convenient, and apparently common, excuse), and he made a somewhat sarcastic remark that I expected him to stay at the dormitory. (I had made reservations for the participants at Columbia's academic residence.) I tried to make him feel guilty, reminding him how I had had to read his poems at the Kościuszko Foundation. "You know that I was really sick," he said. Of course, I had to deal with that matter at the conference. On the opening night, I addressed the full hall at the Kościuszko Foundation: "Many people have asked me 'Is Miłosz really coming?' Last night I found out that he isn't, but the conference's major figure is Wittlin and he is with us." A few people approached me later congratulating me on that concept.

Miłosz was also known to enjoy a little intellectual provocation, to go against the grain of the politically correct or against the excessively patriotic stand. I personally enjoyed his provocations. I remember one or two. At the most lavish and famous 48th International PEN Congress, organized in New York City by the chairman of the American PEN, Norman Mailer, the women writers staged a protest, claiming disproportionately small representation on the panels. There was a moment when everyone had to leave the major conference hall and wait outside because of that protest. I used that opportunity to hunt down Mailer's and Miłosz's autographs. When I approached them, they both thought I was after an interview and had a hidden microphone. Mailer relaxed when he learned that all I wanted was his signature on the book; Miłosz looked slightly disappointed. He asked me whether I knew that Jews thank God in their daily prayers that they were not created women. I knew about it from my father, a secular Jew. And I liked the fact that Miłosz was comfortable talking to me about it. I am aware that many subscribers to political correctness would squirm, but I was touched that he wanted to let me know how familiar he was with Judaism, thus adding one more dimension to our talks. Another example of his prankish provocation is of a different nature. I had an old photo of the Polish-Lithuanian logo, on which the colors on the emblem's banner were reversed. I asked Miłosz what he thought of this, and he replied, genuinely perplexed: "And how should it be?" When I repeated this as a joke later to another Polish poet, he said sarcastically, "No wonder he doesn't know," implying that Miłosz was not a real patriot, because he did not know the colors of the national flag.

In the early 1990s, Miłosz's granddaughter, Erin, now a doctor of medicine and science, was my student, studying the Polish language. From that time until our last conversation, he liked to refer to her as my student. He was quite pleased that she took some Polish at Barnard College. (Many Barnard students attend Columbia courses and Columbia students, Barnard courses.)

He also knew how to be gracious. In 1993, I was conducting a monthly column, What Other People Read, for the cultural supplement of the *Polish Daily News*. I asked several people, both celebrities and ordinary people, about their latest reading. I called Miłosz on the phone, attached the microphone to the telephone, and conducted the interview. Only when I put the receiver down did I realize that the microphone was off. I was devastated.

"Call him back immediately," said my husband. And I did. Miłosz was a bit annoyed, but he allowed me to call again the following day. And he repeated the entire interview. In the interview, the first book he mentioned was Jerzy Stempowski's *W dolinie Dniestru i inne eseje ukraińskie: Listy o Ukrainie* (In the Valley of Dniestr and other Ukrainian essays: Letters about Ukraine). "It is a fascinating book for me because the Polish-Ukrainian relations are very important for us, but our understanding of Ukrainian matters is not sufficient," he said. "Stempowski's interest in Ukraine and Polish-Ukrainian relations parallels my interest in Polish-Lithuanian relations, about which I recently wrote a book, *Szukanie ojczyzny* (In search of a homeland)." The second book he mentioned was *Polish-Jewish Literature in the Interwar Years,* by Eugenia Prokop-Janiec.[8] "Only when one reads this sort of book does one realize and remember how diverse Polish life in the interwar years was. There were magazines, books, and volumes of poetry that were considered Polish-Jewish literature because that's what their authors wanted. Obviously, there was literature written by people of Jewish origin who considered themselves Poles, and there was a literature written by those who wanted to be Jews and considered Polish language as one of the diaspora's languages." For a third book, Miłosz picked Adam Lizakowski's poetry volume entitled *Współczesny prymitywizm* (Modern primitivism). Miłosz liked the fact that Lizakowski "realistically writes about America and Polonia." Miłosz observed, "These are poems that could be considered very controversial, but because they are truly realistic, very often brutal, they are interesting."

I was grateful to him for repeating his interview, and I said, "You are an angel." He sighed the untranslatable "*proszę pani,*" meaning something like "come on."

Another example of him being gracious is of a more weighty matter. I remember a big ceremony for the Bruno Schulz Award, established in the early 1990s by Jerzy Kosiński, then president of the American PEN Club. The award was to be bestowed on another great Polish poet: Zbigniew Herbert. It was a great event—with Elizabeth Hardwick and Helen Vendler in the jury, if I remember rightly—and everybody who was anybody was in the audience. Initially, the condition of the relatively generous (ten thousand dollars, as I recall) award was that the awardee should be present at the ceremony. But Herbert could not come, and he was awarded, anyway. The usual glass-of-wine reception followed. When I met Miłosz, I told him that Mrs. Halina Wittlin, the widow of Józef Wittlin, was in the audience. He immediately asked me to take him to her, and while they talked I brought them their two glasses of red wine. During our conversation, Miłosz told me that he had persuaded the award committee to give the award, despite Herbert's absence. And he was visibly happy that they had complied, although his relationship with Herbert was at that time far from the initial cordiality. Again, I thought that was gracious.

In 2003, when Miłosz was already living permanently in Kraków, Poland, I wrote him a letter asking for intervention on behalf of Tymoteusz

Karpowicz, the prominent Polish poet, who had been (for some time) a professor at the University of Illinois at Chicago. Karpowicz (who died in June 2005) lived in Oak Park, Illinois, in what one might call dire straits. His wife was in an advanced stage of cancer, and he attended to her by himself, despite his amputated arm; they lived on meager resources. I was trying to alert the Polish authorities to the situation but couldn't make any headway. I knew that even though Miłosz respected Karpowicz's poetic achievements—he had published Karpowicz's poems in the first edition of the *Postwar Polish Poetry* anthology—their relations were never cordial, on both sides. Nevertheless, I decided to write to Miłosz. A few weeks later, I received an e-mail from Miłosz's secretary, asking for Karpowicz's bank account number and other data. Upon receiving my letter, Miłosz had talked to the Polish Minister of Culture, who awarded Karpowicz with a long-overdue monetary prize for his contribution in promoting Polish culture in the United States. Karpowicz was an unusually proud person, but I remember how touched he was. He sent me a copy of his letter to Miłosz:

> Dear Sir Czesław,
>
> From the bottom of my Vilnian (still) heart, I thank you very much for speaking up for my legacy and "economic existence" to Minister Dąbrowski. Your remembrance and the financial support come at a dire human time. Many clouds above us are "still not jostled with the horse's nostrils."[9] Neglecting everything else, continuously, I try—as much as I can—to lead out my Eurydice from Hades, myself staying up to my heart in Styx. I wish you, Sir, that your Norwidian horses have most effective nostrils. So there might be more and more clear sky above you.
>
> I embrace you most heartedly,
>
> Tymoteusz Karpowicz
>
> P.S. In your hands I place also my thanks to Ms. Anna Frajlich-Zając for her part in remembering about Karpowicz.

On one of Miłosz's last visits to New York, we sent him flowers from Columbia University's Polish Studies program. I asked my florist on First Avenue to make a European arrangement, and Miłosz (as well as his second wife, Carol, and his granddaughter, Erin) liked it a lot. He stayed at the Wales Hotel on Madison Avenue and had a reading at Barnes and Noble near Union Square. Miłosz had his poems printed boldface in a big font, a gimmick I use now for reading my lectures. He had a great following;

there were so many people that the bookstore limited the autographs to three per person. Some people seeing me with only one book asked me to have two signed for them. I told them, "He will sign my name before I warn him"; they said they didn't care. And that's what happened—he signed their books with my name, and they were happy to have them.

I visited Miłosz four times at his home. The first was for my interview with him in 1980. Eleven years later, in December 1991, while attending a meeting in San Francisco, I visited Miłosz again. I let him know in advance that I was coming, and after arriving, I called to set the time. It was a late Sunday morning; Carol, his second wife, told me that he was in church. Later that day, Miłosz explained to me exactly how I should travel by train from San Francisco to Berkeley, and he waited for me at the station with his car. Carol was out shopping, and Miłosz treated me to a vodka, with his special recipe, herring marinated in mustard with onion and lemon. When I offered to help, he said that during his first wife's long illness he had learned to do everything by himself. Again, it was a very pleasant evening. We talked about Columbia's Polish Studies program, some mutual acquaintances, nothing of consequence. Carol came with a newly purchased coat, of which Miłosz approved enthusiastically. Perhaps the vodka was somewhat responsible for his enthusiasm. But he seemed to be happy. Later Carol drove me to the station.

The next time I visited Miłosz in Kraków, Poland, in 2003, where I went to promote my new book with my husband. Miłosz and Carol greeted us in their new apartment; I saw only the living room, but it was in one of those prewar Kraków buildings with an elegant staircase, big windows, and so forth. I asked him to autograph his book for my friends. We talked about his forthcoming trip to New York for Erin's wedding. I mentioned my essay about him, written for the special issue of *World Literature Today:* "Czesław Miłosz: The Ambivalent Landscape of Return." We complimented him on the apartment.

"It is still not completely furnished, " he remarked.

When we visited him two years later, Carol had already died in the hospital in California, where she was rushed with her devastating cancer. Miłosz, at age ninety-four, had some hearing problems in one ear and walked with a cane, but he was still very active—publishing, writing, editing. He told us that he was afraid of living too long. I think he was afraid to outlive his physical and mental abilities.

While talking to him, I suddenly realized that it was actually from Kraków that he had left Poland as a diplomat, and later an exile. And I said, "You returned to the same town you left from."

"Yes, but only after fifty years, " he replied, with a true note of sadness in his voice.

And I recalled what he had told me in his 1980 interview: nobody chooses loneliness.

Notes

1. Czesław Miłosz, *The History of Polish Literature* (New York: Macmillan, 1969), 280.

2. Both books were later published in English, as Ewa Czarnecka and Aleksander Fiut, *Conversations with Czesław Miłosz* (San Diego: Harcourt Brace Jovanovich, 1987).

3. Anna Frajlich and Jan Kott, "O Miłoszu: Z prof. Janem Kottem rozmawia Anna Frajlich," *Tydzień Polski*, November 8–9, 1980, 3.

4. Cynthia L. Haven, ed., "Nobody Chooses Loneliness," *Czesław Miłosz: Conversations* (Jackson: University Press of Mississippi, 2006), 12–23.

5. At that time in New York, you could find cappuccino only in Little Italy and cut flowers hardly anywhere.

6. See Zbigniew Herbert, *Selected Poems,* trans. Czesław Miłosz and Peter Dale Scott, with an introduction by A. Alvarez (Harmondsworth, U.K.: Penguin, 1968).

7. Czesław Miłosz, *A Treatise on Poetry,* trans. Robert Hass (New York: Ecco, 2001), 23.

8. Eugenia Prokop-Janiec, *Polish-Jewish Literature in the Interwar Years,* trans. Abe Shenitzer (Syracuse: Syracuse University Press, 2003).

9. Quotation from Cyprian Kamil Norwid, "Święty-pokój" [Holy-Peace], in Cyprian Norwid, *Pisma wybrane,* selected and compiled by Juliusz W. Gomulicki, vol. 1: *Wiersze* (Warsaw: Państwowy Instytut Wydawniczy, 1960), 496.

Irony and "Incantation"

ROBERT PINSKY

Czesław Miłosz expressed much about himself with his laugh, a rhythmic booming of pleasure and irony. To my ear, the laugh contained a note of self-mockery and a note of defiance. It echoes for me still as a serious, adult artist's amusement at the childish superficiality of the worldly world, with its powers of reward and humiliation. That rhythmical, expansive kettledrum of amusement—amusement, and something more—with blue eyes firing laser probes to check for accompaniment from his companions, allowed Czesław to express a simultaneous enjoyment and shame that he was himself: a complex, shrewd appreciation by a genius of his own character and appetites, without the moral stupidity of mere egotism. Stringent attention to the world, stringent attention to himself: and, mediating between the two forms of attention, an alert sense of the ridiculous, along with an equally alert awareness of larger matters.

Early in our friendship he showed me some newspaper clippings his brother had sent from Warsaw: a photograph of people lined up in a city square, the queue turning at the corners so that it took up all four sides of the square—they were waiting outside a bookstore to buy Miłosz's poems, in the first government-sanctioned edition available in decades. As I remember, he explained, with that ameliorating fortissimo chuckle, that the edition had been kept small by the Polish Communist authorities.

A second clipping was a two-panel cartoon strip. In the first panel, one man is walking down the street while reading a book, oblivious to a second figure lurking around the corner with a dagger. In the second panel, the corpse of the man who was reading lies in a dark pool, with the dagger in its back. The assassin-thief is now walking along reading the book—he is drawn walking toward us, so the title is now legible, in all caps: "MIŁOSZ POEMS."

Without denying a certain pleasure in such things, Czesław also made clear an element of skepticism: public acclaim, like the public neglect of which he had ample experience, was a matter of petty caprice and of large historical processes, mindless currents that had little to do with art itself. His balanced detachment and pleasure reminded me of the way professional athletes say that one must not be overly elated by victories or overly discouraged by defeats.

For example—as a context for his pleased but nondeluded laughter at those clippings, and at much else—he told me that after years of having his name excluded from official encyclopedias and literary textbooks in Poland, the first sign of rehabilitation was when a certain reference work referred to him—not by name but identifiably to an informed reader— as one member of a certain group not worth serious consideration. He perhaps existed, according to that authoritative text, but if so the fact had no significance. After decades of wintry silence, that anonymous dismissal was the first indicator of a thaw.

Our conversation over those clippings took place in the period after the rise of Solidarity and just before the Nobel Prize—five or six years after Czesław wrote "A Magic Mountain," his poem about being one of the émigré professors who found that they had somehow landed in Berkeley. After surviving the Nazi occupation, witnessing the Holocaust, experiencing exile, writing in *The Captive Mind* about the moral collapse of artists and intellectuals under a totalitarian regime, the poet faced the seeming resolution of life in a half-sleepy, half-irritable neverland, a bland anticlimax he resisted with a spirit of sardonic, flinty comedy. A passage from "A Magic Mountain":

> Budberg, gently pensive,
> Said that in the beginning it is hard to get accustomed,
> For here there is no spring or summer, no winter or fall.
>
> "I kept dreaming of snow and birch forests.
> Where so little changes you hardly notice how time goes by.
> This is, you will see, a magic mountain."
>
> Budberg: a familiar name in my childhood.
> They were prominent in our region,

This Russian family, descendants of German Balts.
I read none of his works, too specialized.
And Chen, I have heard, was an exquisite poet,
Which I must take on faith, for he wrote in Chinese.

Sultry Octobers, cool Julys, trees blossom in February.
Here the nuptial flight of hummingbirds does not forecast spring.
Only the faithful maple sheds its leaves every year.
For no reason, its ancestors simply learned it that way.
I sensed Budberg was right and I rebelled.
So I won't have power, won't save the world?
Fame will pass me by, no tiara, no crown?
Did I then train myself, myself the Unique,
To compose stanzas for gulls and sea haze,
To listen to the foghorns blaring down below?

This English translation by Lillian Vallee appeared in Miłosz's book *Bells in Winter*, published by Ecco Press in 1978, the year before I moved to Berkeley, where I first met Miłosz. The book had made a large impression on me, as on many American poets of my generation. A colleague at Berkeley told me that soon after *Bells in Winter* was published, he had arranged a reading on the university campus by two poets: Czesław Miłosz and Daniel Halpern, the poet who was also, as the director of Ecco Press, Miłosz's publisher. That poetry reading was attended by fewer than ten people—most of them apparently there, the Berkeley colleague told me, to hear Dan.

A couple of years later, after Solidarity, with his poem quoted on the Gdańsk monument, after the Nobel Prize, Miłosz gave a reading on that same campus, where he taught in the Department of Slavic Languages for many years, to a crowd overflowing from the equivalent of a circus big top. Fame had not "passed him by" after all, and in his vigorous seventies he enjoyed the parade without mistaking it for some true Parnassus.

A further coincidental working of history, in particular of Poland and Poles, put him onto still another unlikely and prominent stage. One day I came home to find Czesław in the living room, being entertained by my children, who had let him in. He was just back from Italy and had a new poem for which he had prepared an English trot. He presented the text to me and asked me, what did I think of it?

I hemmed and stalled, trying to take it in: this part looks wonderful, but I'm not sure I understand this other section . . . Miłosz smiled.

"The pope," he chuckled, understanding the absurd magnitude of the implied argument-by-authority, "liked this poem very much."

Years later, after we both had left Berkeley, I saw Czesław Miłosz in his final illness, in a Kraków hospital, a week or so before he died. He was nearly ninety-three.

He greeted me with a familiar mixture of courtliness and attentive self-examination: "I am very moved you have come to visit me. Fortunately, I am conscious."

A little embarrassed, searching for something to say, I asked, "Czesław, have you been composing sentences in your head? Are you writing in your mind?"

He responded, "Nooo," the one syllable prolonged into two or three, in a crooning, Slavic way: "Only absurd bric-a-brac."

Then he chose to give an example of the bric-a-brac, a dream he had that day, in his hospital bed: "I dreamed I was in eighteenth-century Boston," he said. "Arguing with Puritans." Then, "Everybody was in uniform!" the old *basso* laughter ka-booming, with its sense of absurdity and purpose, conviction and skepticism, grief and renewal: an essential sound not just of the twentieth century, but of art itself, in its largest ambitions.

Here is another way of thinking about that laughter: related to something at the core of what I have learned from my friend and his work. I will take an English version he and I worked on, as my example:

Incantation

Human reason is beautiful and invincible.
No bars, no barbed wire, no pulping of books,
No sentence of banishment can prevail against it.
It establishes the universal ideas in language,
And guides our hand so we write Truth and Justice
With capital letters, lie and oppression with small.
It puts what should be above things as they are,
It is an enemy of despair and a friend of hope.
It does not know Jew from Greek or slave from master,
Giving us the estate of the world to manage.
It saves austere and transparent phrases
From the filthy discord of tortured words.
It says that everything is new under the sun,
Opens the congealed fist of the past.
Beautiful and very young are Philo-Sophia
And poetry, her ally in the service of the good.
As late as yesterday Nature celebrated their birth,
The news was brought to the mountains by a unicorn and an echo,

> Their friendship will be glorious, their time has no limit,
> Their enemies have delivered themselves to destruction.

Translation, like certain games, can involve chance as well as skill. For instance, it is in a way lucky for any English translator that "Incantation" does not contain pronouns referring to the earth: because Polish has grammatical gender, calling earth "her" is ordinary, with no risk of the corny or heavy, as there might be—bad luck for you, translator—in English.

And as it happens, as chance has it, the Greek roots of "Philo-Sophia" work in both languages. By luck, the biblical resonance of "everything is new under the sun" also happens to make sense in both languages. In a plainer or more physical example, the like sounds of "beautiful" and "invincible" help give the English version a certain music or conviction, near the outset. Similarly, by something that could be felt as a lucky break, "fist" chimes with "past"; and a similar chiming is emphasized by the pauses (of different kinds) after "are" at the end of one line and "despair" in the middle of the next.

So this time around, our work together went quickly, you might say easily. Not as usual. Czesław immediately approved, as I remember, with no edits or corrections. The poem is one of two by him that I chose to include (with some small changes) in my own book of poems *The Figured Wheel*.

More than once, in quite different contexts, the same question has arisen about the poem: is it ironic? Can these high-minded, idealizing declarations be genuine, or are we meant to understand them as bitterly unreal? If not delusions, then desperate wishful mutterings, refuted by reality yet insistent? Is it ironic? I have heard this question asked by earnest undergraduates and by eminent scholars. My best answer involves a perception of the difference between cultures.

Quite often, in American culture, irony is a matter of corrective deprecation: in its smallest particle, the national double positive—"Yeah, yeah"—that equals a negative of doubt. The irony of Buster Keaton on a railroad handcar, solemnly gesturing aside the locomotive that is heading toward him on the tracks, undermines various kinds of grand scale or delusion: *Look at the physical reality!* and *Come out of the clouds!* the irony of silent comedy yells at its hero. The understatement of Ernest Hemingway, the reticence of Elizabeth Bishop, the desperate allusiveness of T. S. Eliot's Prufrock, all put human life into its place as temporal or unheroic or subject to the doubting correction of *Yeah, yeah.*

It has come to seem to me that Polish irony, as manifested in the poems of Miłosz and also in those of Zbigniew Herbert, is quite different from that, not the diametrical opposite but with a different energy: directed not toward an appreciation of our limited circumstances, but toward the larger limitation of last things. Can I imagine Czesław laughing after reading "Incantation" aloud? Perhaps even punctuating such a reading with booms of that laughter? Yes, I can not only imagine it, I think perhaps I remember it. But not with the irony of Bishop or Eliot, certainly not of *Yeah, yeah.*

The laughter I imagine or remember hearing embodies a different form of irony. This different, Miłosz-laughing form of irony, if I can presume to identify it, is eschatological. Human life, in eschatological irony, is put in the context not of its circumstances (oncoming train engine, decaying culture, existential void, comic misunderstanding) but of eternity.

"Incantation," in other words, is ironic not about the defects of what it says, its propositions but about the limited vision of poet or reader. The answer to the question of irony in "Incantation" must be "yes and no"—pronounced with a certain qualifying, expressive sound.

Note

Adapted from a shorter piece originally written for the Poetry Foundation.

Believers Have This Advantage . . .

In the late seventies, quite by chance, I encountered the great poet in the library of the university where we both taught. I had met him briefly once or twice before, our conversation probably about the weather. At this meeting, I had the opportunity to tell him how much I admired his latest book, which I was in the process of reviewing for a local journal. But I added that *I,* an unbeliever, had been shocked by his flirtation with heresy in some of the poems. He lifted his eyebrows, smiled, and asked me to imagine how *he,* a practicing Roman Catholic, felt about the matter.

Charmed and amused, I thought little of the exchange except to pass it on to appreciative friends—thought little of it, that is, until I had read a good deal more of the poet's prose as well as his poetry. Then the exchange seemed less amusing than strange, strange and disconcerting. Seated before my typewriter, I had the uneasy feeling that my review, so far, was rather thin stuff. Reading more slowly and deeply, I found myself in the company of daemonic powers (in *"Ars Poetica?"*), of skies full of terrifying portent (in "From the Rising of the Sun"), and of a baleful star falling upon and poisoning a third part of the rivers and the mountains (in "Wormwood Star" of *The Separate Notebooks*).

I also ran across passages like this: "There is no doubt in my mind that I hold a deep hatred for life, by its having been created just so, subject to these laws and no other. Such a conviction was always at the heart of Manichaeanism" (*The Land of Ulro*, 255). And this: "Never had the division between man as a unique creature and man as a cypher, the co-creator of the unintended, been so clear cut, and perhaps it was the calling of America, Europe's illegitimate child, to compose a parable of universal significance" (*Visions from San Francisco Bay*, 69).

That parable would no doubt give small comfort to those who read it and even less comfort to Californians, who read it with the understanding that, for Miłosz, California was America essentialized, a place and state of mind in which cosmic forces were at work toward cataclysm—flood, fire, earthquake, or perhaps something greater, some all-consuming catastrophe.

Now, if these had been the fanciful writings of someone in a far-off faerytale place like Vilna or even Kraków, one would have willingly suspended disbelief. But no, they were the work of someone deadly serious and wholly present. The place he wrote of was California, but a California grown suddenly and menacingly strange.

This all would have been less unsettling had one been able to classify the poet's preoccupation with apocalypse with the ranting of salvationist cults—a Slavic variation on transplanted Buddhist or Hindu teachings or simply on drugged vision. Cult California certainly seemed, when Miłosz first saw it, to be tottering on the edge of Chaos and Old Night. But the poet of catastrophe (and he had been this from early in his career) was no ranter. The authority of the poems, the closely reasoned plausibility of the prose allowed no escape into complaisance or the genteel academic amusement I had experienced in the university library.

At this point, unsure where this all was leading, I looked up from my typewriter and out the window at *my* California, so green, so sunny, so benign-appearing, it seemed like Wordsworth's Nature out there, a great healing power, the fount of ineffable wisdom:

> One impulse from [that] vernal wood
> May teach you more of man,
> Of moral evil and of good,
> Than all the sages can.

(Wordsworth, "The Tables Turned")

This might, one could suppose, be called the Sierra Club version, merely one California among many—the wilderness state of Native Americans, the pastoral California of the rancheros, the greed-driven gold rush California, and in our own day, the developers' dream and its near kin, the sleepy state of Lotus Eaters, and, of course, nine-to-five California, little different from nine-to-five Iowa or Vermont. But these Californias lack the grandeur, and terror, of Miłosz's cataclysmic state, a place infested with daemonic forces, actors in a vast eschatological drama of good and evil.

Back at the typewriter, I saw that, daydreaming, I had broken off in midthought: "Believers," I had begun, "have this advantage . . ." For a moment, staring at the page, I couldn't remember what was to come next. What advantage *do* believers have? Then it came to me: they have the advantage of feeling themselves part of a vast, cosmic agon, an agon that gives the least details of their lives, however painful, meaning, and their smallest acts the feel of destiny.

That was how I read Miłosz's great poem, "To Robinson Jeffers." There, two larger-than-life self-exiles, settling for California as home, contest the fate of humanity. Jeffers, in the poem, the atheist worshipper of "God the Terrible," looks to humanity's passing as a purification of beautiful, indifferent nature. Against this nihilism, Miłosz poses reverent memories of his origins rooted in a humble pastoral world where even superstition affirms the preciousness of human life.

A casual reading of "To Robinson Jeffers" can easily miss Miłosz's benign heresy, so gently, so indirectly is it proposed. For implicit in his description of his origins is a view that, where literal-minded orthodoxy has failed to save the past from oblivion, Manichaeanism may offer another means of salvation—imagination, the poet's imagination, not merely an exercise of let's-pretend but a serious product of a deeper consciousness that we sometimes call inspiration, without adding what Miłosz might, the adjective *daemonic.*

Elsewhere, usually in prose, he puts the case more directly: "A possible deliverance [of humans] is offered by the imagination . . . in its construction of a vision of man and the world vastly different from that adduced by eighteenth-century science and its modern descendants" (*Ulro,* 135).

In the poem, however, he makes no overt claims for the saving powers of imagination. The literal-minded reader can take "To Robinson Jeffers" as a great modern polemic against the ancient sin of hubris. But I wonder whether this poem could have been composed by an unbeliever. Not likely.

Having typed this much, I paused again. An unpleasant thought still nagged: if one takes Miłosz with the full seriousness he demands, is one not also bound to accept daemons, at least the evil ones? After all, an unbeliever may believe in the devil but not in God. "I am afraid of the devil, very afraid! Strange admission coming from an unbeliever" (*Ulro,* 255). So reads an entry in the diary of Witold Gombrowicz, Miłosz's friend, countryman, and fellow writer.

But how about us other unbelievers: must we not believe in the devil or, at least, in daemonic inspiration, for better or worse? Well, yes, in some metaphoric sense—say, the personification of bad luck or urgent voices in dreams. That is, one *sort* of believes, but the "sort of" takes away the seriousness of one's belief (and also one's unbelief).

Believers then *do* have an advantage, the advantage of seriousness, of consequence, of an imagination that can grasp and save reality. And one could perhaps have all this if only one could believe, even in heresy, even doubtfully or like the forlorn father in Mark 9:24, who cries out "Lord, I believe; help thou mine unbelief."

Daydreaming again, I woke, my eyes fixed on distance, mere space, then looked down to where the typewriter dutifully waited. And waited still, though one can only hope that whatever comes of waiting is within the scope of the human scale.

Miłosz at Chez Panisse

DANIEL HALPERN

It was just another Berkeley night for the indigenous residents, but for me it was the annual escape from the Manhattan winter, a trip I looked forward to—saying hi to Berkeley pals Robert Hass and Czesław Miłosz. To be sure, there was coffee to be consumed during the day, a lot of it—some cheese, pungent (as in "washed rind"), and good, dense sourdough, purchased down the street from my Berkeley base, the French Hotel. Then there were the long, mandatory walks—very long, by New York standards (New Yorkers walk ten blocks, then look for a taxi or jump into the subway)—through the natural history of the East Bay with Bob (who cares deeply about his landscape), talking about new Miłosz translations and about the man who was Miłosz.

As we walked, I remembered that day in 1980 when Czesław called after he'd heard he'd won the Nobel Prize. His voice: "Dan, I have good news for you. I've won the Nobel Prize." I think I replied, "Not bad news for you, either, Czesław." Then, from the great distance of West Coast to East, that hearty Miłosz laugh, which took in the multitudes—Whitman-esque in volume, Cavafian in subtext. Czesław was a man filled to the top with life. A man who couldn't get enough of it.

For all that, he wasn't an easy fellow to know. Voluble and secretive, his past worn as if an undergarment, he appeared *truly* only through his poems. He was awesome and scary, at times sweet and uncle-ish, affable, and at other times irritable, a man ready to negate the patch of earth you stood on. Well, just a man of the world—but in a way a native-born American could never be. And the poems, they just kept coming until the very end—and they were very good to the end. I was constantly amazed by how his curiosity and passion for life never aged as he aged.

I didn't know him well—he lived a different era, a different air. But there was a moment in Stockholm, during the Nobel festivities, when the avuncular came upon him and he took charge of me at a cocktail party for his old Polish cronies, the ones still around. Now it comes back: the scent of the past hanging over the room, the pungency of marinated mushrooms plucked from Polish fields and brought to Stockholm by his pals. It was a strange but wonderful two hours, there with Miłosz among his comrades as he might have been in prewar Europe. Never an easy man, but a man, for his passion and innate wisdom, undeniable in the world.

Anyway, Chez Panisse. Bob and I met him upstairs. He was a star by then, greeted as a rock star (or Berkeley's version of rock star), as he made his way to the table. Alice said hi and offered up a few greenish *amuses gueules.* We ordered some wine, a chewy petite syrah to go with one of the more happily spiced Chez Panisse pizzas. Bob and I checked with Czesław—he wanted standard pie, but was flexible, allowing a few slices of Italian salami, one or two of Alice's organic California greens, a few multisyllabic, semi-inflammatory peppers, some intensely artisanal cheese . . . You know Alice.

Our food arrived, the cheese boiling on the dough. Bob and I lifted a glass of the inky red—less in celebration than in deference to the roiling, palate-scorching cheese alive atop the pizza, giving it a little respect and time to arrive at a slow simmer. This is the point of the story. Miłosz didn't wait. He was hungry and he ate, filled with that enormously powerful appetite that crossed over into every enterprise in which he involved himself—from the political to the prosodic to the gastronomic. He picked up his wedge of Chez Panisse pizza and partook, heat be damned.

What amazed me that night was not that he didn't stop talking about his confrère Zbigniew Herbert, of whom he rarely spoke, but that he could take the full heat of that wood-oven pizza. Was it a metaphor? A metaphor for what he'd witnessed and endured? I don't have a clue. But he ate the entire slice of boiling pizza, and then looked over at the two of us—sheepishly, I thought—as we awaited the chance to partake of our meal. Maybe it was a quizzical glance he gave us, it's now lost in memory.

Miłosz, he plated himself another wedge and smiled to some distant avatar as we raised a second glass—this time in honor of Miłosz himself, simultaneously reaching for our share of the cooling pizza before it was gone.

Poet versus Camera

Three Encounters

ZYGMUNT MALINOWSKI

1. By the Entrance

Before the usual announcement of 1980 Nobel Prize winners, I received an unusual call from Ewa Czarnecka, pen name for Renata Gorczyńska, editor of *Przegląd*, the literary section of *Nowy Dziennik* based in New York. She told me that there was a good chance that Czesław Miłosz, a prominent, elusive émigré writer and poet, would receive the Nobel Prize. I was a contributing photographer for that paper.

Soon the *New York Times* ran a short article on the front page announcing Miłosz as the Nobel Prize recipient for literature. So it was with great anticipation that we awaited his visit to New York. Miłosz came to Manhattan for an appearance and reading at a large public gathering at the Donnell Library auditorium. Eventually a more private event was planned for the émigré community, organized by the Polish Institute of Arts and Sciences of America (PIASA), a respectable institution with a distinguished history of its prominent members. Bronisław Malinowski (no relation), a renowned anthropologist, was its first president. Founded in New York by several members of the original academy in Kraków during World War II (when cultural institutions in Poland were closed by the Nazis and Poland's culture was decimated), the institute became the Polish Academy of Arts and Sciences in Exile. When the original academy reopened after World War II under the Communist government, PIASA in the States remained an independent, democratic organization. Its headquarters was a stately five-story townhouse on East 66th Street imbued with literary tradition. Its interior of dark wood-paneled walls, covered with paintings and photographs of Polish literary and historic figures, had an aura of greatness. Karol Wojtyla, the future pope, visited the institute; Tadeusz Kantor, the theater director, as well as writers, poets, and artists lectured and exhibited there during martial law in Poland and during the Solidarity era. I myself had a photographic exhibit at PIASA in tribute to the striking workers in the Gdańsk shipyard where a huge monument was erected to commemorate those workers killed. Its inscription was from Miłosz's poem: "A Poet Remembers."

So it was here in New York City that I went to photograph the famous poet. My plan was to arrive a little early so I could photograph Miłosz walking on a city street as well as at the entrance to the institute building with its antique wooden door and decorative wrought iron elements. I knew immediately that I was going to use my Leica and black-and-white film. On the day of the reading, a sunny spring day (not the best according to some photographers, because of the harsh light), my Leica would give me enough detail in the shadows, and if necessary a printer could make minor adjustments.

Shortly before the scheduled event, as I waited in the early afternoon, I saw Czesław Miłosz approaching in the distance on the sidewalk with Renata Gorczyńska at his side. Miłosz had a reputation for being difficult. I heard that he could be stern and unapproachable at times so I waited with a certain amount of trepidation, not knowing if he would cooperate—if he would be a willing subject.

He was wearing a dark overcoat, a dark cap, a white shirt, a dark tie, gray pressed pants, and black dress shoes, with a leather bag hanging over his shoulder. They walked casually. Miłosz appeared at ease and distinguished. As they came closer, my guess was that Renata told him what I was doing there because he seemed pleased.

I had a choice—either to shoot a series of photos, hoping that something would come out that was interesting, or to wait for the right moment—to shoot only when I felt it would be *the* photo I wanted. I opted for the latter.

At that time, I was very much under the influence of André Kertész and Henri Cartier-Bresson, known for photographing at the decisive moment. As Cartier-Bresson Bresson put it, "The decisive moment is the point at which a subject stands revealed in its most significant aspect and most evocative form." So I waited until their features were recognizable before I pressed the shutter. When they came closer, I asked Miłosz if he would pose at the entrance of the institute, and he readily obliged. He seemed in a good mood. Renata opened the door halfway and graciously stepped

PHOTO: © ZYGMUNT MALINOWSKI

inside, holding the door ajar as he faced me, slightly smiling. The sun was over my shoulders and enveloped the façade of the building and his person. The rim of his cap shielded his eyes so he did not have to squint as I pressed the shutter. He had strong facial features and an aura of authority even as he smiled.

I believed that this occasion—the Nobel winner revisiting a supporting institute—would have historical significance, and I wanted to document it in some meaningful way. I chose a wider shot that included the institute's name on the side plaque. It was one photo and therefore risky, but I knew at that moment that I would have the photograph I envisioned if all worked out right. My Leica was manual, and everything depended on setting the right exposure, focus, and timing.

I followed Miłosz inside to the upstairs lecture room, which was filled to its capacity with people young and old. Beside a heavy ornate table, Feliks Gross (PIASA executive director and a professor of sociology at Brooklyn College) and Tadeusz Gromada (secretary general) gave introductory remarks. After the reading, there was the usual book signing and more photos. Adoring fans congregated around Miłosz and some formed a line for book signing. He sat hunched over the table signing each book and smiled at some people as he handed the book back. I photographed him and the book signing, but I knew that the most important moment had already been captured. I knew that those photos would be the photos of the day.

It was a very mysterious process in those days, watching forms take shape under the water, under your fingertips—like Creation! In those days when there were no digital cameras, there was a certain amount of risk in traditional photography. One had to wait for the negatives to be developed to see the results. That was part of life for the photographer, that period of anticipation and uncertainty until the film was developed and photographs were printed.

I was relieved that the images looked exactly the way that I had envisioned them. The photos of Miłosz were delivered to Renata to be used by *Przeglad*. Miłosz by the entrance was used many times: in the front matter of *Polish Review* (the institute's scholarly quarterly journal) and in brochures advertising the institute. Recently, an archival print of Miłosz by the PIASA entrance was acquired at an auction for Seton Hall University.

2. Poet and Two Muses

Early in 1988, I received a call from Wanda Wolinska. Wanda was on PIASA's board of directors. With her usual enthusiasm, she told me that there would be a tribute to Miłosz at the New York University Club and said that if I was interested in photographing the event, I would be the official photographer. I accepted without hesitation. It was going to be a benefit for PIASA, and Wanda was the organizer. This generated a lot of interest from both the Polish and the literary community, especially since the awarding of the Nobel Prize. Miłosz by that time already enjoyed celebrity status; he rarely gave interviews and was not easily accessible, living in faraway California. As the event approached, even the *New York Times* ran an announcement for the upcoming benefit. Wanda also informed me that Miłosz requested that young people should be invited—he liked young people. Such events are meant to generate money, and ticket prices were substantial, therefore Wanda made special arrangements so that students would be admitted free of charge. It seemed to me that the atmosphere was going to be festive. The young are by nature very enthusiastic, and I heard that his lectures in California were very popular with students.

This time, besides a Leica, I chose a Nikon with several lenses and a flash unit to use during the reception, where social interaction lends itself to the use of flash. I planned to get an interesting close-up, a portrait shot. As soon as Miłosz entered the building, I introduced myself to let him know that I would be photographing him and the event. I promised that I would not use flash during the poetry reading so that I wouldn't distract him. He agreed politely, expressing his approval. He seemed serious and concentrated, possibly thinking about the evening ahead. (He wasn't always so accommodating: during one of his readings years later at the Kościuszko Foundation, as soon as he stepped behind a podium, people in the audience started snapping flash pictures, which annoyed him, and he said something to the effect that he was not an exhibit object and straight-forwardly demanded that they stop.)

In an adjacent room with dark wood-paneled walls befitting such a prestigious social club, there was a dark couch with rounded armrests, where the eminent poet would receive his audience; a matching armchair on the side faced the couch. Two marble-top cylindrical coffee tables in front of the couch, a large plant in the corner, and a standing lamp with multiple bulbs completed the setting.

I found him alone, sitting on the couch deep in his thoughts. As I started taking photos, he looked brooding, distant. There was no verbal communication between us. He knew I was there to photograph, and I did not have to give instructions. He seemed to be prepared by the organizers and knew what to expect; moreover, being a Nobel Prize winner gave him a certain satisfaction as a poet, and he acted the part.

To me, it was a perfect setting for the poet: confident in his surround-ings and sure of himself, casually seated, his jacket open, his legs crossed. The entire scene looked right. At one point, he raised his arm and placed his hand on his chin as I took close-ups. His gaze appeared to be far away but inward-looking. As Wanda and one of the co-organizers, Krystyna Olszer, an editor of *Polish Review,* joined him, the entire scene fell into place: Wanda sat on the left in the armchair, and Krystyna was on the far right of Miłosz—the poet in the middle and two women, one on either

PHOTO: © ZYGMUNT MALINOWSKI

side as if they were two supporting pillars. They engaged him in quiet conversation. The composition (and, more important, the mood) was perfect. The dark-paneled room was dimly lit by the lamp, adding a mysterious aura but with just enough light to switch to a Leica and use available light to capture the effect.

It seemed as if an unwritten script took shape—as if a director positioned where each person would sit, arranged and chose the right furniture, and set up the mood lighting. All I had to do was capture the way these women were sitting with Miłosz as the main protagonist, his face chiseled by the sidelights as if he were a Rodin sculpture, his eyes closed for a minute and the lamp lighting the side of his face. Later, when Wanda Siedlecka-Kossak, an art consultant, was reviewing my photographs, we named this photograph "Poet and Two Muses," and it is now in the collection of Wrocław Museum in Poland.

The reading took place in a large, high-ceilinged room with white walls. Rows of chairs were neatly arranged with the podium set up in front with two side tables covered with white tablecloths. On one table was a flower arrangement and on the other a pitcher with water and glasses. Professor Feliks Gross introduced Miłosz as Wanda shook his hand. After the reading, the guests mingled. Among them were Susan Sontag, Tomas Venclova, Stanisław Barańczak of Harvard, Dr. Jerome Krase, the playwright Janusz Głowacki, the late Jerzy Kosiński, and Bolesław Wierzbiański, publisher of *Nowy Dziennik*.

Afterwards, it seemed that there was an endless line of guests who approached, sat next to him, and stayed to chat. A distinguished lawyer in a gray suit, a serious gentleman with a dark bushy mustache, a short-haired woman in a short black skirt and black stockings who was engrossed in a deep conversation with Miłosz and seemed to take too much of his time, as well as professors and their wives. A group of well-dressed university students from Columbia's Polish club gathered around him and exchanged pleasantries. Anna Frajlich, a poet and professor at Columbia University, joined the group. Miłosz was pleased, beaming with a wide grin as he sat in between two women with a glass of wine in his hand, surrounded by exuberant students for a group picture. Anna sat on the side with a shawl over her shoulders; a female student in a long skirt and black hair cut in the flapper style of the 1920s sat next to him and chatted as I took more photos. (Miłosz declined an official dinner invitation after the event—he had made arrangements to go out with the students.)

The earlier solitary photo session resulted in one of the iconic portraits of Miłosz, with his hand over his chin looking into the distance. This

PHOTO: © ZYGMUNT MALINOWSKI

photograph was used as a full-page frontispiece in *World Literature Today* for an issue especially devoted to Miłosz. This portrait photo was in several exhibitions, including Warsaw's "The New New Yorkers and Their Friends" festival. Miłosz, when he finally saw this portrait, requested a copy. I went to one of his several readings at the Kościuszko Foundation in Manhattan with enlarged photo portraits. His new wife was there, as well as the poet Tomas Venclova. After the reading, I asked Miłosz to sign two photos. He looked at the portrait and as soon as he carefully signed them—on the white shirtsleeve of the portrait—asked if he could have a copy. I happened to have a large print, and it gave me great satisfaction to give it to him. When he passed away, the solitary photo was printed on the first page of *Przegląd*. A large poster-size version was commissioned by Brooklyn Public Library for use during a commemoration (September 23, 2004) of Miłosz after his death: He Was and Will Remain, organized by Alla Makeeva Roylance with Anna Frajlich as the principal speaker and actor Erol Tamerman and Izabela Bozek, a writer for *Nowy Dziennik*, reciting his poetry. The same program was repeated again during the Kościuszko Foundation memorial on November 4, 2004, which Dr. Erin Gilbert, Miłosz's granddaughter, attended as an honored guest.

3. A Window onto Union Square

In *1999, on* one of my visits to *Nowy Dziennik*, the current editor of *Przeglad*, Julita Karkowska, told me that Miłosz would be coming to New York to promote his book *Road-side Dog* and would give a reading at Barnes & Noble. This was a high-profile event for which Barnes & Noble allocated one of its prime locations, its large bookstore on Union Square that had a spacious hall for such events. (Most recently, Günter Grass, another Nobel Prize winner, had his reading there.) Its downtown location close to the Village and Soho, where many writers live and many more had their beginnings, ensured a sophisticated and eclectic audience. David Remnick, editor of the *New Yorker*, made introductory remarks and poet J. D. McClatchy read several of his poems before Miłosz arrived. As Miłosz walked briskly into the room, his confident presence caused all eyes to turn to him. He appeared somewhat aloof but not self-important, squinting his bushy eyebrows from time to time. After the reading, he signed books. Again there were young people congregated around him, and he enjoyed having them there.

After the book signing, I went downstairs and asked him to pose for a photograph. I do not recall whether he was already seated on a low, wide windowsill facing the street or whether I asked him to sit there. He had a

PHOTO: © ZYGMUNT MALINOWSKI

purplish outer coat over a brown jacket and a cream-colored shirt with a knit tie. His hair was grayish, thinner, and combed back. He appeared mellow and much older than the last time I had seen him (he was eighty-eight years old), gentler, almost grandfatherly, but still vigorous. There was a slight puffiness in his cheeks and a twinkle in his eyes (he had always seemed abstracted before) as I photographed him. Later, as I examined another set of my photos taken during the reading that day, I noticed an inconspicuous flesh-colored hearing aid on one of the close-up profile shots.

The result of this sitting was a color photo of Miłosz against a wide full-wall window with a view of Union Square. Later an exciting possibility arose that this photo might be used on the cover of *World Literature Today* for the special issue on Miłosz. I corresponded by e-mail with William Reagan, the editor. First he told me that they always use an art reproduction for their cover, but then he later informed me that they had decided to make an exception. My photo of Miłosz appeared in full color on the glossy cover.

I Promised to Speak My Mind

MADELINE G. LEVINE

My collaboration and friendship with Czesław Miłosz began in the most unlikely manner with a rudely dismissive letter from his then–literary agent sometime in the mid-1980s. At the time, I was already a full professor and was serving as chair of our Department of Slavic Languages and Literatures. On behalf of the College of Arts and Sciences at the University of North Carolina at Chapel Hill, I had written to inquire whether Miłosz would honor us by accepting an invitation to appear on campus as a distinguished lecturer in one of our endowed lecture series. My request had been routed to the agent, who most likely dealt with a flood of such invitations. After a considerable delay, a letter arrived rejecting the invitation. Its message, which I paraphrase here, was all too clear: "If you think this great writer will come to your campus for such a measly honorarium you probably also expect to put him up in some junior faculty member's home with a crying baby, diapers on the line, and a barking dog." Humiliated by this response, I informed my dean that I had failed to secure the poet's visit to our campus, and I mourned not only the lost opportunity to bring Czesław Miłosz to Chapel Hill but also the end, as I believed then, of any hopes I might have nurtured of building some kind of personal and professional relationship with him.

Prior to that apparently disastrous misstep, I had had pleasant, but superficial, encounters with Miłosz on a number of occasions. Before I met him in person, he had responded courteously to inquiries I had sent him asking his opinion about translation projects I was interested in undertaking. The first time we met and spoke at any length was at the Miłosz Days celebration held at the University of Alberta at Edmonton in 1981. He was welcoming and friendly but seemed most interested in assessing me, a student of Professor Wiktor Weintraub, Harvard's esteemed scholar of Polish romanticism, against the doctoral students Miłosz could claim as his own. There was an unacknowledged element of competition in his questioning of me—a competition that I am sure was one-sided, for I had never heard anything comparable from Professor Weintraub.

A few years after our meeting in Edmonton, Miłosz had surprised me by telephoning to say that he would be giving a reading at North Carolina State University in Raleigh and inviting me to attend (which, of course, I'd long planned on doing). After the reading, my husband and a colleague and I spent a few delightful hours with Miłosz in a nearby student hangout. We responded to his curiosity about the South, the differences between NC State and UNC, enrollments in Slavic courses, and other matters not at all related to Polish letters. On both those occasions, in Edmonton and in Raleigh, I could see that Miłosz's attentiveness toward me functioned, perhaps primarily, as a device to distance himself from his official hosts and their tiresome adulation. (In years to come, I would observe him behaving similarly at a number of public events, for he seemed both to crave adulation and to be genuinely irritated by it. He would refer to himself as a tame bear with whom tourists like to have their picture taken.) Nonetheless, I had hoped that I would have the opportunity to meet with him occasionally in the future; the contemptuously dismissive rejection letter seemed to erase all such hopes.

Many months later, I came home from work one afternoon to hear from my husband that he had taken a call from Czesław Miłosz and that Miłosz had refused to leave a message, saying only that what he had to say could not be conveyed by an intermediary and that I was not to return the call. When he phoned later that evening, Miłosz astounded me by beginning with effusive apologies. He explained that he had only that day seen a copy of his agent's letter, that he was distressed that someone he considered a colleague should have been addressed so rudely, and so he simply had to apologize personally. He dismissed my protestations that he, after all, had had nothing to do with the letter and insisted that the only way he could make the matter right was to accept the offered honorarium and arrange to give a reading at UNC when his schedule permitted. From this gracious gesture of repairing a hurt that he had not inflicted, our friendship and eventual collaboration began.

Not surprisingly, the poetry reading—held in the spring of 1990, if I am not mistaken—was an extraordinary success. The large campus auditorium was filled to overflowing with a wildly enthusiastic audience of students and community members. After the post-reading reception, the generous proprietors of the one Polish restaurant in town invited Miłosz to a lavish meal with a dozen or so Solidarity-era émigrés from the local university and research communities. Whether it was the engaged response to his reading by the students and community members in the overflow audience, the lively conversation over dinner, the superbly prepared Polish food, or the vodka tumbler that his host kept refilling, by the time I dropped him off at his hotel after 2:00 a.m., Czesław had decided that he would love to return to Chapel Hill for an extended stay. He phoned Carol immediately to share his enthusiasm. A few weeks later, he asked me to see whether I could arrange a visiting appointment for him on the faculty. Administrative hurdles were easily cleared, and by the start of the fall semester of the 1991/92 academic year, he began his one-year residency at UNC as a visiting professor of Slavic and English literatures and an honorary fellow of the Institute for the Arts and Humanities.

It was a year of mixed pleasures and disappointments for Czesław. He had asked not to be burdened with any formal obligations other than giving another public reading. He was looking forward, he said, to having time to write and to accompany Carol on photography trips back to her grandparents' old homestead in Tarboro and around the state. Also, during the first semester, he was suffering from alarming bouts of vertigo. Perhaps he was taken at his word more than he really wished. Later, he would tell me how surprised he was that the university administration hadn't given a banquet in his honor, although he and Carol had stated unambiguously that he didn't want to be subjected to empty formalities. He faithfully attended the weekly lunchtime seminars for the faculty fellows at the Institute for the Arts and Humanities, but he usually had more to say about the luscious desserts he ate there than about the intellectual content of the seminar discussions. (That was a discovery for me: his gustatory enthusiasms were not just a poetic trope!) He was as eager to meet with my students in the classroom as I was to invite him in. He charmed a small group of Polish literature students by talking to them about *Pan Tadeusz* as if they really had read it all in the original and understood its subtleties, although he knew very well that this wasn't so, and he shocked them by flatly declaring, "Lithuanian is an impossible language that no one can speak." He took over my Dostoevsky class when it was time to focus on *The Devils,* and he delighted in the give-and-take with the students, patiently trying to disabuse some of the more advanced graduate students of their notion that relying on a Bakhtinian approach with an emphasis on chronotopes and the narrative's dialogic structure was the surest path to understanding that novel's essence. He told me that it felt good to be in the classroom again, if only for a short while. It surprised and no doubt pained him, too, that although he had befriended a number of faculty members from our Department of English, he was never invited to teach an American poetry class or to meet with the creative writing students or English majors. We discussed it one day toward the end of the year when it was already too late for me to carry a message to my English colleagues that he did, in fact, want to be "disturbed." "Small fish," he explained to me derisively, "feel uncomfortable when a big fish is introduced into their pond." He could be very cutting about English departments in general, as witness his remarks in *Rok myśliwego,* which he would later soften for the English version, *A Year of the Hunter.*

But that was a trivial hurt compared to the great wound he received that year when he first read Zbigniew Herbert's barely disguised attack on him in the poem "Chodasiewicz." I remember sitting with Czesław on a bench on campus in brilliant sunshine while he read the poem aloud to me, then had me read it for myself to be sure I understood. He kept repeating over and over again, with a look of utter despair on his face, that he could not understand how Herbert could have been so cruel, alternating those comments with critical remarks about the work as a piece of bad poetry. By that time I had spent many hours with Czesław, listening to him read his newly written poems from the notebook in which they were penned in blue ink. He wanted me to like them all, and I usually did, but when I once owned up to disliking a particular poem he had written that morning, he reminded me that, like Picasso, as an old artist he had to try out new styles and themes or risk just repeating himself endlessly. Visiting with him and Carol at their rented townhouse or sitting with them on our front porch, I had become familiar with his bouts of exaltation and his black moods, which sometimes alternated with each other in the course of an afternoon. I already knew the refrain that I was to hear every time we talked about a new translation project and even after a project was well under way ("Who needs another one of my books in English? Think of all the trees . . . !"), and I'd seen the giddiness with which he rushed to embrace one of the huge oak trees in our woods. I had noticed the sorrowful look on his face and the subdued tone when he talked about the steadily diminishing ranks of those who really understood what Poland was like in the 1930s, and I had heard him express his frustration at feeling at times that he was writing into a vacuum. But those had always seemed to be fleeting, perhaps even well-rehearsed, moods, a ritual performance that enabled him to move ahead. I had never seen him as profoundly distressed as he was that long afternoon when he shared the "Chodasiewicz" poem with me, a conversation—no, an uninterrupted lament—to which he returned obsessively for some time afterward.

By the spring of 1991, I had already completed work on the first book of his that I would translate: *Beginning with My Streets: Essays and Recollections* (1991). Jane Bobko at Farrar, Straus and Giroux had been urging Miłosz to commit to publishing a new collection of his essays. He had submitted a plan for such a volume at some point in the 1980s but then had gotten cold feet. Meanwhile, Carol had almost persuaded him to go ahead with the book and had suggested that he ask me to be his translator, a proposal that Jane approved. Miłosz called me to ask whether I would like to translate the book *if* he should agree to its publication—and also to explain that he wasn't sure he wanted to go ahead with the plan. (The trees that would have to be sacrificed!) When I asked why, exactly, he was reluctant to agree to publication, he told me that an anonymous reviewer commissioned by Jane Bobko had suggested dropping a few of the essays, arguing that they were repetitive or simply not as compelling as the others. The reviewer had recommended publication with some revision of the proposed contents. I took a deep breath, gathered my courage, and confessed that I was that anonymous reviewer—and mentally took leave of my not-yet-assumed role as prose translator for Czesław Miłosz. His response astonished me. Since he'd won the Nobel, he said, almost no one would tell him that something he wrote wasn't good enough. So, if I would promise always to speak my mind, he would agree to publication. I gave him my word.

Over the dozen or so years that I worked as his translator, preparing a total of five volumes of his prose writings for English publication, the nature of our collaboration slowly changed, evolving from solely focusing on his texts to a genuine friendship that grew to include my separate friendship with Carol. For the first book, *Beginning with My Streets*, once he had established the selection and order of the essays, we settled into a working rhythm. I would translate several essays, then send him a list of queries about references or lexical items I wasn't certain I understood. That would be followed by a lengthy telephone conference, which was often something like a private seminar as Czesław filled in the political or cultural background for me; sometimes, we debated turns of phrase or specific word choices. After I completed the first "final" draft, he gave the manuscript to Arthur Quinn and Leonard Nathan to vet for him (I believe both these friends gave him their comments in writing). I flew out to Berkeley, and fortified with Carol's great food and good cheer, we spent the better part of a day going over the translation line by line, accepting some of the editorial comments, rejecting others, and making additional changes as we went along. I did a final polishing when I got home and sent the translation back to Berkeley for approval; finally, the manuscript went off to John Glusman at Farrar, Straus and Giroux, who had taken over the project. When the galleys arrived, we corrected them together in my UNC office, since that was the year when Czesław and Carol were living in Chapel Hill.

A Year of the Hunter (1994) followed on the heels of *Beginning with My Streets*. For this translation, Czesław introduced a new requirement. Concerned that he had allowed himself disparaging comments in the Polish that would be hurtful to individuals who would discover them in the English translation, he asked me to alert him to anything that I thought was mean-spirited or potentially offensive. I did draw up a short list that we discussed; certain minor discrepancies between the original and the translation can be attributed to that exercise. It turned out that what underlay this worry was the anguished reaction of his friend Rose Mandel to Czesław's depiction of her husband, Artur, in an advanced stage of Alzheimer's. Rose, hurt and feeling betrayed, had broken off the long friendship that had bound Czesław and Janka, Rose and Artur. Miłosz wanted to remove the passage from the translation; I argued for leaving it in, believing that anyone who read it would be moved by the poignancy of the description and surely would not see it as a caricature. Furthermore, the damage to the friendship had already been done. We revisited this issue many times before the book finally went to press with the offending passage intact. Miłosz worried more about this book's Polishness than he had with *Beginning with My Streets*. At one point, he actually considered deleting the haunting tale with which the book ends, the story of the one-time actress Stanisława Umińska and the wartime performance of the Christmas pageant in the convent she headed as Mother Superior. He thought it "too Polish"; I was certain it would appeal to readers as if it were an embedded short story. In fact, he thought so, too, but he needed to hear that stated firmly by his "expert on American readers," as he took to calling me.

Miłosz adopted a strangely aloof attitude toward the translation of *Abecadło Miłosza* and *Inne abecadło*. He had agreed to a contract with Farrar, Straus and Giroux that called for the two Polish volumes to be consolidated into a single volume, reduced in size by roughly 15 percent, but he refused to make the cuts himself or to give me any guidance as to which entries he wanted to preserve and which he considered expendable.

We argued about this, but he was adamant. When I sent him the list of entries I proposed to omit, with my rationale spelled out for each, his only response was that his list would have been different and that he found some of my choices surprising. But he refused to tell me which of my proposed cuts he would have preferred to restore and whether I was planning to include entries that he would rather have excised. Although he responded to my usual list of queries, this time he did not ask to see the manuscript of *Miłosz's ABC's* (2001) before I sent it to the publisher.

Miłosz was much more engaged in planning the retrospective collection of essays that Bogdana Carpenter and I coedited. His usual ambivalence was expressed this time by sudden, sometimes dramatic, shifts of conviction as to which of his many writings should be included. Carol got involved in advising him, too, but of course she didn't have access to his untranslated Polish corpus, so her advice and ours were at odds. For a time, it seemed as if the project might not come to pass. In the end, however, Czesław expressed his pleasure at the volume Bogdana and I had crafted from his writings, especially once *To Begin Where I Am: Selected Essays* (2001) started receiving laudatory reviews.

The last book that I translated for him was *Legends of Modernity: Essays and Letters from Occupied Poland, 1942–1943* (2005). Surprisingly, this was the one translation about which he expressed no ambivalence; he was eager to have it available in English. But he was already in failing health when I began working on it and had neither the time nor the interest to respond to queries and offer advice about difficult passages. He didn't live to see the book come out, but I was told by Agnieszka Kosińska, his devoted personal secretary, that he knew I had completed the translation and that she had received the manuscript I had prepared for him in extra-large type.

I saw Czesław for the last time in June 2003, in Kraków. He insisted that we go out to a restaurant in the Rynek for lunch (a complicated production—getting down the stairs of his apartment building, taking a taxi, walking slowly into the square—tactfully managed by Agnieszka, who went with us), but the old gusto was gone. Mostly, he talked about his loneliness, how much he missed Carol, how shocking her death (followed soon afterward by his brother's) had been for him. The bust of Carol he had commissioned wasn't completed yet, but he showed me the photograph it would be based on, indicated where exactly it would be placed, and spoke about his hope that he would hear her laughter warming the room when he looked at it. He was ready to die, he said, for he had outlived his life, but he also felt that he was still needed by his sons.

Despite the pervasive sadness of this visit, there were also moments when Czesław brightened with his old curiosity. He wanted to know if there was any interesting political news from the States that he might have missed, and I finally came up with one topic that intrigued him: the Christian-Zionist support for Israel and the fundamentalist rancher who was trying to breed an all-red cow that would, according to rabbinical lore, hasten the coming of the Messiah. That was the last time I heard Czesław laugh—not the hearty laughter of old, but a genuine laugh nonetheless. I cherish the memory of that moment.

"Pretending to Be a Real Person"

HELEN VENDLER

It was in late 1983, if I remember correctly, that the *New Yorker* asked me to review two of Miłosz's collections, *Bells in Winter* (1978) and *The Separate Notebooks* (1984). I had not liked, when I read it, *The Captive Mind;* I did not know, while reading it, that the political and intellectual paths taken by Miłosz's contemporaries, scorned in that book, were paths that Miłosz himself might have followed. The denigration expressed toward those he profiled was (I later felt) implicitly directed against himself and his own susceptibility to the temptations to which they succumbed. Then came the Nobel Prize, which brought Miłosz as a poet to my attention, along with the superb 1981 issue of *Ironwood* devoted to his poetry. That sent me to the 1973 *Selected Poems* and the 1978 *Bells in Winter.* By then, I could see the tip of the Miłoszian iceberg and longed to know what the other nine-tenths was like. I felt honored to write about *Bells in Winter* and *The Separate Notebooks,* to sketch out for myself, in the *New Yorker* essay (March 19, 1984, 138–46), the contours of Miłosz's daunting power. (It was not until the *New and Collected Poems, 1931–2001* that I could take some measure of the whole, although I knew that that collection was not by any means a *Complete Poems.*)

Miłosz had come to Harvard in 1981–82 to give the Charles Eliot Norton Lectures (later published in 1983 as *The Witness of Poetry*). I was invited to a party given for him as he began the lectures, and I looked forward to being in the presence of the author of *Bells in Winter* and *Selected Poems.* I didn't approach him, but after a while my host, Teresa Gilman, asked me if I had yet met him. When I said no, Teresa brought me up to where Miłosz was conversing with someone. She said, "Czesław, this is Helen Vendler, I wanted to have her meet you." Miłosz looked at me under beetling eyebrows, frigid and unsmiling, and said, with some acerbic disapproval, "Ah, the pope of poetry"—and nothing further. I was so taken aback that I couldn't say a word, and he turned away and resumed his conversation. I drifted off, not knowing what to think. What had given him this idea of me?

Later I surmised that some poets in California were not sympathetic to the poets I admired, and perhaps they felt that I had neglected (as in fact I had) the West Coast. Whatever had filtered through to Miłosz, in any case, had not been in my favor. I was sorry about this, admiring his work as I did (by that time passionately). And I was pained at being so characterized when we met; I certainly didn't regard my reviews as infallible doctrine *ex cathedra;* I was merely doing my best to spread the word about contemporary poets whose writing, to my mind, deserved recognition.

So I attended the rest of Miłosz's intensely felt lectures regretting our distance from each other but exhilarated by the immersion in his mind. Unlike *The Captive Mind, The Witness of Poetry* was primarily about poetry, not about political choice. Miłosz's remarks on poetry and the social order were among the first contemporary meditations I had encountered that issued from a strong poetic self rather than from an extrapoetic standpoint. His rhetoric in the lectures, as always, was compelling (it leaps off the pages of the published book), but poetry, not rhetoric, governed the direction of his remarks. From then on, I read every book of his that I could find. I continued to prefer the poetry to the prose, but the prose helped me with the poetry. I read his *History of Polish Poetry* to understand better the world from which he came. (Over the long run, his writings directed me to Zbigniew Herbert and Anna Swir and Wisława Szymborska, as well as some earlier Polish poets.) My Harvard colleague and friend Stanisław Barańczak, whose indomitable energy in translation was a wonder to us all, kept me aware of Polish poetry with his book on Zbigniew Herbert and, later, with his translation (with Seamus Heaney) of Jan Kochanowski's *Laments.* Somehow I found myself slipping, through reading Miłosz's poetry, into the ambiance of Polish verse. I eventually met John and Bogdana Carpenter and read their Herbert translations; I read Barańczak's anthology of two decades of Polish writing under the Communist regime.

It was during the period of his Norton lectures that Miłosz at last could return to Poland: his books could be published, he could see his friends, and he received an honorary degree given him by Lublin Catholic University. I have never seen anyone change so entirely. The somber exile appeared transformed by joy; he smiled as he had not before; he allowed himself to be proud to be known once more in his native country. I saw, then, a new Miłosz—one with an unbounded capacity for happiness. But we did not converse. I was afraid of a further rebuff.

The next time I saw Miłosz, after the appearance of my 1984 *New Yorker* piece, he understood the depth of my delight in his work, and he was ready to think me a friend rather than an enemy. We were at Donald Davie's house in Nashville after a Vanderbilt University symposium in Miłosz's honor. Donald and Miłosz were old friends, and Donald and I were old friends; somehow that made it all right for Miłosz and me to be friends. There in Donald's living room after the official portion of the day had ended, we sat on the floor and drank and talked and laughed and I could experience both Miłosz's powerful charm and Donald's dry warmth; it was a very happy evening. Miłosz and I shared a back seat in the car that returned us to the hotel. He was asking me about my youth. I told him that when I was in my women's Catholic college, the nuns had told the other students to keep away from me and my two close friends; we were a "bad element." When this was reported to us, none of us could understand it; there we were, all living at home with our parents, all virgins, all studiously getting A's. We felt hurt. (Later, of course, after all three of us—atheists one and all—had gotten Ph.D.'s in English and were college professors, we understood; in spite of our polite and irreproachable behavior, the nuns saw something other than subordination in our level and inquiring gaze; they knew we were rebels before we knew it ourselves.) Hearing this tale, Miłosz threw back his head and laughed uproariously. "When I was fifteen, in high school," he said, "one of the priests said to me, 'Miłosz, you have a *criminal* face!'" He hadn't known why he deserved such a remark, either; but his superiors sensed his intellectually independent future before he did.

Perhaps because of my early affection for Blake's *Songs of Innocence,* I loved unreservedly Miłosz's twenty-poem sequence "The World", which I had read in the English translation of Robert Pinsky and Robert Hass. I suggested to Andrew Hoyem, who issues beautiful limited editions from his Arion Press in San Francisco, that we try to do an *en face* edition of "The World," which I eagerly wanted to write about. Andrew was interested by the idea, and I proposed it to Miłosz, who to my joy agreed. (We were, of course, communicating by letter, since I was in Cambridge and he in Berkeley.) But Miłosz wrote that, before the Arion printing, he wanted to retranslate "The World" himself. Originally, he said, he had let himself be persuaded that it would be a good idea to have a rhymed translation, because the original was written in rhymed stanzas. Now, however, he felt that it was more important to retain the simplicity of the original Polish diction, and he wanted to restore that transparency before the sequence was republished. So we waited, but not too long—and once we had the adjusted translation (indeed more beautiful than its predecessor), I could write my introduction. Miłosz approved it, and the book was printed in 1989, containing, as a frontispiece, Jim Dine's dry-point portrait, done on Mylar, of a bristly eyebrowed fierce Miłosz.[1] I appreciated the sequence all the more after having tracked it, word for word, in the Polish against the English, trying as well as I could to see the sequence of its sounds, the placing of its line breaks, and the character of its syntax. The redefinitions, at the center of "The World," of the theological virtues of Faith, Hope, and Charity brought into the Blakean atmosphere of the sequence touching talismans of Miłosz's youthful catechism. In its deliberate naïveté of expression, reflecting its origin in childhood belief and Blake's *Songs of Innocence*, Miłosz had created in "The World" an autobiography in style—from simplicity to complexity—as well as in narrative. Miłosz liked the edition and was glad to have *The World* as a freestanding poem between hard covers, with each poem given its due in both languages.

In June 1989, Miłosz came to Harvard to receive an honorary degree. He had by then returned frequently to Poland, and he spoke with depth of feeling about being there and about seeing Szetejnie again. He often said I should come one day, and I said I would; but it did not happen. Later, in 1992, I wrote in the *New York Review of Books* (August 13, 1992, 44–46) an essay on Miłosz's 1991 *Provinces* and his prose collection *Beginning with My Streets*, mentioning also the introduction to Miłosz's work by Leonard Nathan and Arthur Quinn. That book disappointed me, because I wanted, from critics who could read Polish, remarks about Miłosz's individualities of style, but these commentators spoke mainly of Miłosz's themes.

My former Harvard graduate student Robert Faggen, who had become a professor at Claremont McKenna College, convened a conference there in honor of Miłosz in April 1998, and it was there that I met Miłosz again. In that atmosphere, he was unbuttoned, funny, willing to pose for pictures, generous in his responses to the speakers. We were at ease together there, and we had more time for conversation later in 1998, in Santa Fe, where I was to be Miłosz's interlocutor in a Lannan Foundation video. Thinking that I should do him the courtesy of letting him see the questions I was about to put to him, I gave him a copy the night before, asking him to delete anything he didn't want to discuss. He and his second wife, Carol, and I got into the cab to go to the foundation the next morning, and he said, with a rumbling laugh, in his deep voice with its pronounced accent, "You ask *very good* questions," and said I could ask them all. The video was imperfect in production (I was told by the Lannan people), but they issued it anyway. I've never been able to bring myself to watch it (although I own it), so I don't know how well it succeeded, technically speaking. But it was comfortable to sit with him in the studio and talk: again he was openhearted and free in his remarks, and nothing came out "canned" or "tailored."

I had heard by then that there was a long sequence he had written called *Treatise on Poetry.* I begged him to publish it in English so I could read it. "But," he said, "it deals with Polish poets that people here don't know at all, and about aesthetic quarrels among modern writers." "I don't care," I said. "You still should do it; you can add notes giving readers any information they would need." In a year or so, to my enormous surprise, I received in the mail a typescript of the translated treatise, accompanied by a provisional version of explanatory notes. I made some suggestions with respect to the notes for the benefit of readers, and he adopted them, I think, though I've never checked. When *A Treatise on Poetry* appeared in 2001, I had the great pleasure of writing about that formidable poem in the *New York Review of Books* (May 31, 2001, 27–31). I know that there is a "Treatise on Morals" as yet untranslated; I am still waiting for that.

In 2000, a couple of years after the Lannan meeting, I was telephoned by a staff member at Amherst College, who said that she was hoping to arrange a visit by Miłosz to the college. He had asked if they would invite me to be his interlocutor for the conversation with the students after his reading. The staff member clearly found this somewhat peculiar, as in fact I did, too; he was so vivid a conversationalist that I thought he would do very well with the students without any help from me. But I of course agreed, and Carol and he and I met for lunch in Amherst before the afternoon reading. By this time, with uncertain balance and impaired sight, he used a cane because he found walking difficult; Carol looked after him with discretion and a complete absence of any patronizing solicitude. We had a merry and affectionate lunch, talking mostly about Kraków and the transformation of the old barn in Szetejnie into the Miłosz Center. At the end of lunch, I asked him whether he wanted to do his reading first and then have the conversation (as I thought he would, since the poetry should have pride of place) or whether he wanted to have the conversation first and then the reading. "Oh," he said, again bursting out with laughter, "let's have the conversation first so I can pretend to be a *Real Person!*" And he did that very successfully. We conducted a quasi-reprise of the Lannan conversation for the students and then opened the floor to them; they rose vigorously to the occasion, and he answered them in good spirits. He then gave a resonant reading, mostly of recent poems, reproduced in very large type because of the worsening of his macular degeneration. The thought of oncoming blindness had depressed him greatly, but he had recently been helped, Carol told me, by one of the machines that can magnify on a screen a book placed beneath it. In that way he had been able to continue to read Polish books in small print. He had apparently tried having persons read to him in Polish, but he hadn't found that satisfactory—probably because, like most rapid readers, he found oral reading too slow.

In 2001, when my essay on *A Treatise on Poetry* appeared, Miłosz was in Kraków. Afraid that he would not see an American journal there, I sent him a copy of the essay, wanting him to know how grateful I was that his brooding intellectual sequence now existed in English. By return mail, he sent me a beautiful book of photographs of Carol and himself visiting scenes in Vilnius and Poland. Their happiness together was by then the linchpin of his life.

We all expected, of course, that he and Carol would return from Kraków. Then there was her illness and her travel to consult doctors in California while he remained in Kraków; then came the news that her illness was terminal, followed by his rapid flight to California; then her sudden death and his desolate return to Poland. After Carol's death, he sent me his elegy for her, "Orpheus and Eurydice," printed in a small booklet in five languages—Polish, English, German, Russian, and Swedish. In it, he is the Orpheus who descends to a modern Dantean hell to find, and lose, Eurydice. In the elegy, he dwelt on Carol's having called him "a good man": he was never sure he deserved that epithet.

I thought he would live forever. The sheer force of his personality seemed inextinguishable. Even now, his death seems not to have happened, although I saw, with pain, in the Kraków newspaper sent me by a friend, the coffin with its affixed and inscribed bronze tablet: MIŁOSZ.

Notes

1. Czesław Miłosz, *The World*, with an introduction by Helen Vendler (San Francisco: Arion Press, 1990).

Miłosz as Buddhist

JANE HIRSHFIELD

Since hearing the news of Czesław Miłosz's death, I've been remembering an afternoon we sat outside his house on Grizzly Peak, in
Berkeley—a half-timbered Tudor of an architectural style known locally
as "Storybook Cottage." That afternoon, he carried a newly arrived copy
of the *New Yorker* magazine. He wanted me to explain the cartoons, whose
references were not part of days spent more in the company of Schopen-
hauer than amidst ordinary American culture. Once a joke became clear,
his great laughter was unaccented yet somehow thoroughly Polish. Afterwards, in a change of direction entirely characteristic, he asked me to
describe the Buddha's teachings on suffering and liberation.

Miłosz's sympathy for the dharma arose, I think, out of the central role
compassion played in his own understanding of human life. The story
of Shakyamuni's devotion to solving the problem of suffering had long
drawn Miłosz to Buddhist thought, and the Mahayana idea that an awakened person might refuse the freedom of nirvana until every last creature
and grass blade might also enter was greatly of interest. Still, the equally
important idea of *sunyata* (the essential "emptiness"—more accurately,
"spaciousness"—of all that appears to be objective, reified existence, including the illusion of a fixed and entirely separate self) filled him with
undisguised horror. For him, a world devoid of the eternal, individual
human soul and its salvation, one in which, as he put it that day, dinosaur
consumes dinosaur and meat-eating wasps devour the body of a mouse,
was a realm of unimaginable hell.

I've been asked to describe what he was like—not the poetry, but the
man. I didn't find the two to be much separate. He knew himself well, and
the poems describe without sentiment even the wolfish concentration of

his eating. The trickster humor is, of course, present also, as is the historical and theological way he parsed the world. Born into an age before Freud, Miłosz spoke without any reference to psychological dynamics, an absence both noticeable and startling. In person, as in the poems, he thought by argument. Disagreement was, I believe, for him a sign of intellectual respect— he only bothered to debate what he found of interest. He remembered with his senses (his fierce accuracy in this recalled a preserving monastic scribe of the Dark Ages) but almost always also by the imprint of praise or rebuke. Ideas resided for him in the minds of men and women vividly present and consequently still responsible for their thoughts' repercussions, no matter the century of their birth. Weil, Sartre, Merton, Pope John Paul II, Adam Mickiewicz, Walt Whitman—his relationship with each was personal, his engagement a conversation held across a round café table.

I knew Miłosz only during the last fifteen years or so of his life. Of his body's diminishments, the encroachments of deafness and loss of vision were, I think, equally difficult, since he lived by conversation during the hours he was not at his desk. Perhaps it was the gallantry of a Polish man of his generation in the presence of a woman, but I heard no complaint about either infirmity beyond a brief apology for the inconvenience. Meanwhile, over the years, magnifying glass and hearing aid were each in turn exchanged for increasingly powerful models. His handsomeness, despite his contrary protestations, was undeniably discernable to the end.

I saw the return to Kraków, to its café life with friends and the easier hearing of his home language, bring Czesław a clear and obvious happiness, as did his love for his wife Carol, during the years I knew him. Thirty-seven years younger, she died two years before he did. At her memorial mass in Berkeley, the erectness of his carriage as he sat beside his son Tony was, I understood, that of a man too long practiced in the bearing of losses too large. When I saw him beforehand, he said to me simply, "It was she who was supposed to do this for me." It is the only moment I can remember him looking bewildered.

The late poems held increasing references to the idea of the coldness of poets. The assertion arose, I think, in part in answer to the continuing force of his passions, for persons, for words, for ideas. Only a person of enormous heat notices the constraint placed on heat by art. He championed with a special delight to American readers the work of Anna Świrszczyńska, poet of erotic love and of the female body, along with Zbigniew Herbert, Tadeusz Różewicz, and Wisława Szymborska. To Polish readers, in turn, he brought his collection of "useful poems"—titled, in English, *A Book of Luminous Things*—by Walt Whitman, Kobayashi Issa, Carlos Drummond de Andrade, and poets of Scandinavia and ancient China.[1] This role as ambassador between literatures was part of the larger work of preservation that included the hats and dresses of an earlier era; the Polish librarian, Miss Jadwiga, who died in the Warsaw Uprising; the alchemical childhood vision of a black-smith. In conversation, too, it was the people and places of his earlier life he most wanted to discuss: Simone Weil, Witold Gombrowicz, his older cousin Oscar. Miłosz's labor of transmission was not only a fidelity to ideas and de-bate but also the mark of his gratitude for what he himself had been given.

I was, I believe, the youngest and the last of Czesław's American poet-friends. I met him only after he had already turned seventy-five, when we were both invited to a group picnic on Angel Island, in the middle of San Francisco Bay. Not long after, he invited me to dinner after translating one of my poems into Polish. He showed me how largely it is possible for a person to live, even in old age, rapacious for knowledge, experience, and—though it is not a term he would use—the understandings of wis-dom. His investigation of good and evil was not conceptual but personal and pressing. I came to see him as joined in the pursuit of Einstein's own final question: Is the universe benevolent or not? The last time I visited him, in Kraków, in 2002, I asked if he had come to any conclusion, since the poems seemed to me to argue one side as strongly as the other. He told me no, he hadn't, that what he called that day his moods of blackness con-tinued to alternate with the rarer times of feeling an existence luminous beyond question. One held dominion, and then the other.

In these days following his death, I've pondered the resonance between a thought that reappears throughout Czesław Miłosz's work and the San-skrit phrase that closes the central text of Zen. The Heart Sutra's final words are *gate gate paragate parasamgate bodhi svaha* (gone, gone, utterly gone, completely released now, freed one, *svaha*). The last two untranslatable syllables are a *darani*, a sacred incantation of liberation and the breath's exhalation, meaning, I believe, something very close to the poet's own recurrent wish for the dead—and also I believe his hope for those who, living, serve as their witness. "I put this book here for you," he ended the early poem "Dedication," written while still in his thirties, "so that you should visit us no more." Decades later, the wish for liberation from pain is spoken in words more simple still: "Peace to you," he said in one poem; in another, "Breathe freely, you who suffered much." *Svaha*.

Notes

Slightly adapted from a piece written for the poets' memorial gathering in Kraków that followed Czesław Miłosz's funeral.

1. Czesław Miłosz, ed., *A Book of Luminous Things: An International Anthol-ogy of Poetry* (San Diego: Harcourt Brace, 1996).

Miłosz at San Quentin

JUDITH TANNENBAUM

I taught poetry at San Quentin in the 1980s. The prison was maximum security during that time; most of my students were serving some kind of life sentence. These bare facts hold a great deal of nuance and consequence, including the reality that I was able to work with most of my students intensely and for many years.

Of course, I often brought them poems I loved. One writer I cherished was Czesław Miłosz, and I introduced his work to my students soon after I began teaching at the prison. I told them that Miłosz had been born to the Polish-speaking class in Lithuania in 1911 and that he had lived through much of the horror that the twentieth century had to offer. He lived through World War II in Nazi-occupied Warsaw; he first served, then broke with, Communist Poland; he spent most of his life in exile. I talked of how Miłosz's poems conveyed both the cruelty he had witnessed and the joy of being a creature with consciousness, alive on this planet, able to witness. I let my students know I loved the poems' ability to express the limitations of being human, while always remaining on the side of the human.

When I brought in a few of his poems to class, Elmo—a fine writer and thinker, himself—had arguments to pick with Miłosz. Elmo read from "Bobo's Metamorphosis": "But metaphor seemed to him something indecent."[1] He asked, "Why is this man afraid of the power of language?"

Elmo referred to Carolyn Forché's poem "The Colonel" and said, "When Forché had to describe a bag full of severed human ears the Salvadorian colonel shook in her face, she wrote, 'They were like dried peach halves. There is no other way to say this.'[2] Metaphor was the most accurate description she could find."

"But, Elmo," I argued. "Your own beloved Neruda once wrote, 'The blood of the children ran in the street / like the blood of children.'³ Even Neruda, metaphor maker extraordinaire, saw a horror so profound, the only way he could convey it was to let the fact stand for itself. He knew comparing the spilled blood of children to anything else would cheapen the truth.'"

Elmo acknowledged my point but let me know that his preference was for a poetry of passionate language. Miłosz's poetry seemed distanced to Elmo.

"There *is* distance, but there's passion, too. That's what I love about Miłosz. Look at what follows the line you quoted: 'By looking he wanted to draw the name from the very thing.' Does that sound like a dispassionate wish to you?"

Elmo certainly understood what I was saying, but he wasn't drawn in by what seemed to him a mental passion. Instead he wanted to be overwhelmed and seduced by the energy of a poem's language. I was attracted to, and distrustful of, both passion and distance, and so I treasured Miłosz's paradoxical vision.

Astounded at the nerve required even to think the thought, I decided to ask the Nobel Prize winner—a Berkeley resident—if he would come to our class as a guest. On the afternoon I planned to call, I flitted around the apartment like a nervous teenager. Like a teenager I sat on my teenager's bed, needing Sara's "Go ahead, Mom, make the call now" encouragement to dial the number. Miłosz himself answered the phone and said yes, he would visit our class on March 17. All I had to do, then, was to prepare Miłosz's security clearance and gate pass, and to pray. I prayed that there would be no lockdown on March 17 and no students in the hole and that the afternoon count would clear early.

The hole. At one time, that's exactly what it was: a dungeon with neither windows nor lights, where prisoners were confined as punishment. Such forms of punishment were common in American prisons throughout much of our history and in use at San Quentin, in one form or another, as recently as the 1950s. By 1986, however, being thrown in the hole meant being confined to a cell in one of the prison's lock-up units.

And count. Three times each day, almost all else at the prison stopped for institutional count. This cell-by-cell check confirmed that all prisoners were present, that none had escaped or been stabbed or left buried in a laundry cart somewhere.

Some men were given permission not to be in their cells but instead to attend a class, job assignment, visit, self-help group, or special event. This permission—being "outcounted"—consisted of listing an inmate's name on a "movement sheet" that had been signed by the captain. Guards had to account for all prisoners, whether by seeing their breathing bodies through the bars of the proper cells or by noting their faces when taking their IDs and checking these against the movement sheet.

Afternoon count began at 4 p.m. and, depending on how smoothly it went, took an hour or so to complete. When the count had cleared, the men were released from their cells for chow. If all went well, the men listed on the sheet for what was called "6:20 movement" left the dining hall and were walking across the upper yard toward the classrooms and chapels by 6:30.

We then had about two hours before evening count began. Depending on their custody level, some students stayed in class until the count cleared—most often around 9:30. Others had to return to their cells before evening count, therefore missing a third of each class.

On March 17, there wasn't a lockdown but Elmo, who had planned to interview Miłosz for the *San Quentin News*, had been rolled up—taken from his cell and put in the hole. And afternoon count had cleared very late.

Under normal circumstances, our class would have been canceled. However, Jim, the man who put the arts program together at San Quentin, left Miłosz and me to sit at the officer post and walked across the plaza to convince the captain that this visit from a Nobel Prize winner was not normal circumstances. Jim must have been persuasive, for the captain agreed.

We had a long wait, however, before class would begin. Miłosz sat at a desk going over the material he'd brought to share with the men. He read to me from an interview with a political prisoner in Uruguay. The man spoke of his effort, in prison, to recall lines from Homer. He ached to lose himself in literature and spent most of his time reconstructing in his mind the work he loved, line by line.

I told Miłosz that my students said they could not afford to lose themselves. I told him how, when I had declared one task of a poet to be that of attention, my students had laughed. "Judith," Gabriel had said, "if attention is what it takes, then we're all master poets. We *have* to pay minute attention in here. We all notice if the trash can on the upper yard has been moved six inches from one day to the next. Our lives may depend on such detail."

Jim nodded and mentioned an inmate who had come to the Arts-in-Corrections office to borrow some brushes to paint. Jim said, "He came back today, and when he looked at the box on top of the bookcase where the brushes had been, he told me, 'Someone's stolen three brushes.' I climbed up to check and saw, sure enough, three brushes had fallen behind the box."

Officer Weichel walked into the officer post, told us that inmates were just now being released for chow, and asked if, while we waited, Miłosz would like to see a cell block. I hadn't yet been inside such a unit, so I silently hoped, "Yes, let him say yes," until Miłosz said this "yes" out loud.

Weichel walked us to North Block and rang the bell. A disembodied voice responded, and after explanations from Weichel, we heard a key turning on the other, unseen, side of the thick black door. Once on that side, we stood in a vestibule with dim light and a high ceiling, its paint peeling.

Weichel led us inside, where I saw five rows of cells, one on top of another. Bars formed the front wall of each cell. From where we stood, we could see heavy wire mesh placed over these bars. Officer Weichel pointed to this black screening and said, "Officers were always having to do the 'San Quentin Shuffle' to avoid being struck through the bars by some inmate-manufactured weapon. The mesh makes a stabbing less likely."

North Block was "the hole," one of the security housing units (SHUs) where prisoners found guilty of serious disciplinary infractions were sentenced to a term of confinement. Gang activity, assaults, inciting others, manufacturing weapons, and drug charges were among the many reasons a man could end up in an SHU unit such as North Block.

The overripe smells of dinner and sweat filled the space. A man on the third tier yelled out his next move in checkers to his opponent two tiers below. A man on the second tier stood handcuffed, wearing only his shorts, while two guards searched his cell. Some men were singing, some were hooting at me, and some were debating the news with others three cells over. Across from the tiers of cells, gun walks jutted into the blocks. Officers sat there or walked, patrolling, looking across into the cells for possible trouble.

The reverberating noise, false light, and moist, dungeon-y odors nearly made me faint. *This* is where we lock up human beings? Public money is being used to create *this*? We expect men spending time in a place like *this* to be capable of being responsible citizens-in-the-world in the future? In the following days, I told friends, "We give animals in zoos more space and respect." Miłosz's stunned response was, "What does a man do here if he wants to study?"

Miłosz described European prisons, which had no bars but solid doors. The primary rule in those prisons, he told us, was silence. What does someone do here if he wants to read, Miłosz asked, if he wants to write? Weichel said every man was given earplugs when he entered San Quentin. Miłosz and I nodded, as though this were a solution.

We walked back to Four Post, subdued, hardly talking. Once we were there, the officer told us that the men in my class were just being released and we could go to the classroom to meet them. What with late chow and no Elmo, only five men showed up. In the hour granted us by the captain, Miłosz talked about good and evil.

Leo protested, "There's no such thing; good and evil are subjective."

"You say that because you're an American." Miłosz nodded. "But to any twentieth-century European, evil is not subjective."

Leo stuck to his position, and Miłosz shrugged: he understood this view. Miłosz told us about a philosopher friend. When she was little, she asked her father, "Is that tree real or am I only imagining it?" He told her it was real because he saw it and her mother saw it, too. But, the little girl said, maybe they were all imagining the same tree. Her father took her then to a hot stove and said, "If you put your finger in there, it will be real heat." Miłosz said, still, she was never completely convinced.

I kept out of the conversation, but Miłosz's talk of good and evil certainly caught my attention. Evil, after all, was a word often used to describe these prisoners engaged in debate, many of whom had killed another human being. I had never thought of these men as evil, though. It wasn't that I saw evil in subjective terms, as Miłosz said Americans do: I knew that if I came upon one man torturing another, I would view the torture as evil.

But my life hadn't caused me to come upon torture. Miłosz was right: I was an American—a white, middle-class American born to liberal and kind parents. I'd never witnessed bombs falling on my city or the incineration of human beings in gas chambers or a round-up of free people who would be sold as slaves. I'd never experienced rape, kidnapping, child abuse, or a gun held to my head. I'd only once seen a beating, had otherwise barely seen one person's hand raised to hit another. My daughter, the person I loved most in the world, was alive and unharmed. Bigotry seemed evil to me: racism, classism, and sexism were evil. Misuse of power was evil. But I'd never met a person, not even at San Quentin, who was evil and only evil. From what I'd observed so far in life, every human being was capable of doing both good and bad, but no one I knew could be summed up forever by his worst act or best intention.

Miłosz declared that if there were no objectivity, everything would be a jumble. He said we need to perceive order and that art, therefore, requires removal and distance. To a room filled with protests, Miłosz replied that art was not life; life, unlike art, Miłosz agreed, requires "moral indignation."

Miłosz's broad face, his Eastern European–accented English, and his language of formal discourse were all strange to the men in this room. They were honored by Miłosz's visit and shook his hand with enormous respect. Still, they left confused.

I walked Miłosz out through the plaza, through Count Gate and Scope Gate and down the long path to East Gate. Above the bay's soft play over rocks, that Mediterranean sound, Miłosz asked, "Who is the most intelligent man in the class?" The question surprised me, as earlier in the evening his first question to me—"At what university did you study?"— had surprised me.

Elmo was the one I assumed Miłosz would consider the most intelligent, but Elmo had not been in class. I stuttered. Miłosz said, "I think that young black man by the doorway."

Miłosz meant Spoon; he had chosen the one man in class who had said nothing, who sat off by himself, surrounded by a circle of chairs. But Miłosz was right, Spoon had a deep poet-intelligence, and our guest recognized this in Spoon's silent face, hidden as it was behind shades.

Notes

Excerpted and adapted from Judith Tannenbaum, *Disguised as a Poem: My Years Teaching Poetry at San Quentin* (Boston: Northeastern University Press, 2000). Copyright © University Press of New England, Lebanon, NH. Reprinted with permission.

1. Czesław Miłosz, *The Collected Poems, 1931–1987* (New York: Ecco, 1988), 165.

2. Carolyn Forché, *The Country Between Us* (New York: Harper and Row, 1981), 16.

3. Pablo Neruda, "A Few Things Explained," in *Residence on Earth* (translated by Frances Mayes in *The Discovery of Poetry* [New York: Harcourt Brace Jovanovich, 1987], 94).

"On the Border of This World and the Beyond, in Kraków . . ."

JOANNA ZACH

It was not when he came to Kraków, and then divided his time between our city and Berkeley, that Miłosz chose this place. No, he really chose it later, when he returned from the funeral of his wife in 2002, knowing that this was going to be the place of his own final departure. Aboard a plane from San Francisco, he already had in mind a poem "in memoriam Carol." It just came to him right then, line by line. He would tell me later that it is very difficult to come to terms with such poems: no matter how deep and genuine the pain, form makes use of an emotional situation for its own purposes, which makes it "morally suspicious." This only shows that he was never able to compromise his ideals, haunted by a contradiction— perhaps a false one?—between art (perfection) and love (devotion). Hence the feeling of guilt or falsehood, precisely because shaping emotions into form requires distance.

But if you measure honesty by the respect for both truth and intimacy, "Orpheus and Eurydice" is a very honest poem: "I don't know—said the goddess—whether you loved her or not. / But you have come here to rescue her."[1] Once, in a conversation, he said, "We speak of love as if we knew what it is, while there is only a multitude of individual cases, quite different from each other." Be that as it may, I believe the following words to be both a powerful confession and one of the pinnacles of world poetry:

> Only her love had warmed him, humanized him.
> When he was with her, he thought differently about himself.
> He could not fail her now, when she was dead.[2]

Simone Weil said that death of our beloved is so terrible, precisely because it reveals the failure of love. It proves our affection to be insufficient to overcome the power of death. That's the ideal behind the poem. Orpheus knows only songs of life. He is a poet of the senses, "having composed his words always against death."[3] There is nothing in Hades he could make a song of, and toward the end of the journey he already knows he is defeated:

> He was, now, like every other mortal.
> His lyre was silent and in his dreams he was defenseless
> He knew he must have faith and he could not have faith.[4]

I cannot separate my understanding of this poem from what Miłosz said that day he gave me a copy . . . There was nothing I could do but to turn to the piece of poetry and to speak of Orpheus. I realized that his situation was not entirely hopeless. He had lost Eurydice, but it was the journey itself that finally gave him the strength to embrace life once again. What did he learn? Perhaps a secret of love, which is not to be revealed in words: "But there was a fragrant scent of herbs, the low humming of bees, / And he fell asleep with his cheek pressed to the warm earth."[5]

He was alive, and as long as one lives, there is time to make use of, and space to inhabit. In the words of another poem:

> day draws near
> another one
> do what you can.

> ("On Angels"[6])

ᕙ

I met Miłosz in 1989, and after that my meetings with the poet were regular though, for some years, infrequent. That changed toward the end of his life, so that I had the chance to see him more and more often, including the time he spent in a hospital. He made me feel that what people say to each other is always important, irrespective of the subject matter, because, by merely using words, they contribute either to clarity and order or to chaos. That was the first step into what turned to be a kind of initiation. I had found a Master, and I was eager to learn. But I had to start with a humble respect for thoughts and words. Right at the beginning, Miłosz disarmed my affectation with a broad smile. "That's all for today," he declared. "We are not going to save the world."

Now, when I ask myself what I learned from him, this is what comes to mind: with every sentence you write or pronounce in public, you must be prepared to pay a cost, for otherwise everything turns into a game and intellectual life loses its gravity, that is, a meaning. And he was paying. Behind his taste for order and measure, there was a deep understanding of the follies of the twentieth century. I saw a man struggling till his last days for the clarity of consciousness, and I remember his words: "endurance comes only from enduring."[7] We are fragile, inwardly vulnerable, our mind being contingent on our motor centers. The division of time, of the day's labor, turns into a philosophical premise for any sort of activity. What Miłosz wrote about man as an organizer of space, both internal and external, became indeed his everyday practice. His powerful sense of vocation and his desire for truth, his knowledge acquired at the highest cost, and his curiosity—all that would have crushed him, if not for an enormous effort to maintain the equilibrium or, simply, to be useful. Three months before he died, he telephoned me from the hospital to announce, "I know what I shall write about, as soon as they let me home."

There is a theory that says lyric poetry can be written only at a young age, maintaining that it is a product of hormones, or at least of vitality. When vitality declines, comes "the age of mind," the time for crop rotation. That day in a hospital he wanted me to take a pen, as he was ready to dictate a poem. (I tried to count: if he wrote his first poems at high school, say, at the age of thirteen, and now he is ninety-three . . . that makes eighty years of constant literary activity. Amazing.) We stopped after a few lines. I could not help him. I realized he was too feeble, too weak to continue, and poetry requires physical strength. At least to that extent, it is a product of the flesh. But let me recall another day, some time earlier. When I came to him, he confessed, "This morning I started to record a new poem, but suddenly I realized it was too gloomy, upsetting. One must not sadden people." I understood. On the one hand, there is a natural desire to commune with a reader, to follow a free movement of thoughts and feelings. On the other hand, there is a sense of responsibility toward one's fellow men. He did not want to burden anyone with his own despair. Some might speak of the conflict between self-discipline and sincerity. But "with pen in hand," one wants to keep one's self-respect. Besides, it was poetry that always protected him against the force of inertia, and now he felt abandoned. He once wrote that "no one puts words on paper or paint on canvas doubting; if one doubts, one does so five minutes later."[8]

In his last volumes, the image of the poet changes. The hawklike Lithuanian from the Berkeley hills descends, step by step, into a realm of ordinary suffering, with a clear aim to humanize the laws of nature. There is something new in his poetry written in Kraków: an effort to come closer to the reader and approach himself in a more direct way. He went as far as to admit his solitary fears and mock the parameters of deep old age. But he never permitted himself to indulge in self-pity or hopelessness. Thus he fought his last battle against nature: that is, decay. In all he wrote, there is a consistent aversion to reducing man, both in literature and in philosophy, to animal drives and needs. Why should we bow to the laws of nature? Just because it has been a common practice? In his striving toward the "purity of despair," Miłosz would find a close ally in Northrop Frye, who said that "humanity's primary duty is not to be natural but to be human."[9]

When I think of Miłosz's poetry, I think of the light. You may call it the light of reason or the light of faith, but truly, you cannot say where the light comes from. "Yet the books"—as he wrote—"will be there on the shelves, well born, / Derived from people, but also from radiance, heights."[10] And I am very grateful to him for all those poems in which there is a powerful sense of beauty, shining above a broken life.

◖

I have never regretted that I did not ask him questions that I might or probably should have asked. I had the chance to ask him about every poem that I had cherished for many years before I met him, yet I was happy with what he told me about a few of them without asking. It takes a long time to learn something about a man, and it takes a long time to understand a poem. But nothing bears fruits without patience. He certainly changed my views on literature, but even that cannot be easily rendered into conceptual knowledge and put into practice. Miłosz was an exceptionally learned poet, but it is not necessarily the author who gives the best interpretation of his own work. The answers we get are answers of the moment, while the potential of the mind constantly changes. In the act of writing, there is so much compressed energy that a good poem, or at least a masterpiece, is always "richer" and "wiser" than its author.

◖

At the end of June, when he was no longer able to work, I asked him for a favor, and he permitted me to read (instead of a newspaper) his own poems. I would not exchange the memory of that experience for any other.

We had, in fact, two or three sessions of these readings. Sometimes he wanted to speak, sometimes not. Now and again he looked surprised: "Was it really I who wrote it?" But most of the time he was just attentive. I quickly learned where to stop, so that he could rest or reflect upon the shadows of the past. I started with "The Song," the poem he wrote at the age of twenty-three in Vilnius:

> Earth flows away from the shore where I stand
> Her trees and grasses, more and more distant, shine.
> Buds of chestnut, lights and frail branches,
> I won't see you anymore.[11]

He remained silent. There was a grapevine climbing the wall behind the window. High summer. The first voice in "The Song" is a female voice, accompanied by the chorus. I always loved this poem, as it seemed to me that through the female voice Miłosz achieved an emotional nakedness that goes far beyond experience based on the opposition of the sexes. Whoever "she" is—the poet's anima, the "other self," or a persona that represents one of the inner forces in conflict—that day she had to play the role of a departing soul. But at the same time, she was so distant, so pure, that I hardly felt a connection between her and the young poet of amazing talent or to the old Orpheus listening to her voice.

Notes

The title derives from Czesław Miłosz, "In Kraków," *Second Space: New Poems,* translated by the author and Robert Hass (New York: Ecco, 2004), 6.
1. Czesław Miłosz, "Orpheus and Euridice," *Second Space,* 100.
2. Ibid., 99.
3. Ibid., 100.
4. Ibid., 101.
5. Ibid., 102.
6. Czesław Miłosz, *New and Collected Poems, 1931–2001* (New York: Ecco, 2003), 275.
7. Czesław Miłosz, "A Magic Mountain," *New and Collected Poems,* 336.
8. Czesław Miłosz, *Native Realm: A Search for Self-Definition,* trans. Catherine S. Leach (Garden City, N.Y.: Doubleday, 1968), 273.
9. Northrup Frye, *The Double Vision: Language and Meaning in Religion* (Toronto: University of Toronto Press, 1991), 27.
10. Czesław Miłosz, "And Yet the Books," *New and Collected Poems,* 468.
11. "The Song," *New and Collected Poems,* 7.

In Gratitude for All the Gifts

SEAMUS HEANEY

Those who knew Czesław Miłosz couldn't help wondering what it was going to be like when he was gone. He more than held his own, writing away for all he was worth in Kraków, in his early nineties, in a flat where I'd had the privilege of visiting him twice. On the first occasion, he was confined to his bed, too unwell to attend a conference arranged in his honor, and on the second he was ensconced in his living room, face-to-face with a life-size bronze head and torso of his second wife, Carol. His junior by some thirty years, she had died from a quick and cruel cancer in 2002, and as he sat on one side of the room facing the bronze on the other, the old poet seemed to be viewing it and everything else from another shore. On that occasion, he was being ministered to by his daughter-in-law; perhaps it was her hovering attentions as much as his translated appearance that brought to mind the aged Oedipus being minded by daughters in the grove at Colonus, the old king who had arrived where he knew he would die. Colonus was not his birthplace, but it was where he had come home to himself, to the world, and to the otherworld; the same could be said of Miłosz in Kraków.

"The child who dwells inside us trusts that there are wise men some-where who know the truth":[1] so Miłosz had written, and for his many friends he himself was one of those wise men. His sayings were quoted, even when they were wisecracks rather than wisdom. A few days before he died, I'd had a letter from Robert Pinsky, telling of a visit to the hospital where Czesław was a patient. "How are you?" Pinsky asked. "Conscious," was the reply. "My head is full of absurd bric-a-brac." It was the first time I'd ever detected a daunted note in any of his utterances. A couple of years earlier, for example, I was told that a similar inquiry from Pinsky's fellow

translator, Robert Hass, had elicited the reply, "I survive by incantation"—
which was more like him. His life and works were founded upon faith in
"[a] word wakened by lips that perish."² This first artistic principle was
clearly related to the last gospel of the mass, the "In principio" of St. John:
"In the beginning was the Word." Inexorably then, through his pursuit of
poetic vocation, his study of what such pursuit entailed, and the unremit-
ting, abounding yield of his habit of composition, he developed a fierce
conviction about the holy force of his art, how poetry was called upon to
combat death and nothingness, to be

> A tireless messenger who runs and runs
> Through interstellar fields, through the revolving galaxies,
> And calls out, protests, screams.

("Meaning"³)

With Miłosz gone, the world has lost a credible witness to this immemo-
rial belief in the saving power of poetry.

His credibility was and remains the thing. There was nothing disin-
genuous about his professions of faith in poetry, which he once called
philosophy's "ally in the service of the good," news that "was brought
to the mountains by a unicorn and an echo."⁴ Such trust in the delicious joy-bringing potential of art and intellect was protected by strong
bulwarks built from the knowledge and experience that he had gained
firsthand and at great cost. His mind, to put it another way, was at once
a garden—now a monastery garden, now a garden of earthly delights—
and a citadel. The fortifications surrounding the garden were situated on
a high mountain whence he could view the kingdoms of the world, recognize their temptations and their tragedies, and communicate to his readers
both the airiness and the insights that his situation afforded. Somewhere,
for example, he compares a poem to a bridge built out of air over air,
and one of the great delights of his work is a corresponding sensation of
invigilating reality from a head-clearing perspective, being liberated into
the authentic solitude of one's own being and at the same time being given
gratifying spiritual companionship, so that one is ready to say something
like "It is good for us to be here."

Miłosz was well aware of this aspect of his work and explicit about
his wish that poetry in general should be capable of providing such an
elevated plane of regard. Yet as if to prove the truth of William Blake's
contention that without contrarieties there could be no progression, he
was equally emphatic about poetry's need to descend from its high vantage

point and creep about among the nomads on the plain. It was not enough that the poet should be like Thetis in W. H. Auden's poem "The Shield of Achilles," looking over the shoulder of his artefact at a far-off panorama that included everything from kitchen comedy to genocide. The poet had to be down there with the ordinary crowd, at eye level with the refugee family on the floor of the railway station, sharing the smell of the stale crusts the mother is doling out to her youngsters even as the boots of the military patrol bear down on them, the city is bombarded, and maps and memories go up in flames. Awareness of the triteness and tribulations of other people's lives was needed to humanize the song. It wasn't enough to be in the salons of the avant-garde. Certain things, as Miłosz says in "1945," could not be learned "from Apollinaire, / Or Cubist manifestoes, or the festivals of Paris streets."[5] Miłosz would have deeply understood and utterly agreed with John Keats's contention that the use of a world of pain and troubles was to school the intelligence and make it a soul. The discharged soldier of "1945" has received just such a schooling:

> On the steppe, as he was binding his bleeding feet with a rag
> He grasped the futile pride of those lofty generations.
> As far as he could see, a flat, unredeemed earth.

And what, in these drastic conditions, has the poet to offer? Only what has accrued to him through custom and ceremony, through civilization:

> I blinked, ridiculous and rebellious,
> Alone with my Jesus Mary against irrefutable power,
> A descendant of ardent prayers, of gilded sculptures and miracles.[6]

Tender toward innocence, tough-minded when faced with brutality and injustice, Miłosz could be at one moment susceptible, at another remorseless. Now he is evoking the dewy eroticism of some adolescent girl haunting the grounds of a Lithuanian manor house, now he is anatomizing the traits of character and misdirected creative gifts that led some contemporary into the Marxist web. From start to finish, merciless analytic power coexisted with helpless sensuous relish. He recollects the fresh bread smells on the streets of Paris when he was a student at the same moment as he summons up the faces of fellow students from Indochina, young revolutionaries preparing to seize power and "kill in the name of the universal beautiful ideas."[7]

No doubt the intensity of his early religious training contributed to his capacity to let perpetual light shine upon the quotidian, yet this religious

poet was inhabited by another who was, in a very precise sense, a secular
Miłosz, one afflicted by the atrociousness of the saeculum he was fated to
live through. The word *century* (usually preceded by the definite article
or the possessive pronoun, first person singular) repeats and echoes all
through his writing. It was as if he couldn't go anywhere without en-
countering, as he does in his poem "A Treatise on Poetry," "The Spirit
of History . . . out walking" wearing "[a]bout his neck a chain of severed
heads."[8] And it was his face-to-face encounters and contentions with this
"inferior god" that darkened his understanding and endowed everything
he wrote with grievous force.

His intellectual life could be viewed as a long single combat with shape-
shifting untruth. "The New Faith" upon which the Communist regimes
were founded was like the old man of the sea, a villainous fallacious Proteus
who had to be watched, wrestled with, held down and made to submit. Just
how much stamina and precision this entailed can be seen in the almost
inquisitorial prosecution of argument and accusation that characterizes
The Captive Mind, the book he introduced like a bell and candle between
himself and his Polish contemporaries who had succumbed to the Marxist
tempters. The sense of personal majesty that developed around him in
old age derived in no small measure from his having survived this ordeal,
which had sprung him into solitude and left him a wanderer, as capable in
the end of self-accusation as he had ever been of accusation.

Once, after a poetry reading in Harvard where he had seemed, as I later
wrote, to combine the roles of Orpheus and Tiresias, he said to me, "I feel
just like a little boy, playing on the bank of a river." And the poems convinced you that here too he was telling the truth. In fact, Miłosz gave the
lie to T. S. Eliot's line that humankind cannot bear very much reality. The
young poet who started out with his peers in the cafés and controversies
of 1930s Warsaw was present when those same young poets were dying in
gunfire during the Warsaw Uprising, their memorials little more than graf-
fiti in the rubble of the devastated city. The old man, the sage of Grizzly
Peak Boulevard in Berkeley, veteran of the cold war, hero of Solidarity,
friend of the pope, was at once the child "who receives First Communion
in Wilno and afterwards drinks cocoa served by zealous Catholic ladies"
and the poet who constantly heard "the immense call of the Particular,
despite the earthly law that sentences memory to extinction."[9]

I know Miłosz's poems only in translation, but they come through so
convincingly in the "target language" that you forget that their first life
is in Polish. Reading him in English, you are in thrall to a unique voice, a
poetry cargoed with a density of experience that has been lived through

and radiated by an understanding that has rendered it symbolic. It's not just that one trusts the ear and the accuracy of those poets who have done the translating, although their contributions in this regard have been indispensable. It's more that one can hardly not intuit the sheer weight of human presence, prose content, and musical transmission that must subsist in the original away beyond our linguistic reach. The poetry as a whole is eminently comprehensible, equally well supplied with occasions of surprise and recognition. It can move from sumptuous evocation to solo articulation. Its easy-as-breathing cadences, its often unexpected simplicity (as in a bewitching early poem such as "Encounter"), and its equally unexpected but persuasive obliquity ("Far West," for instance) convince you of the truth of Miłosz's frequent claim that his poems were dictated by a daemon, that he was merely a "secretary." Which was another way of saying that he had learned to write fast, to allow the associative jumps to be taken at a hurdler's pace. When he tells us that his poem *"Ars Poetica?"* was written in twenty minutes, I believe him and rejoice.

Part of the secret and much of the power came from his immense learning. His head was like one of those Renaissance theatres of memory. Schoolboy Latin, Thomist theology, Russian philosophy, world poetry, twentieth-century history, the dramatis personae of the age, many of whom were his close companions—you have only to read a few pages of his copious prose to realize how present all of this was to him and how flimsy and inadequate the old cliché "a well-stocked mind" turns out to be in his case. The poetry is the fine flower of an oeuvre that extends to autobiography, political argument, literary criticism, personal essays, fiction, maxims, memoirs, and much else that is original, frolicsome, ominous, and more or less unclassifiable. Other poets have written voluminous prose. Among his near contemporaries in English, one can think of Hugh MacDiarmid and W. H. Auden, both gifted with vigorous intelligence and a rage for order. By comparison, however, MacDiarmid, for all his compendiousness, seems to protest too much. Auden is closer, in that he too is compelled to examine the middle state of human life and can never forget the border states of beast and angel. Yet compared with Miłosz, Auden tends toward don-speak, doesn't appear to suffer as much from the complicating drag of the contingent: you get serious speculation, but it tends to lack the interesting impairment of specific personal gravity. I love Miłosz because there is such a guarantee in his tone, a guarantee that the performative prose-writing persona is being kept under constant scrutiny by a more penitent, more punitive side of himself. What we get in the prose, as in the poetry, is the speech of the whole man.

Yet Miłosz was always impatient with "the insufficiency of lyric," as the poet Donald Davie expressed it[10]—indeed, the insufficiency of all art, being deeply conscious of the unattainability of the reality that surrounds us. His yearning for a more encompassing form of expression than is humanly available was a theme to which he returned again and again. "Arranging colors harmoniously on a canvas is a paltry thing compared with what calls out to be explored."[11] Yet he also exulted in the certainty that he was called as a poet "to glorify things just because they are,"[12] and he maintained that "the ideal life for a poet is to contemplate the word 'is'."[13] In pursuit of this ideal, he brought poetry beyond the chalk circle of significant form and opened it to big vistas and small domesticities: his poems sometimes have the head-on exclamatory innocence of child art ("O happiness! To see an iris"[14]), sometimes the panoramic sweep of synoptic historical meditation, as in "*Oeconomia Divina*":

> I did not expect to live in such an unusual moment. . . .
> Roads on concrete pillars, cities of glass and cast iron,
> airfields larger than tribal dominions
> suddenly ran short of their essence and disintegrated. . . .
> Out of trees, field stones, even lemons on the table,
> materiality escaped.[15]

Yet by diagnosing the onset of this lightness of being, Miłosz effectively halted it for his readers, and much of his staying power as a poet will continue to reside in his exemplary obstinacy, his refusal to underprize the thickness of the actual and the sovereign value that can inhere in what we choose to remember. "What is pronounced strengthens itself. / What is not pronounced tends to nonexistence."[16]

Thinking of Czesław during these past months, seeing him in my mind's eye marooned on his bed, visited by friends yet always with his eye fixed steadily on the life-obliterating wall ahead, I couldn't help but see him also in the light of two works of art that have about them a typically Miłoszian combination of solidity and spiritual force. The first is Jacques-Louis David's painting, in the collection of the Metropolitan Museum of Art, of the death of Socrates. The sturdily built philosopher is on his high bed, bare to the waist, finger in the air, sitting upright and expounding to his crowd of friends the doctrine of the immortality of the soul. The picture could well carry as an alternative title or caption the words "I permitted myself everything except complaints"—a remark made by Joseph Brodsky, one that Miłosz quoted with high approval and which could apply with equal justice to Miłosz himself. And the other work, probably brought to mind by that tableau of Miłosz face-to-face with the bronze likeness of Carol, is an Etruscan sarcophagus in the Louvre, a mighty terracotta sculpture of a married couple, reclining on their elbows. The woman is positioned on the man's left side, couched close and parallel, both of them at their ease and gazing intently ahead at something that, by all the rules of perspective, should be visible in the man's outstretched right hand. But there is nothing to be seen there. Was it a bird that has flown? A flower that has been snapped away? A bird that is approaching? Nothing is shown, yet their gaze is full of realization, as if they are in the process of settling for the bittersweet answer Miłosz provided to his own question to life:

> Out of reluctant matter
> What can be gathered? Nothing, beauty at best.
> And so, cherry blossoms must suffice for us
> And chrysanthemums and the full moon.[17]

I was in our back garden, in sunlight, among flowers, when the call came. There was a fullness about the morning that was Californian, an unshadowedness that recalled his poem "Gift," written in Berkeley when he was sixty:

> A day so happy.
> Fog lifted early; I worked in the garden.
> Hummingbirds were stopping over honeysuckle flowers.[18]

Thanksgiving and admiration were in the air, and I could easily have repeated to myself the remark he once made to an interviewer, commenting upon his epigram "He felt thankful, so he couldn't not believe in God."[19] Ultimately, Miłosz declared, "One can believe in God out of gratitude for all the gifts."[20] So when the cordless phone was carried out and I heard the voice of Jerzy Jarniewicz, I knew what the news would be, but because I had been long prepared, I wasn't knocked askew. Instead, there was an expanding of grief into the everlasting reach of poetry. In the Dublin sunlight, the figure of the poet in his hillside garden above San Francisco Bay merged with the figure of Oedipus toiling up the wooded slope at Colonus, only to disappear in the blink of an eye: when I looked he was there in all his human bulk and devotion, when I looked again he was not to be seen—and yet he was not entirely absent. There and then I could have repeated the words of Sophocles' Messenger as he reports the incident that, for all its mysteriousness, has the ring of a common truth:

He was gone from sight:
That much I could see. . . .
No god had galloped
His thunder chariot, no hurricane
Had swept the hill. Call me mad, if you like,
Or gullible, but that man surely went
In step with a guide he trusted down to where
Light has gone out but the door stands open.[21]

Notes

Previously published in the *Guardian,* September 11, 2004.

1. Czesław Miłosz, "If Only This Could Be Said," in *To Begin Where I Am: Selected Essays* (New York: Farrar, Straus and Giroux, 2001), 324.

2. Czesław Miłosz, "Meaning," *New and Collected Poems, 1931–2001* (New York: Ecco, 2003), 569.

3. Ibid.

4. "Incantation," *New and Collected Poems,* 239.

5. *New and Collected Poems,* 490.

6. Ibid.

7. "Bypassing Rue Descartes," *New and Collected Poems,* 393.

8. From Section III, "The Spirit of History," *New and Collected Poems,* 128.

9. "Capri," *New and Collected Poems,* 588.

10. Donald Davie, *Czesław Miłosz and the Insufficiency of Lyric* (Knoxville: University of Tennessee Press, 1986).

11. Ewa Czarnecka and Aleksander Fiut, *Conversations with Czesław Miłosz* (San Diego: Harcourt Brace Jovanovich, 1987), 307.

12. "Blacksmith Shop," *New and Collected Poems,* 503.

13. Czarnecka and Fiut, *Conversations with Czesław Miłosz,* 266.

14. "O!" *New and Collected Poems,* 683.

15. "Oeconomia Divina," *New and Collected Poems,* 263.

16. "Reading the Japanese Poet Issa," *New and Collected Poems,* 350.

17. "No More," *New and Collected Poems,* 158.

18. "Gift," *New and Collected Poems,* 277.

19. Czarnecka and Fiut, *Conversations with Czesław Miłosz,* 265.

20. Ibid.

21. Translation by Seamus Heaney from Seamus Heaney, *The Door Stands Open* (Dublin: Irish Writers' Centre, 2005), no pagination (a limited edition).

Missing Miłosz

NATALIE GERBER

He was exquisitely polite to everyone, great and small, rich and poor,
and had the gift of listening with attention to everyone.

—Czesław Miłosz,
from "My Grandfather Sigismund Kunat"

As the years go on, I miss Czesław Miłosz more and more.

Now, as an assistant professor of English at a mid-sized state college in
upstate New York, I teach an entry-level world poetry course that satisfies
a core curriculum requirement. The students come from a range of majors
and, not infrequently, are intimidated by or resistant to reading poetry.
Few have much experience with verse, and almost none have read poetry
that overtly wrestles with conscience and historical circumstance, as does
Miłosz's, or, for that matter, poetry that requires its reader to work as hard
as his does to understand both its literal meaning and its ethical import.

To students who have little experience with verse or whose favorite poets
purport to be canonical American writers such as Frost and Dickinson,
I teach a handful of Miłosz's poems relevant to World War II, the Holocaust, and the postwar period. Though the students are genuinely drawn
to Miłosz's work, dazzled by his writing as "great literature," and believe
that they do understand the poetry and its lessons, at the same time—used
to a culture that conditions all of us to read carelessly—they misread it and
mistake its core lessons, its vital distinctions, at who knows what cost.

For example, it is not easy for my students to tease apart the distinctions so carefully made by the speaker in "Dedication," yet the poem suggests that the failure to do so was a matter of life and death for the person(s) it addresses:

> You whom I could not save
> Listen to me.
> Try to understand this simple speech as I would be ashamed of another.
> I swear, there is in me no wizardry of words.
> I speak to you with silence like a cloud or tree.
>
> What strengthened me, for you was lethal.
> You mixed up farewell to an epoch with the beginning of a new one,
> Inspiration of hatred with lyrical beauty,
> Blind force with accomplished shape.[1]

Year after year, the majority of my students fail to see the poem's insistence that "inspiration of hatred" and "lyrical beauty" are *not* the same, or that "accomplished shape" must *not* be equated with "blind force," as that gives power over history to immoral regimes. The students not only fail to read with precision but also, and more so, worry me that as citizens they may fail to pierce through political rhetoric.

Yet I can empathize with them. For many years, I was dazzled rather than educated by both the poems and my fleeting personal connection to Czesław Miłosz. It wasn't until I became a teacher and sought to pass on the lessons of his poetry to others that I discovered what it was that Czesław taught me through his poetry and his presence.

ᐁ

When I was a graduate student at UC Berkeley in the late 1990s, I knew Czesław Miłosz briefly and, I suppose now, superficially.

From February 1999 to May 2000, I assisted Czesław and his second wife, Carol, with general literary tasks, from answering correspondence and arranging his rare public appearances and interviews to taking dictation and preparing his papers to be archived. I was given this position by Robert Hass, for whom I had served as an assistant during his tenure as U.S. poet laureate from 1995 to 1997.

In part, my role was household steward during the Miłoszes' extended visits to Kraków. Back at their U.S. home in the Berkeley hills, I fed the cat, took in the mail, and discouraged the two deer from their comfortable habits of eating the plants and napping on the small, jeweled lawn over-looking the San Francisco Bay.

In another part, my role was assistant and confidante to Carol, an amazing, levelheaded, tough-as-nails woman whose vivacity and business acumen were in equal measure. She was business partner and legacy manager as well as wife, a witty and worthy conversationalist and companion to her husband. I knew her perhaps better than I did him, as we shared Diet Cokes and talked about color choices for painting and refurbishing their Kraków apartment, her serial attempts to quit smoking (I believe she finally did), and the seemingly trivial engagements of day-to-day living, interspersed with stories about dining with dignitaries and other Nobel laureates. Amid all of this were her brilliant salvos for managing Czesław's business affairs. In my recollection, in large part over dissatisfaction with the promotion of his titles worldwide, she skillfully maneuvered the change of literary agent from Sterling Lord Literastic to Andrew Wylie. This transition was in progress when I began working for the Miłoszes. In fact, one of my first tasks was assisting Carol with the review of long spreadsheets listing the languages and countries of publication for each of Czesław's books, as she and the new agent considered whether there were gaps in translation or in rights that needed to be addressed.

From outward appearances, Carol was the dynamo responsible for the careful and hands-on management of Czesław's titles, while Czesław was somewhat more retiring in the actual business side of his literary estate. Though this is perhaps not uncommon (I now know) among artistic figures and their partners, my perception of this situation deeply affected me. I had few strong female role models; Carol, a former associate dean at Emory University and an objectively and effortlessly glamorous woman, became one for me. Conversations in which she shared her own challenges in completing her dissertation helped me immeasurably when I was facing the challenges of completing mine. My desire to emulate her intelligence, acumen, and glamour also took a somewhat lighter form: somewhere in the back of my closet is the tailored Gloria Vanderbilt black velour dress shirt I bought to match the one she occasionally wore. An expensive purchase for me at the time, it epitomized what I saw as aspects of her: the design cut into the material—indented lines between rows of velour—had a masculine energy that she made strongly and powerfully feminine.

I saw Czesław perhaps less than one might suspect for someone serving as an assistant. Often Carol and I would review the week's business—upcoming readings, interview requests, incoming correspondence, tasks associated with the forthcoming *New and Collected Poems, 1931–2001* (Ecco, 2003)—and then Czesław would appear briefly for a specific task. Not unlike the poetry anthology he had recently coedited with Bob Hass, he had a luminous air, although pinpointing its source is difficult. Perhaps I can say that he exuded moral authority, that is, wisdom. Slow movement coupled with deliberate speech heightened attention to his features—his famously bushy eyebrows as they arched and fell, the often playful light in his eyes that signaled his sense of humor and his patience. Even so, I was intimidated in his presence, aware of my own limited knowledge before a gaze that was frank, naked, and forgiving.

This forgiveness—manifest in a personal anecdote I'll shortly tell—had its counterpart in an unassuming demeanor evident in his correspondence. He took both pleasure and responsibility in exactly wording the letters he would send, and his words were bare of any egotism. He often appealed to the generosity of his correspondents even as he invoked his own human frailty. As an example, in reply to an invitation to join a program in Sweden at which he was asked to read poems in Polish and English and then lecture on Russian and Polish literature, he first apologized for writing in English (a fact necessitated by his dictating his replies to me) and then, with characteristic humility, wrote, "Your program seems to be so full that it nearly scared me." Also, he wrote, "Reading poetry in Polish and in English is, of course, fine. But as to the rest, you must be lenient."[2] Such modesty and gentleness on his part were abundant in the brief letters written to individuals from around the world who sent their manuscripts to him. Invoking his schedule and his failing eyesight (for reading, he used a special optical device that magnified text), he often promised nonetheless to spend a few minutes with a manuscript and found kind words to say of a finely titled book, such as *Love Is an Observant Traveler,* or of someone's success in publication.

Perhaps Czesław's legendary kindness is evidenced by the following anecdote. While I assisted Czesław, he was working with Robert Hass on *A Treatise on Poetry,* the first complete translation into English of *Traktat poetycki* (1957), his epochal poem of World War II and postwar life in Poland and in exile abroad. Czesław was drafting the notes to accompany Bob Hass's translation of the poem, and I was asked to proofread these notes to correct any infelicities in English; for example, Polish lacks determiners, so Czesław's use of *a* and *the* in the manuscript often needed to be reversed. I vigorously made such suggestions on wording and on the need for numerous and encyclopedic notes, which seemed to me—as perhaps a typical young American reader, reasonably well educated but utterly ignorant about the historical events, personalities, and references in the poem—modest or too few.

Czesław patiently sat side by side with me reviewing my copious emendations and queries. Where I asked for the birth and death dates for a writer or for a standard spelling for a name that appeared with variations through the text, he graciously and unassumingly complied. The process took hours. However, in response to my many requests for additional information, Czesław simply said that I must be very harsh on my undergraduate students (I was currently teaching an undergraduate composition course), a true and lateral statement that startled me and settled the matter. A year later, after I had moved to the East Coast, when the book came out and the Miłoszes kindly sent me an autographed copy, I saw that Czesław had reworked the notes with Bob and that they remained, in contrast to the long-winded notes I had requested, comparatively short and instructive. They were also largely factual or recollective, in telling contrast to the famously knotty and befuddling authorial notes accompanying *The Waste Land*, the poem to which Helen Vendler would liken *Treatise* in its significance for World War II and the postwar period in her lionizing review of the new translation in the *New York Review of Books*.[3]

While I am not sure whether this story says more about Czesław or about me, to me it illustrates his equal perceptiveness and kindness, his direct and humane nature. Czesław could have quite simply dismissed my suggestions by pointing out the obvious—that I had overstepped my bounds as an assistant, that he was a Nobel laureate and I was a mere graduate student, that I was no longer proofreading but rewriting. Instead, he addressed his complaint to me in my capacity as a teacher and so preserved my dignity.

Miłosz's gentle rebuke to my fastidious suggestions taught me about the essential aims of poetry and that the exactitude I expected missed the point. In my suggestions, I sought to reconstruct the geography and history of the poem. But, as in Miłosz's careful wording, the narrator of the poem intends rather "to humanize time" (as he wrote in *A Treatise on Poetry*), evidenced in his author's notes, which emphasize what cannot be found in encyclopedias or historical registers—the seemingly trivial details of an everyday life that Czesław both partook of and keenly observed. Like the "pin, seashells, a glass lily" that one note identifies as objects typically found in middle-class apartments at that time and which perished, along with their wearers, or were mutely preserved in glass cases where they cannot testify to their provenance, these details become luminous in the poem, poignant images of a world that is lost except to individual memory.[4] Through Czesław, I came to value a poem for its ability to humanize time—to make available to readers a range of experiences, feelings, and actions that might otherwise remain beyond their reach. Inevitably, this altered how I teach.

      Czesław Miłosz died in August 2004, which happened to be the month that I began teaching full time. News of his death reached me in my office as I was finalizing syllabi for my fall courses. Beyond the evident, public loss, I felt that something had been lost personally to me, but I was hard pressed to name it. Because I hadn't known Czesław well, was what I felt simply loss of a gratifying personal "connection"? As I look back now—a decade after I first met Czesław, and with five years' experience teaching some of his poems—I realize that what I miss most is his unswerving conviction that humanizing time is more than a matter of luminous detail, that this humanization in poetry is a realm for "serious combat, where life is at stake"[5] and that it is built upon a firm conviction in a present moment in which our feelings, thoughts, and actions are inevitably shaped by our conceptions of the past.

     Most readers today, including my students, take for granted that poetry is indirect and that it is primarily concerned with conveying personal feelings. But Miłosz's presence, like his work, testified against such assumptions. In person, as in poetry, he sought direct speech as a moral imperative. As one example, when an interviewer presented him with a flattering, innocuous question about his work, Czesław steered the conversation back to urgent matters of ethics, suggesting, for example, how our choice of philosophy affects our orientation toward history. While the "lyric" pleasures of poetry were never banished, their allure was admonished. Like his poems, he gave no corner to merely beautiful, beguiling speech. It is this spirit—a man who wore the public mantle of his work lightly but assumed its historical burden with utmost seriousness and responsibility—that I miss and that I want to convey to my students to deepen and to humanize their relationship to poetry.

     For this reason, I like to teach Czesław's poem "A Confession" in the postwar Polish poetry unit I designed for my world poetry class. It is a lighter poem than his others, and its autobiographical veneer is quite appealing to my students. Nonetheless, the poem leads to the kinds of distinctions that I find compelling throughout Miłosz's work. Beneath the speaker's self-effacing meditation as to why he should have been called as a prophet, given his indulgence in sensual pleasures, lies a deeper discussion as to the false and dangerous divisions we make between prophets, demagogues, and ordinary people. If we exclude everyone who exhibited human frailty, who would be left? We need not look back as far as World War II to witness the dangers and errors of assuming that leaders or great men are beyond judgment. The kinds of ethical questions spurred by this poem become a powerful introduction to a unit in which we look at poetry as witness and discuss its blending of personal response with historical record and what it offers that more concrete or supposedly objective (that is, impersonal) forms of writing do not.

On a side note, the poem also captures my sense of Czesław as a man who benignly acknowledged his own and others' *human* frailties at the same time that he refused to absolve anyone's *moral* failures. I wish that I could do more to make this "personal sense" of Miłosz infuse my students' experience of his work. At the same time, I have learned that this personal sense does not necessarily lie in reminiscence or a biography but arises more from some quality of Miłosz that we might happen to capture through such means.

When I first started teaching, I told my students that I had once worked for Miłosz, thinking that my firsthand experience might help them connect to the texts and make a great and formidable author more approachable. But that strategy proved to be more personally flattering than effective, as conversations quickly became derailed by curious inquiries that went off topic. Today I direct my energy instead to the careful reading of the poems themselves. Most often, I find myself tempering the students' tendencies to read bitterness, anger, and sarcasm in place of a self-searching and ironic consciousness in Czesław's postwar poems. One obvious reason for these tendencies is, as I mentioned earlier, that the students tend to read carelessly and so miss the extended syntactic patterns that govern statements, as in the excerpt from "Dedication." Or they tend to skip over portions of lines or stanzas that suggest a more abstract response; for example, in their reading of the poem "A Poor Christian Looks at the Ghetto," most students tend not to account for the line "Ants build around the place left by my body," which challenges their perennially popular idea that what the speaker fears from the guardian mole (which the students mistakenly take as a symbol of the Nazis) is physical death and not some kind of moral accountability.[6]

I also suspect that the students project their own emotional experiences onto the poems, rather than probing those articulated by the poems themselves. As the generation that grew up in the aftermath of the Monica Lewinsky episode, anesthetized to political scandals, these students—now subject to a steady media diet of nationalist aggressions, ethnic hatreds, and genocides—don't presume that the morally complex and personally engaged stances taken by speakers in Miłosz's poems are even possible. Instead, most of them believe they are powerless to affect the world and so view it with anger or cynicism; they do not, as Miłosz's poems so scrupulously do, include themselves in their vision of world events.

So, even as I nudge my students to account for every word on the page to achieve a complete reading of the text, I also strive to explain why the more careful distinctions that emerge from these readings are so important. Indeed, why should these students in a rural university some sixty-plus years after many of these poems were written care that "blind force" is *not* the same thing as "accomplished shape"? that reading "wise books" is not "the same / as leafing through a thousand works fresh from psychiatric clinics"?[7] or, for that matter, also from "Dedication," that "poetry which does not save / Nations or people" is no more than "A connivance with official lies, / A song of drunkards whose throats will be cut in a moment, / Readings for sophomore girls"?[8] I point out that we, too, are living through times marked by escalating nationalist aggressions and invasions into sovereign countries. Because these students can relate personally to the events of 9/11, I draw parallels between their experiences of that event and Miłosz's experience of horrors in his lifetime. I remind them how World War II began, with an unforgettable September attack, the invasion of Poland on September 1, 1939, and how that event might have looked ordinary, external, and impersonal against the landscape of one's personal life. And then I show them the passage—at the end of "Part Two. The Capital: Warsaw, 1918–1939" in *A Treatise on Poetry*—in which Miłosz reminds us so wrenchingly of this truth as he portrays a personal tryst in Warsaw, taking place on a beautiful September night that proves to change the course of history:

> A beautiful night. A huge, lambent moon
> Pours down a light that only happens
> In September. In the hours before dawn
> The air above Warsaw is utterly silent.
> Barrage balloons hang like ripened fruit
> In a sky just grown silvery with dawn.
>
> On Tamka Street a girl's heels click.
> She calls in a half whisper. They go together
> To an empty lot overgrown with weeds.
> A watchman on duty, hidden in the shadows,
> Hears their soft voices in the bedding dark.
> I do not know how to bear my pity.

Or how to find words for our common plight.
A little whore and a worker from Tamka.
Before them, the terror of the rising sun.
Later I would ask myself more than once
What became of them in the coming years and ages.[9]

As we discuss the poem, I suggest that one seemingly insignificant decision that appears in the notes to this poem—Miłosz's acknowledgment that he is the night watchman, as evidenced by his decision in the translation to change the third-person pronoun *he* to the first-person pronoun *I*—might be a key place for the students to begin their investigations of the power of language and of individual consciousness, of witness, and of the weight of memory.[10] I remind them that poetry is not merely lyrical expression freighted with individual emotions and experiences (which is what today's undergraduates, like yesterday's, privilege) but a salutary aim that reminds us (as he writes in "*Ars Poetica?*") "how difficult it is to remain just one person" and that challenges us not to take refuge in private fancies, as romantic poetry does, but to participate in and be answerable to history in one's own voice.[11]

In short, I encourage them, as Charles Altieri once remarked apropos of poetry in general, to imagine that they are the "I" for whom this poem is true. This might not only improve their reading but also expand their range of available emotions and experiences. Such an exercise, of course, has application well beyond the literary, as it may help these students to remain open in the face of our contemporary onslaughts rather than preclude their own efforts, as a great majority of us, myself included, are inclined to do.

I am somewhat optimistic that the questions I am asking today as a teacher are better ones than the ones I once asked Czesław about *Treatise*. Perhaps I have helped a few students to approach Czesław's poems more freely and more seriously, not as canonized texts preserved on the page but, as Boris Pasternak once said of books, as examples of "burning, smoking conscience" directly relevant to how we live today.[12]

Notes

1. Czesław Miłosz, *New and Collected Poems, 1931–2001* (New York: Ecco, 2003), 77.
2. These references are to letters that I typed from dictation for Miłosz (electronic files in my possession): both quotations are from a letter to Leonard Neuger, March 20, 2000. The title of the poetry volume, *Love is an Observant Traveler*, is from a letter to JonArno Lawson, March 15, 1999.
3. Helen Vendler, "A Lament in Three Voices," *New York Review of Books* 48, no. 9 (May 31, 2001): 27–31.

4. Czesław Miłosz, *A Treatise on Poetry,* trans. Robert Hass (New York: Ecco, 2001), 66, author's note 5.

5. Czesław Miłosz, preface to *A Treatise on Poetry,* 1.

6. "A Poor Christian Looks at the Ghetto," *New and Collected Poems,* 63–64. This poem is part of a group of poems called "Voices of Poor People."

7. Czesław Miłosz, *"Ars Poetica?" New and Collected Poems,* 240.

8. "Dedication," *New and Collected Poems,* 77.

9. Miłosz, *Treatise on Poetry,* 25.

10. Ibid., 94, note to p. 25.

11. *"Ars Poetica?" New and Collected Poems,* 241.

12. Pasternak quoted in Edward Hirsch, *How to Read a Poem and Fall in Love with Poetry* (San Diego: Center for Documentary Studies in association with Harcourt, 1999), 14.

Job and Forrest Gump

CLARE CAVANAGH

My life story [is] the triumph of foolish Jan over his wiser brothers.

— Czesław Miłosz, *A Year of the Hunter*

Why not concede that I have not progressed, in my religion,
   past the Book of Job?

With the one difference that Job thought of himself as innocent
   and I saw guilt in my genes.

I was not innocent; I wanted to be innocent, but I couldn't be.

— Czesław Miłosz, "Treatise on Theology"

In the summer of 2002, I conducted a series of interviews with Miłosz in preparation for a biography I was just beginning. Miłosz's attitude toward the project was, perhaps inevitably, mixed. He had given me his blessing, but he worried nonetheless about the shape his life would take in the hands of a young (at least by his standards) Slavist from California, that is to say, the Land of Ulro. I called him as soon as I got into Kraków. We said our hellos, but his next remark was a shocker. "I must convince you not to write the biography," he told me. My heart stopped. "I can't, I've already spent my advance!" I yelped. (This wasn't entirely true, but I was damned if I was taking that line off my vita without a fight.) "Then you must make it a comedy," he replied. "It's the story of Forrest Gump."

I'd handed him just the set-up he'd been looking for, and he roared at his own joke.

I did not first meet Miłosz in California, where I grew up and went to college just a couple of hours from the famous house on Grizzly Peak Boulevard in Berkeley, or at Harvard, where I attended his Norton lectures as a graduate student in the early eighties. We were in the same room several times at various gatherings in Cambridge, but I couldn't bring myself to ask him to sign my *Wiersze wybrane,* the selected works, which I had just begun to read in Polish.[1] The Nobel Prize, the famous bristling eyebrows, and, above all, the poems: it was too much for an awestruck would-be Slavist to tackle. (I was likewise shy of approaching even the pre-Nobel Seamus Heaney, whom I would pass every so often on the way to class.)

I learned only later that even Nobel Prize–winning poets rarely minded being waylaid by overly enthusiastic students. Miłosz would glow whenever I passed on the reactions of my undergrads or grads, the alumni and retirees for whom I occasionally lecture at Northwestern, or the miscellaneous Miłosz fans whom I encountered on a fairly regular basis. I remember telling him about the grad student who jumped up and down squealing as if she'd seen Elvis when I gave her the copy of *Second Space* he'd autographed for her, and the two successive administrative assistants at Northwestern Gender Studies—both nice, smart, gay artists (God knows how many fans have yet to come out of the closet, I told him)— who had wanted to meet me just because I knew Czesław Miłosz. The response was the same every time. He would beam, turn pink, and say, *"Nie może być, nie może być"* (You don't say, you don't say). It was like giving a kid a bicycle for Christmas. The reactions keep coming—the student who cries watching a film of Miłosz reading, the yoga teacher who reads Miłosz to her meditating students. I wish he were there to tell.

From the start we spoke, I should mention, in a macaronic mix of Polish and English. I followed his lead, of course—what else do you do with Czesław Miłosz?—and he switched languages unpredictably. The subject, his mood, his health, how friendly he was feeling that particular day, hour, or minute: we could go back and forth a dozen times in the course of an afternoon. Sometimes we even did Russian: he recited Osip Mandelstam's poem "Lamarck" for me from memory one day, with obvious relish. Or sometimes I would switch from English to Polish because I found it easier to ask what Wisława Szymborska calls "the most pressing questions are naïve ones" in a language I know less well than my own.[2] If you don't feel smart enough even in English—and around Miłosz that could happen in any language—you might as well give up on sophistication and subordinate clauses and get straight to the point in Polish. He was infinitely patient, I should add, though, with nonnative speakers. As is true of so many Poles, he was delighted that a non-Pole had taken the pains to learn their impossible language. (I call them the anti-French.)

I'd missed my chances in Cambridge and California. I first met Miłosz only years later in Kraków, after I'd already earned my spurs as a Slavist and a translator. But even so, it was touch and go. The poet Bronisław Maj, whom Miłosz admired and had translated, told me over and over just to give Miłosz a call when I got into town. But it seemed presumptuous, like calling Goethe to ask if I could stop by for coffee. So before I went over in the summer of 2000, I finally sent him and Carol a cautious e-mail asking if they might possibly find time for me during my next visit. I still have the e-mail they wrote back. I never got over the shock of finding that address in my inbox; I miss it now. When I finally visited, he was in grand form, and I took to Carol immediately. ("When I met Carol, I said to myself, 'He really is a smart guy,'" I told him after she died. "But she picked him," his assistant, Agnieszka Kosińska, objected. "But he let himself get picked," I replied. He beamed.) I'd dressed up for the occasion but was taken aback when Czesław began to admire my feet. No one has ever admired my feet, and with good reason. "Are they really so perfect?" he asked. Weakening eyesight and the this-worldly inclinations of the planet's most unlikely Manichaean work wonders on the unpedicured. I was taken aback—what on earth do you say?—but Carol saved me. "He wants to know if you're wearing stockings," she explained. I was.

This was Miłosz in his Gumpian mode, the Miłosz of the unexpected, unearned (so he thought) happy ending. He'd found a wonderfully smart unpretentious wife who looked after him and his interests with both intelligence and joy. He'd returned part time to Poland after decades of exile. He had his lovely, large Kraków apartment—"you could roller skate across it," he boasted—and the house on Grizzly Peak. He was lionized in both his native and his adoptive land (though Poland and the returning prophet treated one another with suspicion as well as warmth). We moved on to topics that were more literary. Miłosz and Robert Hass were just then working on his volume *To* (This), and Carol wondered how the title's demonstrative pronoun should be translated. She didn't know much Polish, but she'd sensed the problem. "'That' is too far away, but is 'this' too close?" she asked, pointing. "You think like a translator," I said. Or at least like this translator; I spend a lot of time behind closed doors waving my arms and trying to figure out just how near or far the words should be from wherever I happen to be sitting.

Then she went off on other business, and Miłosz and I talked about many things: Polish poetry, poetry in English, Polish literature in translation, the "Miłosz school" and the "Barańczak school" of American translators, that is, the generations of Slavic graduate students who'd fallen under the influence of one poet or the other. I belong to the second camp, but he didn't hold it against me. We got on to Philip Larkin, whom he loathed. I tried to defend Larkin, but since Miłosz liked me, he decided I agreed with him, anyway. This went on for an hour or so, and when we'd finished, Miłosz turned to me and said, "Good shop talk." Good shop talk with Czesław Miłosz!

Miłosz had left me a message when I got back later that day to the friends' house where I was staying. He wanted to do an interview with me (a phone call from Czesław Miłosz! an interview with Czesław Miłosz!) and asked me to call back. So I summoned up my nerve and called. Carol answered the phone. "I'm sure he'd love to talk," she said, "but he and [his friend, the American Slavist] Alexander Schenker have just put away a bottle of Scotch between them, and I doubt you'll get much out of him." I asked when I should call back. She said around nine the next morning. So I called the next day at nine, and there he was, bright-eyed and bushy-tailed so far as I could tell. I couldn't have done it in college, let alone at eighty-nine.

But why should Miłosz want to interview me, and not vice versa? My Irish surname and American street address give me a peculiar advantage in Poland; I translate and teach Polish literature by choice and not by virtue of genealogical and patriotic obligations. Miłosz wanted me to help prove to his mistrustful countrymen that they were not, in Słowacki's phrase, simply the "parrot of nations," endlessly imitating the literary fashions of the West.[3] What he had long called "the Polish school of poetry"—by which he meant the great Polish poets of postwar Poland (Zbigniew Herbert, Tadeusz Różewicz, Miron Białoszewski, Wisława Szymborska, and others), whom he'd worked to promote from his earliest years in American exile—was neither a compensatory figment of his poetic imagination nor a self-serving device designed to exaggerate his importance in the eyes of doubtful compatriots. As an Irish American Slavist from California, I could say what I knew to be true from my own experience without risking accusations of self-aggrandizement or defensiveness: that Eastern European poetry, with Poland arguably occupying pride of place, has held for decades now a privileged position in Anglo-American and Anglo-Irish writing alike. The interview was in fact called "The Polish School of Poetry" when it appeared in the Polish daily paper *Rzeczpospolita* (The Republic) early in 2001. The irony of Miłosz's using me to establish his credentials as a bona fide founding member of the "Polish school" didn't escape me. I still had no clue, though, as to how problematic his status as the Polish poet par excellence was among some of his own countrymen. I never would have guessed it from seeing the headlines, fireworks, and festivities that accompanied his ninetieth birthday in Kraków later that year or from reading the interviews with Carol in the Polish equivalents of *Elle* and *Cosmopolitan* (nice work if you can get it). I didn't realize that I'd already become for some Polish poets and critics what I am still, unapologetically, today: a Miłosz apologist. I didn't know back then that there was anything to apologize for. Now I know. In Poland, Miłosz has been taken to task for many sins: his rejection of rabid nationalism; his resolutely complex, decidedly non-Polish form of Catholicism (he loathed the notion that "Polish" and "Catholic" were virtual synonyms); his early affiliation with the Polish Communist Party; and perhaps above all, his enormous international fame. Many younger poets particularly— and who wasn't younger than Miłosz?—found living in the shadow of the Great Man intolerable.

And that brings us to the Jobian side of the equation. In July 2002, I was already at work on the biography and stopped by the apartment at Bogusławskiego 6 as often as I thought was decent. (Miłosz would ask my friends, "Why doesn't Clare call?" when I tried to keep from pestering him. What could I say? Because he's Czesław Miłosz, and he's great, and I don't have a clue what a biographer is supposed to do with a nonagenarian living legend.) Carol wasn't at home. She'd been ill for several months with an as-yet-undiagnosed ailment and was being treated, I believe, in California then. Czesław said at least they knew it wasn't cancer. I was interviewing him—on literature, on his Lithuanian ancestors, on whatever he wanted to talk about—when he got the phone call telling him that it was cancer after all. "I think we will not talk any more about literature today," he said, and he didn't look like the great, rather fearsome Czesław Miłosz then, just the oldest, saddest man in the world. I asked if I could hug him, and he said yes, so I did, and after that he said, "We are friends, ya? We are friends?" And he gave me a present, a photo album called *Serdce Litwy* (Heart of Lithuania), for which he'd written the text; it's signed and dated "July 26, 2002." Carol died a few weeks later. He called me from California to tell me, and I didn't know what to say, and he couldn't hear me when I did speak. Even if I had said the right thing, I hadn't said it loud enough.

This was the anti-Gump, the poet whose loved ones pay for his art, for his success, for his survival: and he pays too, by losing them time and again. This is where the "child of good fortune" meets Job, as Miłosz writes in

Second Space, which ends, in the Polish version, with a valedictory for his "ridiculous / Contradictory life."[4]

While Carol was still alive, we kept up an e-mail correspondence, albeit rather one-sided. I would write him about the Miłosz enthusiasts among my students and my *emerici,* the retirees I taught in my alumni classes, or the kid who slept in the front row at my lectures until we got to "A Poor Christian Looks at the Ghetto," which woke her up for the rest of the course. Or I would write him about whatever Miłosz work I happened to be reading at the time, and he would send back preemptive warnings: "Remember, *The Issa Valley* is not autobiography!" "Remember I am a poet, not a politician!" (This was vis-à-vis *The Captive Mind* and Miłosz among the pro-Soviet French intellectuals in the 1950s: "The worst decade of my life," he told me.) My favorite e-mail came, though, early in 2002 when I'd been complaining about having to serve as department chair in the coming academic year. "I sympathize out of sincere friendship for you," he wrote in Polish. "I spent thirty years at Berkeley pretending to be the village idiot so that I wouldn't have to chair." Miłosz the village idiot. Yes, and George W. discovered quantum physics. I wrote back that I'd tried that tack, too, but the competition in my department was too stiff. This wasn't entirely fair, but I wanted to make him laugh. Anyone who has heard his laugh will understand.

After Carol died, he stopped writing back—his health, his eyesight, his spirits didn't permit. But I kept writing and visiting. Writing was the easy part—all I had to do was to pick up one of the books, and I would want to go online immediately. It took me a few years to get over the urge to write to him every time I read his words. And I had a never-ending supply of Miłosz jokes for him, because my precocious son—he was seven or eight at the time—never stopped making fun of my obsession with "your poet-friend, Czesław Miłosz." I would repeat them whenever I went to visit, and Miłosz roared every time. My son, Martin, was, and is, obsessed with politics, and out of superhuman motherly devotion I watched a State of the Union address with him one night. When I started criticizing Bush after the talk—what's a mother to do?—he said, "So who do you want for president, Czesław Miłosz?" I was driving Martin to school sometime in 2003 when he decided to quiz me on presidential history. He asked me who'd been the youngest president ever elected. I said, "JFK." He said, "No, he was the youngest president ever inaugurated, Teddy Roosevelt was the youngest one ever elected." Or maybe it was the other way around. In any case, I got it wrong. The next question was easier, though: "If Kennedy was alive today, who would be older, him or Czesław Miłosz?" Miłosz loved that one.

His favorite story, though—he told it to friends who told it back to me—was when Martin and his friend Teddy went with me to the local Barnes and Noble. Martin took Teddy straight to the poetry shelves, showed him the *Collected Poems,* and said, "My mom knows that guy." (I don't remember whether Teddy was impressed.) And then Agnieszka Kosińska would tell about her own son yelling when she got home, "*Mamo, jakiś Miłosz do Ciebie dzwonił*" (Mom, some Miłosz guy called you). I doubt that Amazon.com had in mind the happiness of aged Polish poets when it started the practice some years back of listing in their searches not just the author's works but all the American books in print that cite him. One time I carefully printed out almost all of the then-eight-hundred-plus references to Miłosz in everything from self-help manuals to foreign policy studies to give him when I visited. (My printer gave out before it reached the end, which thrilled him.) He read them all, along with the many four-star reviews that his readers had given his books on Amazon. And he read every word, good or bad, that came out about him in the Polish press. But more on that later.

The visiting got more difficult. I knew he had black moods when Carol was alive, but Carol was famous among his friends for driving them away. But I really saw the doubts, the moods, and the black sides—he could give Jehovah a run for the money when it came to striking terror—only after Carol died. Sometimes it would be yet another younger poet attacking him; "He called me 'Moscow's dancing bear,'" I remember Miłosz saying bleakly about one young writer. The attacks came on a fairly regular basis, and he took them all to heart. I suppose this was the reverse side of the childlike joy at every compliment. I once gave a Kraków cabdriver Miłosz's street address—I never mentioned his name—and he recognized it right away. "Are you going to visit Czesław Miłosz? Please give him the best regards of the cabdriver in the red Mercedes," he requested. Miłosz beamed.

Sometimes the doubts ran deeper—his life, his poetry, his soul. And sometimes the doubts were about me: "You will produce not my life, but only some facsimile," he said with a scowl in the summer of 2003. He spent several weeks that summer putting me through the biographer's equivalent of boot camp. I'd come armed daily with the best questions I could muster, written with the help of a small army of poets, professors, and Miłosz specialists. And every day he gave the same response: "*Takie oczywiste pytania*" (Such obvious questions). Then he would invite me for another session the next day, when yet another set of questions would be dismissed and after an excruciating hour or two, I would be sent home to think up some "questions no one's asked me yet." Questions no one has ever asked Miłosz. It was like Rumpelstiltskin in Polish, but worse.

Finally, after a sleepless night spent reading and rereading *Druga przestrzeń* (the then-untranslated *Second Space*), I went in and asked about the poems and about religion. Those were the questions he wanted. And that was what I'd wanted to talk about, too, but I'd thought biographers were supposed to do something different. We talked about "Father Seweryn" and "The Treatise on Theology"—I said I'd been surprised by the Virgin at the end, and he laughed and said, "I was, too." He asked me to turn the tape recorder off, and he talked about Carol's Southern Baptist childhood, and Catholicism, and the mass, and the afterlife. I can't yet bring myself to repeat everything he said about Carol and the afterlife—maybe I am a bad biographer after all, but it feels like violating a friend's confidence. A Polish friend of mine, not raised as I was in the church, insists that Miłosz was an orthodox Catholic at the end. He wasn't. He was a practicing Catholic, though, which is something very different. He watched mass every day on the television when he couldn't attend. He disagreed with the church on some things—birth control for one—and had nagging doubts about others. There was no prototype for the priestly speaker in "Father Seweryn," he told me; he'd simply imagined that some priest out there must be tormented by the same seesaw of disbelief and faith, or at least the hope of faith, that he himself experienced almost daily.

And I told him that he'd helped me to return to the church after a fashion, because if he could call himself a Catholic, then what the hell, I could too. We called ourselves the "confused Catholics." Once, earlier, when I'd visited, Miłosz had asked, in one of his black moods, "Why do I still have so many doubts at my age?" "If you didn't have doubts, I wouldn't have any use for you," I told him. And it's true. I'm so grateful for his doubts.

"I didn't deserve such an old age," he told friends not long before he died. When I last visited him, in July 2004, he wasn't talking much. I saw him first in the hospital; later, when he'd gone back home to Bogusławskiego 6, he asked me over to say goodbye. I meant to send him an e-mail when I got back to the States; I had a good joke for him. The priest at my church was chewing out the parish parents for letting their daughters come to mass in shorts and tank tops. "When I'm saying 'Body of Christ,' I don't want to be thinking, 'Christ, what a body!'" he bellowed. That would have been something for Miłosz.

Notes

1. Czesław Miłosz, *Wiersze wybrane* (Warsaw: Państwowy Instytut Wydawniczy, 1980).

2. "The Century's Decline," *Poems, New and Collected, 1957–1997,* trans. Stanisław Barańczak and Clare Cavanagh (New York: Harcourt Brace, 2000), 198–99.

3. Juliusz Słowacki, *Grob Agamemnona* (1840), as quoted in *Skrzydlate słowa,* ed. Henryk Markiewicz and Andrzej Romanowski (Warsaw: Panstwowy Instytut Wydawniczy, 1990), 621.

4. Czesław Miłosz, *Druga przestrzeń* (Kraków: Wydawnictwo Znak, 2002), 115.

Last Poems and *Ars Moriendi*

AGNIESZKA KOSIŃSKA

One day in 1996, my professor of poetry at Jagiellonian University, Teresa Walas, told me that Czesław Miłosz's wife was looking for a secretary for her husband (who was spending more and more time on visits in Kraków from Berkeley) for helping with correspondence in Polish and English and for administrative matters. I had an interview with Miłosz's American wife, Carol Thigpen-Miłosz, in English, at U Literatów (The Literary Café).

Things seemed to go well, because I was invited to visit the Miłosz household on Bogusławski Street, where the Nobel laureate was supposed to look me over. He was sitting on the couch in Carol's study, with me standing across from him, when I introduced myself. Miłosz shook his head and yelled to his wife in English, "Carol, I don't need any secretary." Then a moment later he asked, "What can you actually do? Can you type? Do you know Russian?" My affirmative answers paid off immediately. "That means I can dictate something to you." Miłosz did not delay at all.

That day we had our first working session. It consisted of editing letters of the poet to Jerzy Andrzejewski, Jarosław Iwaszkiewicz, and other writers for a collection of correspondence from the years 1945–50, which was eventually published in 1998 under the title *Zaraz po wojnie* (Immediately after the war). It was a great undertaking, but very difficult, and laughter saved me; these letters were loaded with tragedy, but often they were quite comic. Miłosz also laughed with his infectious and resounding laughter.

I left this meeting all sweaty and a bit irritated. Miłosz worked quickly, he was impatient, and he did not seem to realize that I was hired for a totally different task, but we were united by our common sense of humor

and our similar intimation, generally speaking, of the absurdity of existence, which caused us to constantly burst into a laughter that was totally
incomprehensible to people around us. Carol would rush into the room;
concerned, she would ask, "Folks, what are you laughing at?" These common character traits were the basis of our relationship right up to the end.

From that first day until 2004, I was Czesław Miłosz's secretary and had
the opportunity to be both witness to and participant in his creative process.

Miłosz was a poet who got up early in the morning, and in a notebook
with thick, white unlined pages he would write his poems with a fountain
pen—a Waterman or Pelikan with dark blue ink. I would always see these
pages when I came to work in the mornings. Often it was a note, fragment,
sketch, or sentence, but just as frequently it was a nearly finished work.
Then, a little later, he would type verses into the computer, his dear old
Mac, with tiny stickers marking Polish letters that constantly fell off. He
would copy them either from his notebook or from memory, doubtlessly
remembering perfectly what he had handwritten a few days earlier.

Either he or the both of us would print out what he had typed on a
small printer that didn't always spit out the pages the way he wanted and
often jammed. I tried to collect all that came from his pen and printer, even
sometimes what he had condemned to the garbage bin. I put loose papers
in order. I stapled, labeled, and dated them. Well, if I could keep up . . .
"Dear Agnieszka, what are you deliberating about like that?" he would
ask, amused, while observing me bustling around; he was already prepared
to move on to the next task. He did eventually wait for me to finish this
arduous process of collecting and ordering, because it did not take that
much time, and the end result aided the creative process.

The printout was put in a folder, which was deposited in either the top
or the bottom drawer of his desk on the left side. One never looked into
this part of the desk, unless he clearly asked you to look.

Like any good nobleman, he lorded over his poetic domain. He took
poems out of folders and read them, sometimes with the help of a looking
glass or a reading machine, sometimes with my help. He would hand-cor-
rect the computer printout, most often with a fountain pen, more rarely
with red and navy blue crayons that I bought at his request just for this
purpose. The poem once again migrated into a folder. Sometimes Miłosz
asked me to handwrite the printed-out poem with the corrections. The
new version once again ended up in the appropriate folder in his desk; with
time, to make things more simple, I established new folders for newer and
older versions of poems and kept them on my own shelf.

Sometimes he gave me a page and would simply say, "Please read." I
had to find the appropriate tone, division into verses, and breathing rate;

what was most difficult in that half minute or so of rather loud reading was that I had to develop my honest opinion about the poem—all of that had to be worthy of that special moment. He also had the habit of reading new poems during meetings with friends, either at home or when he was visiting them.

He would finally pull the poems out of their folders and ask, "Who are we going to give it to?" Then I read the poem out loud, and if I knew the poem's handwriting was too troublesome for editors, I would retype it into his computer or Carol's computer, depending on which I was using at that moment. Then we would again check the layout of verses and strophes, spaces and punctuations, lowercase and capital letters, and finally indentations. He had his own punctuation habits for his poems, and they did not always square with standard Polish punctuation. Breaking lines at the appropriate point, in this and not that place, was also important; it was usually regulated by breathing or a specific design of the author. This is how Miłosz prepared his poems for print, including those in the collection *Wiersze ostatnie* (Last poems).

I sent them out, most often by fax, to journals that he usually worked with: *Kwartalnik Artystyczny* (Artistic Quarterly), *Zeszyty Literackie* (Literary Notebooks), *Tygodnik Powszechny* (Universal Weekly), and *Odra.* He always asked for a final, preprinting correction of the poem, and we always did one. In the Krakówian archive of Czesław Miłosz, just as in the editorial offices of the above-mentioned journals, you will find these computer printouts of poems, written in large fonts and full of spelling mistakes; the final versions; and the printouts after corrections, too.

When his hand, and later his eyes, started to fail, neither event changed the poet's life all that much. He dictated what he thought was worthy of dictation. He heard and remembered the verses that he had continually worked over in his head during a period of seventy years. Precise maps of the poems were in his mind, and you could read their paths off his face when he traveled over them. We continued to work on versification in the mornings. He dictated off the top of his head and, more rarely, from loose pages covered with hieroglyphs of computer printouts, because for the most part he could not see them anymore. Poems off the top of his head usually were a development of notes from notebooks that were numbered and dated, first by him, later by my hand.

He would usually simply say, "Please write this down." Whenever the mix of a roguish look and a beaming beatitude appeared on his face, I always knew that it was time to write poems. He usually dictated by lines. He also usually marked capital letters and, unwillingly, the commas, which came few and far between. In the end he would say, "Please make something out of this." My corrections were always painstakingly reviewed and accepted: I read slowly, line after line, and asked about everything twice. If there was a change, I revised it, first by hand and later on the computer. The printout would make it into one of the folders, both his (in the desk) and mine. When it emerged from the folders, it once again underwent the trial of reading out loud.

Until Carol's death in 2002, my work as a secretary consisted of a series of literary undertakings—both editing and taking dictation. Miłosz dictated just about everything: essays, letters, notes for interviews. With time, he also started dictating poetry. At times, when dictating, he marked paragraphs, parts, verses, and punctuation; but eventually he would simply say, "Clean this up somehow." He, of course, always accepted the end result. My most "independent" book is the collection of articles *Spiżarnia literacka* (Literary cupboard), published weekly during the years 2003–2004 in *Tygodnik Powszechny*.

I also worked on things connected to the poet's life—the institution which the Nobelist undoubtedly was. This had not been easy for Carol, who knew neither the language nor Poland nor the native manners. She patiently tolerated this whole tornado; Carol was a very understanding life-companion, yet despite all her best efforts, one person could not manage it all. This is why I took over the poet's office.

On top of taking dictation, I had to manage the day's schedule in the office, in the library, and in the archives of the poet. I had to take phone calls in between, send faxes, or listen to Carol's patient questions, plus I had to read the correspondence, which flowed in from all over the world. I also took care of contacts with the media, and I managed the Miłoszes' travels, because Miłosz, even though he was past ninety, did not turn down literary meetings. Quite early on, my employer confided to me matters connected to publishers and publishing contracts. There were other, more quotidian tasks, for example, buying a new winter jacket for Czesław, which, as we all used to say, bordered upon a miracle, because he neither wanted to part with his favorite old jacket nor wanted to waste time trying on the several new jackets we brought back from the store after pestering everyone, telling them that we would return them if they didn't fit.

After Carol's death, the situation changed so that, at Miłosz's behest, I became, using his words, something like a *majordomus*. My son captured the situation quite pithily: "Kind of like a wife, but not for bed."

Wiersze ostatnie came into being in 2002 and 2003 in Kraków. Miłosz did not dictate any poems in 2004.

The year 2004 was an exemplary *ars moriendi*. Czesław Miłosz designated that year for putting in order his earthly, especially his literary, estate. At Miłosz's request, I made an inventory of his poetic stock. I read him almost all the poems that later made it into *Wiersze ostatnie*. He added the following commentary to this reading: "None of these poems are designated for hasty publication." From our conversation it appeared that "hasty" meant immediately after his death.

Miłosz detested being hurried, and he disliked chaotic rushing, especially when it came to poetic material. He had his own internal rhythm and an unshaken consciousness of form, which he only dismissed when it was necessary. You could say that when he was ready, he was ready for certain. Living in a rush culture of quick and easy publishing, we have great difficulty in understanding what it means to do poetry for over seventy years in humble service to one's own daimonion.

Now, after the poet's death, I take care of his Krakówian heritage, meaning, all that I have lived with daily for the past fourteen years: Miłosz's residence in Kraków and his furniture, paintings, trinkets, clothes, archives, and library. Everything remains just as it was when he was alive, when I used to come to work for him. Now you can come and see how this kind of man lived.

For me, working with Miłosz, being with him all day long, was like being locked in a submarine: it was a total submersion in Miłosz's world, coupled with incredible pressure from within and without. Now, six years after his death, I continually test myself against the saying of Simone Weil that Miłosz liked to cite, "Distance is the soul of beauty," and I try to understand what I saw and heard while working with him.

Translated by Artur Sebastian Rosman.

"The Stakes in His Poetry Are Really High"

Interviews with Robert Hass

CYNTHIA L. HAVEN

March 17, 2000: "Czesław is fun. A lot of fun."

I met Robert Hass at his home in Inverness, on the Pacific Coast near Point Reyes, about an hour and a half north from his office at UC Berkeley. As a backdrop to our conversation, jazz is playing loudly throughout this austere and immaculate house of weatherworn wood, part New England and part dacha, and the trees swing dramatically outside the window—signs of a California spring.

CH: In *Twentieth Century Pleasures,* you wrote an essay, "Reading Miłosz." That was written in the mid-1980s. How has your perception of his work changed since then?

RH: What I said then is not exactly wrong, but I've learned a lot more about him since then. I know his work better. I think I got the general outlines right—but I have a more distinctive sense of the phases of his work.

CH: How did you begin your collaboration?

RH: I started working when Czesław asked me what I thought of the translations of his poetry that I'd seen. I said you could tell from them he had an interesting mind. He said, "What?" [Hass imitates Miłosz's peremptory tone.]

CH: When did this occur?

RH: This is probably about 1978. We were neighbors in Berkeley. I'd been aware of his work for a long time because one of my best friends from grammar school ended up studying Slavic languages at Berkeley. He turned me on to *The Captive Mind* about 1960. So I knew him, and found him quite an intimidating figure.

CH: It's funny, because he's not intimidating when you speak to him, is he? He's only intimidating from a distance.

RH: He was more so, then. He had a fierce, hawkish, standoffish formality. In those days, when he gave public readings, which was rare, he liked to have somebody else read the English. I thought at the time it was because he was concerned about his accent. I came to understand . . . basically, his English is perfectly good. He has a strong accent, but he's not hard to understand. It was his way of insisting on his Polishness. On being true to himself. Quite unnecessary, really. Anyway, there was an international literary festival in San Francisco, and Miłosz was asked to read. We had met, actually, because we shared a publisher—Daniel Halpern at Ecco Press. My publisher was bringing out a volume of his poems.

I'd been in a room with him [Miłosz] before, but I hadn't introduced myself. So we met socially. Then he asked me if I would read his poems.

CH: And that was when you got what was probably an intimidating "What?"

RH: [chuckles] Yes. Then I said there was a flatness in . . . what would be an example? An example would be, you could say the line, "From where I stand, the earth declines" or you could say "Earth falls away from the place that I am standing." And one of them has a rhythmic flow, and softness: "The earth falls away from the place where I am standing." It's not just a question of which sounds good—in English, either—it's a question of what's going on in the original language, what phrasing. Polish is quite different from English. So there's a feeling you get reading some things that you're getting a more or less word-for-word translation, but you can't tell what's going on in the poetry. Some early translations were really quite good. But in some of them, it's really hard to know what's going on. So anyway, I started correcting some translations of his poems.

   And then at that point, I asked him about works of his I'd read about—essays about Eastern European poetry, and poetry written during World War II and poems of the Holocaust that weren't in English. One, in particular, I was extremely curious about . . .

CH: Which one?

RH: A poem called "The World." It's a long poem written in a series of short poems—very simple, in the style of a children's primer in Polish. I asked him if it had been translated, and he said no. I asked if I could have a whack at it, if there was a trot, a literal translation. He said, "Well, if you want." Lillian Vallee, a graduate student at Berkeley who had helped him translate *Bells in Winter,* had done a literal version of the poem, so I went to work on it. And a magazine, *Ironwood* magazine—it's gone now, but it was a very good literary magazine—decided they wanted to do a special issue on Miłosz. At the same time, my friend Robert Pinsky moved to Berkeley, so I enlisted him, and we worked on a translation of "The World" together for *Ironwood.* In the middle of this work, Miłosz won the Nobel Prize.

CH: That must have changed the scale of things.

RH: It changed the scale of things.

CH: Were you shocked?

RH: Well, no. I was surprised, but not shocked. Two years before, he'd gotten the Neustadt International Prize for Literature, which is always thought of as a kind of indicator of the Nobel Prize. But yeah, I was surprised and delighted.

   A friend, a woman named Renata Gorczyńska, was the cultural editor for a Polish-language newspaper in New York, an American Polish-language newspaper. She came out because Czesław was getting four bags of mail—four duffle bags of mail every day—from Poland.

CH: All congratulatory letters?

RH: He said he'd gotten a letter from almost everybody he'd been to school with. Everybody in his third-grade class wrote "Dear Czesławi, My goodness!" letters. He was a banned, an underground, writer in Poland, so people knew of him, but they didn't really know his work particularly. The poets did, and political people did, but ordinary people didn't. They had no access to his writing.

Anyway, Renata came out, and I thought, "Oh great!" It was difficult to impose on Czesław, and I wanted somebody to read the poems aloud to me and talk to me about how they felt to a Polish-language reader. So I asked her if we could get together and do that. And she said yes and then said, "Have you seen the poems this guy is writing *now?*" Renata is a blonde with—in whatever year that was, 1980—red-framed glasses, slightly smoky glasses. She'd been the jazz DJ for the Polish equivalent of BBC radio, playing American jazz. She came to Long Island for a broadcasting conference at Stony Brook and jumped ship, defected, and had gotten this job with this Polish-language newspaper. She was somebody who grew up reading Miłosz in samizdat editions.

Once she got here she could read the poems that were being published by his Polish publisher, which was a small émigré press in Paris called the Instytut Literacki. It had been Miłosz's publisher since 1950. And they also published a magazine called *Kultura,* which was the place that translated his poems. So anyway, Renata, when she got here, could read the Instytut Literacki volumes—so she knew what he was up to. So she said to me, "Have you seen the work this guy is doing *now?*" And I said, no, the only poems that had been translated were the poems from the forties to sixties, mostly. She said, "Well, listen," and she started doing sight translations of a group of poems called *The Separate Notebooks,* which are quite amazing.

I was working with Robert Pinsky on "The World"—and I was working with her on doing the new poems, in order to get them ready for the *Ironwood* issue.

So that is how I got started working on Miłosz. I didn't expect to be doing it for twenty years. But there was this huge body of work, and I was interested to see it in English. I have a little Polish, but not enough to translate poetry. For several years, I worked with Renata, just from time to time. And then Czesław and I got started working together and after a while we fell into a rhythm. We'd get together once a week on Monday morning and he would either already have done a first translation, or we would sit down and do a translation—either of new poems or one of the *Collected Poems*, the older poems.

CH: So how would the team work?

RH: He would do a first translation. In that first translation, you're also establishing the "rhythmic regime" of the poem, in a certain way. Renata would read aloud to me endlessly, and I could hear the original rhythms and interrogate her about things. Czesław didn't particularly want to do that. He wasn't interested in giving me Polish lessons. But I learned a little about the prosody of Polish poetry from her.

So we would sit down, and sometimes his translations were terrific, and there would be nothing to do except a kind of light editing—figure out what's an *a* and what's a *the* because it's bewildering for him, "a bird and the tree" and "the bird in the tree." He doesn't instinctively get it.

Sometimes there would be all kinds of problems in translation. Sometimes it would be the right word, right level of diction, how to translate a very idiomatic expression from one language to the other. Sometimes he would do a fast, awkward translation and we would really be starting from scratch. It varied. Basically, our collaboration was different in a few cases where—like with this long poem—I needed a literal translation. Then I needed to do it by myself. I knew what the meter was, but I couldn't sit there, word for word, with him saying, "No, no, no, that's not what I said," because it had to have a rhythmic flow in forty pages. So I had to have some freedom to get the sound of it. I would take it home and work on it. A lot of times, we did it together. And [for] a lot of it, I was just trying to help him with the tone and diction, sometimes with the rhythm of his translation.

So by accident, in the course of this, at an age when I was really too old to have a master anymore, I got to apprentice myself to this amazing body of poetry.

CH: When did he cease to be intimidating?

RH: Oh, immediately. There are great differences between us, but we were both raised Catholics. I went to a Catholic college, so we had rather similar educations. And the more I worked on it, the more I saw how differently he thought about things than I did, indeed, than Americans did.

CH: Such as . . .

RH: Well, let's see. What were the main things? I think American thought is far more pragmatic than European thought. I think that most people are lazier thinkers than Czesław is.

I thought of him as being someone of enormous philosophical rigor and severity—and I've come to see over the years that that is not true. He's a poet, not a philosopher. A lot of his ways of thinking about things are very instinctive.

An example of the difference would be one conversation when he asked, "What are you working on?" I said, "I've agreed to write this essay on American nature writing, and I don't know where to start." He said, "Oh, well, nature to me, of course, is pure horror." And I said, "You were just talking about going up to the wine country and how spectacular the hills were, and the colors of the vines." And he said, "Oh, beauty—different story." [Laughter.] Some of us asked him if he'd read Flannery O'Connor, and he said no. Had he read so-and-so? "No." And finally he said, "You know, I don't agree with the novel." *That's* a different way of thinking.

CH: Of course, however, that's not European. That's *him.*

RH: That's him. So, anyway, there were things I got about his work—and there's also a lot to learn about him. And it's been fascinating to do—because his life spans the century. When he was a kid, the Russian revolution went through his grandparent's farmyard. In the middle of the thirties, in the middle of the rise of fascism and the depth of the Depression, he graduated from high school and he and a couple friends canoed from Warsaw to Paris on the European rivers. His uncle, Oscar Milosz, was a great figure in French literary life, so he had an entrée to that whole world and saw it from the point of view of an ironic young man.

CH: To ask a big question, how do you see his influence on American literary life—or even, more broadly, Western literature?

RH: It's hard to say, exactly. You see quotations from his poetry everywhere. It's not that American poets aren't serious, but in the various poetries of the nineteen-fifties and after, there was a certain kind of playfulness. I think it's because Pound and Eliot and the Modernists seemed kind of heavy. There was an impulse in the next generation of poets to lighten up—not that they weren't serious; "Howl" is a serious poem. Miłosz's poetry can be playful—but the stakes in his poetry are really high. I think, among other things, people are just moved by that.

He's an old man now. In Poland, of course, the younger generation—one part of the younger generation—is figuring out how to get out from under this very great generation of poets whose moral seriousness—Szymborska, Miłosz, Herbert, and Różewicz—

CH: What a team!

RH: They were the greatest poets of the twentieth century. So the younger generation is reading Frank O'Hara. There was an article in one of the Polish literary magazines about the O'Hara-ization of Polish poetry. These kids didn't grow up with either the Nazi occupation or with semi-imposed propagandistic dictatorship. They live in a different world. There are United Colors of Benetton stores in Kraków and Warsaw.

CH: Apparently the same thing is happening in Russia: a literary lull after the great poets of this century. Czesław kept insisting on how very different Poland is from Russia. And yet . . .

RH: The differences are . . . [Pause.] What happened in Russian poetry, in fact, is that there was this tradition of dramatic performance. The poets who were heroes of the young in the nineteen-fifties, sixties, seventies were figures like [Yevgeny] Yevtushenko and [Andrei] Voznesensky—who made big rhetorical gestures in their poetry and recited it dramatically before crowds. They were, in some ways, tolerated as pressure gauges or something, to let off the steam. And their trick was to see how far they could go, without getting shut down.

There's the alternative exile figure of Brodsky. He was writing intellectually complex and difficult poetry, some of it based on English and European models. He was very interested in the metaphysical poets. He was interested in Auden. He was interested in the Russian poets who were banned or underground, like [Osip] Mandelstam and [Anna] Akhmatova.

CH: But Miłosz is also a very dramatic performer.

RH: By *our* standards, but he's not standing up there like
Yevtushenko: "And I am the first tree . . ." [Laughter.] It's like
the difference between Whitman and Auden.

    Writers like Miłosz, Herbert, and Szymborska, a Czech
writer like Miroslav Holub, to some extent [Serbian poet]
Vasko Popa, and others had their irony, their minimalism,
their use of parable, the kind of moral relationship to history,
their dryness of tone, the passionate seriousness—all of that
got absorbed by a lot of American poets. How it influenced
anybody very specifically, I'm not sure I could say.

CH: Who would you put under that influence?

RH: Oh, gosh, I know that for C. K. Williams, for example,
Herbert was an important poet. I know that for Charles
Simic, who was born in Serbia but grew up in Chicago,
Herbert and Miłosz and Popa were important poets. A poet
like Mark Rudman, who wrote a book-length poem called
Writer—that's a mix of verse and prose—I'm sure that he was
formally influenced by Miłosz's *Separate Notebooks.*

    It's very difficult to demonstrate influence. Influence is
a difficult subject. People say all kinds of things about it,
but short of clear-cut imitation, it's very hard to pin down
influence.

CH: More particularly, we could point to a West Coast influence.
He's been here for forty years. Is there perhaps a West Coast
legacy, in particular?

RH: It's true. But if you look at poetry in California in the last
twenty years, one of the main movements has been language
poetry—to which Miłosz is hostile. Another has been the
emergence of—how can I put it?—ethnically identified poetics.
He's not unsympathetic to it, but he's a little wary of anything
that smells of nationalism. The problem with being a Polish
poet was—you couldn't look at a tree, you had to look at a
Polish tree, because of the political situation, for years. He saw
a whole generation kill themselves in the Warsaw Uprising,
because they believed that rhetoric and the Russian romantic
political poetry, so he's pretty allergic to that stuff.

    Jane Hirshfield and Czesław are friends. She admires
him, but again, it's sort of hard to pin down influence.

Linda Gregg, who lives in the East now, but was a friend of Joseph's, audited Czesław's courses when he was still teaching in the late seventies. I know she's written poems—she wrote a poem called "The Gnostics on Trial," which is kind of a response to Czesław's dourness of that time. She was responsive to him, but again, it would be hard to say that there was a formal influence. She lives in Northampton, Massachusetts—but she was born out here, and I think living here at the time.

Because his books sell well—you know lots of poets are reading him—but how he's influenced them? It's hard to say. Robert Pinsky and I both translated him. But even with me, again, even though I've been soaked in this work for twenty years, it's hard to say where the influence is. I can certainly identify it. This is a different thing than influence, in a way, but sometimes a phrase that will come to my mind to describe something will be a phrase that I've used in translating Czesław, his line. You can point to his ambition and seriousness—but Pound and Eliot were ambitious and serious, Wallace Stevens was ambitious and serious.

CH: They were, but . . . well, could the "Four Quartets" have been written without the two world wars? In an article on Miłosz, Vendler wrote, "There are no direct lessons that American poets can learn from Miłosz. Those who have never seen modern war on their own soil cannot adopt the tone . . ." Perhaps part of that seriousness is rooted in historical circumstance—whether it's the bombing of London or the capitulation of France—

RH: Oh, no, but the French didn't experience what Czesław experienced. It was a society that essentially collaborated. The Poles thought existentialism was an improbable bad faith doctrine coming out of a collaborationist culture. They just never bought it.

The French have since reacted against it—but this idea that everyone makes themselves and defines value through each gesture of radical freedom was bound to seem like a joke to people who had no freedom, who were living under the Generalgouvernement of the Gestapo.

I don't know enough about this to be talking about it, really. The French experience as opposed to the Polish experience.

CH: Isn't this part of what you called the high stakes in Miłosz's poetry, and why people are moved by it?

RH: Seamus Heaney has written about the effect of reading Mandelstam, Miłosz, Herbert, and the Eastern European writers on the English-language writers of this period. They press their noses longingly against the window of people who have had dramatic historical experiences.

CH: Back to your own relationship with Miłosz. How has your relationship changed? You found him intimidating at first, then less so.

RH: A lot of it was just—Czesław is fun. A lot of fun. We laughed a lot. He likes to eat and he likes to drink. He's very funny. So it was just fun, being around him. In that way, our relationship changed. Another change was . . . I can think of different examples. When he was working on the anthology *A Book of Luminous Things,* he said he was organizing the poems into categories. And I said, "Oh, that's interesting. What categories?" He said, "Travel, place, women's skin, nature, cities." And I thought, "What's the principle of organization here?" There wasn't a principle of organization. That's different from what one would have thought. One would have expected some clear, theoretical thing.

Even great writers, and he's undoubtedly a great writer, have half a dozen themes, preoccupations. In one part of his mind, the world was so cruel. He thinks maybe the gnostics were right and it is a diabolical creation. Your average American—well, there is no average American as far as religious belief is concerned—would be inclined to believe the world was created by a good God or they are agnostic about it.

CH: Maybe they don't own a cat. I think of his poem "To Mrs. Professor in Defense of My Cat's Honor and Not Only." Watching a cat with a mouse makes some statement about the world and creation. What, after all, is the point?

RH: It's in American poetry, too—in Jeffers, and in a poem like Frost's "Design"—a kind of echo of Blake:

> Tyger! Tyger! burning bright
> In the forests of the night,
> What immortal hand or eye
> Could frame thy fearful symmetry?

But Czesław would say,

[Recites the whole of "Theodicy" from memory.]

> No, it won't do, my sweet theologians.
> Desire will not save the morality of God.
> If he created beings able to choose between good and evil,
> And they chose, and the world lies in iniquity,
> Nevertheless, there is pain, and the undeserved torture of creatures,
> Which would find its explanation only by assuming
> The existence of an archetypal Paradise
> And a pre-human downfall so grave
> That the world of matter received its shape from a diabolic power.[1]

So there's that temptation of thought. A few years ago, he started taking lessons in Lithuanian.

CH: A few years ago?

RH: Yeah.

CH: Wasn't it one of his native languages?

RH: No. He heard it spoken by the farmworkers in his childhood. Lithuanian was to Polish what Irish was to English. So he never really learned the language.

CH: Just a few years ago, then?

RH: I thought maybe he was starting to believe he might go back there, sometime.

CH: I thought he had.

RH: This was before he went back. But I asked him why and he said, "In case it's the language of heaven." [Laughter.]

CH: So has he changed over the years?

RH: Not much. There have been changes in his work. I think that public life changed him enormously.

CH: After he got the Nobel?

RH: Um-hmm.

CH: How so?

RH: Well, lots of things have changed. His wife died—Janka, his first wife.

CH: Then he married Carol?

RH: Yeah. After a couple of years.

Carol was a dean at Emory University and he went and gave a
reading there. She was taken with him and then she came out
on vacation after Janka's death, and they—she pursued him,
basically, I think.

CH: I can believe it—she seems a very strong woman. She seems to
be one of the powerful organizational forces around him, one
of the forces that allows him to keep going.

RH: Interesting. I don't want to talk about his private life. Also,
Carol is a southern woman. Her family, I think, has a lumber
business in Atlanta. So she is very gracious. She had a
professional career and a professional life, without ever having
become the kind of feminist who couldn't tolerate Czesław.
She likes her life with him. There are difficulties.

CH: How could there not be?

RH: She's very good at it. She's smart enough and traditional
enough.

CH: Always playing second fiddle can be hard.

RH: It seems not to be a problem for her.

CH: How long have they been married?

RH: Fifteen years? That long? I forgot what year. At least ten years.

CH: Watching you come into Berkeley's Morrison Reading Room
with him last month was a moving experience. And as he read,
I noticed that you were mouthing the words of his poems—
your translations—as he spoke. So you have formed with him
. . . how would you describe it? A partnership? A symbiosis?

RH: We're good friends. He's my father's age, but it's not a father-
and-son relationship. Nor are we exact contemporaries.
We've just become friends—you get to know somebody quite
well. In an odd way with writers, the person and poet are
somewhat different people.

CH: Is that true with Czesław?

RH: Sure.

CH: How do you see the difference?

RH: Let's see—is there a way to say this? Parts of his poetry, like parts of anybody's poetry, are written with the social personality. And I've gotten so I kind of recognize the difference. Not that you can't write poetry out of your social personality. One of the themes of his poems is the feeling of permanent estrangement from himself. There's one poem in which he sees himself as Cabeza de Vaca—come back from travels among the Indians and suddenly sitting at a dinner table with a bunch of people with lace.[2] You know that poem? Anyway, and part of him always felt like literature was embarrassing—he calls it a tournament of hunchbacks in one place. So there's that side of him.

CH: Tsvetaeva said you have to have a Quasimodo complex to be a poet . . .

RH: Yeah. So there's that side of him. The other is the big dramatic Dostoevskian theological questions that really are not operative, for whatever reasons, so much anymore in life. He's tormented by the idea that all of these religious people—wearing out the stones kneeling in places and wearing out the toes of statues of saints for thousands of years—are all deluded.

CH: He thinks they are deluded?

RH: He hates the thought that they *might* be.
This is where he's not so much a rigorous thinker as a playful one. I walked over one morning and he was looking at a book of the history of women's underwear. He was completely delighted because there's this huge section on late nineteenth and early twentieth centuries' undergarments. These things that he saw that his aunt and his mother had on the line—I don't know where he saw them—suddenly could be rescued. He truly thinks it's horrible that everything just passes away, into oblivion. He hates it. Another poem says: if I find out at the end, if it's really true, that this all means nothing—that a bird on a tree is just a bird on a tree, that we die and that's it, and that all this human anguish, suffering, all of this has meant nothing—even then, at least there will be one messenger, that "runs and runs / Through interstellar fields, through the revolving galaxies, / And calls out, protests, screams."[3] There's that terrific sense of urgency, and one of the things that goes with it is: if he can't remember and get down

on paper the hairstyle of his piano teacher who was crushed in a bombing when she was an old lady, if her life goes unmarked into oblivion—then oblivion won.

He doesn't think literature is eternity—[recites theatrically] "so long as this may live"—he thinks it's a pathetic makeshift, and that language can't really get at experience, but he thinks it's the only tool at his disposal.

So anyway, one morning he's likely to be looking through a book about nineteenth-century women's underwear; the next week, he found this book about medieval theologians who simply could not believe that there could be no time in heaven. They thought that if there were no time, there would be no sunrises and no sunsets, and no morning and no afternoon, and it would be boring. So they invented some quantity, they gave some Latin name to this thing that was like time but not time, that allowed for diurnal change in eternity. This idea pleased him a lot.

CH: Joseph Brodsky said he got almost a sensual pleasure from saying no.

RH: [laughs] He's good at setting limits. He protects himself. That's one of the ways he's been so extraordinarily productive.

CH: He seems to have a lot of people around to do precisely that— protect him and protect his time.

RH: For years, he didn't. He was living in intolerable obscurity and loneliness. There was a poem in which he wrote, "I fashioned an invisible rope / And I climbed it and it held me."[4] He had to invent the idea that there was still somebody to read his poems. His few comrades—"you whom I could not save"—died during those years.[5] I think he felt quite alone. What he did was teach literature, teach Polish literature, and develop this little network of graduate students. He was the first Polish literature professor in the Slavic Languages Department [at Berkeley].

CH: He has certainly increased the visibility of Polish literature— that's a real and indisputable influence.

RH: Yeah, yeah, oh yeah. His first book he did here was *Postwar Polish Poetry,* and that was the one that introduced people to Eastern European poetry.

In Argentina, Witold Gombrowicz, in his diaries, wrote
about *Captive Mind,* in that famous passage where Czesław
describes himself as having a copy of *The Waste Land* in his
back pocket, and diving into the street because Germans were
raking it with machine-gun fire, and the bullets were hitting the
cobblestones, which lifted like bristles on a hedgehog's back.
Gombrowicz says, in effect, "What a crafty s.o.b. We've had to
act like a minor literature in relation to London and Paris for
the last two centuries. At one stroke, he shifted the moral center
of European literature one thousand miles east." Gombrowicz,
who didn't know Miłosz yet, saw this as sheer literary politics.
Not in a bad sense—but as a way of staking a claim for Eastern
European writing. He's a novelist and playwright, probably *the*
major novelist and playwright in Poland . . .

CH: What is Miłosz working on now?

RH: He just finished working on the translation of *Treatise on
Poetry.* We just finished working on that. He's also written
a bunch of new poems, not a huge number, which we've
translated, and I think he's assembling that book.

Being back in Kraków has given him access to archives that
he didn't have access to before, and so he was able to go into
the archives in the university library in Kraków and read all
of the underground publications from the war years—also the
newspapers. I think he went in first just looking for things that he
vaguely remembered reading and he ended up putting together
an anthology of editorials and writing and political essays from
about 1937 to 1946 [*Wyprawa w dwudziestolecie*], documenting
the arguments that were going on inside Polish culture—right-
wing, left-wing, various sorts of left-wing, literary. Everyone, of
course, had more or less rewritten their story over the years.

Then he wrote a commentary on it. It's caused a great stir
in Poland. It's a bestseller in Poland.

CH: When was it published?

RH: This last year. He's been there about half a year for the last
few years.

All the people wanted to deny the intensity of anti-
Semitism. That's been the headline story. They say "these
emphases are not accurate." The various kinds of left-wing
posturing, right-wing posturing . . .

CH: That book was a wonderful thing to do!

RH: It was a great thing to do! The amazing thing about it—a lot of people, famously, get the Nobel Prize and go into the tank. It feels valedictory, somehow. Czesław was just off and running. And he continues to find projects, forms, in which to invent and discover. *Road-side Dog* is an example. He was going through a period where he thought he couldn't write poetry, so he woke one morning with the memory of the dog barking on the road outside the manor houses and started writing these little pieces of prose. And then the subject came to him, "Subjects to Let." That gave him something. When he did *Unattainable Earth,* he got this idea because he was translating stuff into Polish from other languages—D. H. Lawrence, for example.

Bits of ideas from other writers written in journals, poems, and so on. So *that* gave him a form.

CH: So in retrospect, *Road-side Dog* was filling in a dry spell.

RH: Yeah, yeah.

CH: Is there anything else he's working on?

RH: I asked him, "What are you are working on?" He said, "Nothing, really." But who knows what that means? I've never known him not to be working on something.

CH: Are there any new themes emerging in his poetry?

RH: I think of Whitman's "Sands at Seventy," as he called the last section of *Leaves of Grass.* I think the stuff he's writing now—is it valedictory? I don't think he's going to write another long poem.

CH: What do you consider a long poem?

RH: Whether it's a long poem, or a series of poems, but there's a way in which you get into . . . You know, to write a book of poems is to wrestle with an angel, and the first part of the task is to figure out what angel you are wrestling.

CH: That's good. You just made that up?

RH: Yeah, yeah. You know, you scratch in the sand for a while, writing out of your obsessions. And after a while, you figure out what it is you are doing or need to do.

CH: So you don't think there will be another book?

RH: Contractually, what is supposed to happen is a new collected poems. I think the present plan is—the twenty or so pages of new work will be at the end of that collected poems, rather than published as a separate book.

CH: What is there about these poems that might be different?

RH: Nothing.

CH: No new shift or new . . .

RH: Maybe it's the equivalent of sitting down to music you've been haunted by and continuing to kind of tease it out on the piano, see how the melody sounds this time. I think, sometimes, you stand back and see differently. I think I'm too close up to see.

May 29, 2008: "I miss him every day."

This interview occurred in Robert Hass's Berkeley home, within walking distance of Miłosz's Grizzly Peak residence. Miłosz had died in 2004.

CH: Your latest book, *Time and Materials,*[6] melds the historical and the intimate in a way that reinforces what you've said in the past—that to be fully human is itself an act of political subversion. You take on the Iraq War, the destruction of our environment, and the effects of globalization on the developing world, without losing your focus on your usual themes of memory, and how we relate to each other.

RH: During this period, it wasn't possible to overlook another round of violence, as if we had learned nothing. I think that's why it comes into my poems. It's always a torment to know whether poetry can or should address these matters. I had, between these two books, a twenty-five-year apprenticeship to Czesław's struggle around this issue.

I remember when we were working on translating a poem of his, which was kind of a rant, about Sarajevo. I was struggling to find the most persuasive English for something that didn't feel to me as if it was probably particularly persuasive in Polish. We were also under a time constraint, because the op-ed page of the *New York Times* wanted it. And he looked at me and said, "I know this isn't a very good poem, but sometimes it is better to be a little ashamed than to be silent."

CH: And yet we live in a world where . . .

RH: There's a certain fastidiousness, also. It's not as if American poets are apt to ignore politics or not address the subject. They do all the time. It's all preaching to the choir. That's the problem: the air of self-congratulation that is apt to accompany any moral indignation. Even the sort of Dostoevskian solution, which would be to express torment at one's feeling of self-congratulation after expressing moral indignation. And then the intellectuals, if noticing one's revulsion from one's self-congratulation . . . it's endlessly self-reflexive.

It's wonderful about poetry—it can be about anything. It's paying attention to turns of mind you do not know.

CH: You said to me eight years ago that Czesław's late poetry was equivalent to sitting down to music you've been haunted by and continuing to tease it out on the piano, to see how the melody sounds this time.

RH: My reaction is somewhat superstitious: one doesn't want to give up the treasure by shining too bright a light on it.

CH: A quote from Miłosz: "Consciousness, that means nothing." What did he mean by that?

RH: I think he meant that the first fact for us is consciousness, awareness, the composed scene in the mind at every living moment of experience. Then awareness of the scene—and an awareness of the awareness.

Philosophers had a very hard time talking about this because it's hard to know where to stop. But the ordinary sense of consciousness, as mental awareness that *is the world* for us, including all the bodily sensations, before we have any meaning for it. It's the given. As life is a given. Then we have to figure out what it means. But the first meaning is no meaning. It's being.

CH: It just means that you are alive and breathing—basically, is that what he's saying?

RH: Well, no. Because that would be the beginning of a reductive account of it. You're not just alive and breathing: you're seeing; feelings, colors are streaming in. Your whole history is sitting there, or it can be removed, et cetera.

CH: Something else you said eight years ago: "At an age when I was really too old to have a master anymore, I got to apprentice myself to this amazing body of poetry." That was four years before he died. How do those years look now?

RH: It was a great gift. I miss him every day. Even though he had moved to Kraków in the last years, and the collaboration got to be more complicated. We had to do it by e-mail and phone, and I didn't miss that obligation at the end, of having to get his work done to a certain schedule, but I just miss him. He was an endlessly entertaining and interesting companion. One of the things that is a comfort to me about losing friends who are writers is that their books are still there. With Czesław, there's stuff I haven't read yet. There are still some things that haven't been translated. I can haltingly read a little bit of Polish now, but I can't read well enough to read prose. So it's a great pleasure—like that book *Legends of Modernity,* essays written in the 1940s. That was a big surprise to me. I didn't even know it existed.

CH: I know it's still a big question, but can you describe how he influenced you?

RH: I can't really. He was.

CH: It must look different to you now than it did eight years ago, when I asked the same question.

RH: One of the things that you do with any writer you study is that their questions become your questions, in some way. Their way of formulating thoughts and thinking about possibilities becomes some of yours. Some of them are current for you and some are not. One example is that thinking about the word *consciousness.* His formulation of that came to my mind. There were other fathers for me [pauses], though Czesław wasn't really a father figure for me at all. His work ethic was certainly impressive. His willingness to take on serious and seemingly impossible subjects.

CH: Like?

RH: World War Two.

CH: Okay.

RH: One of the features of his poetry that is really striking is the way that he can go from close-up to long-range very swiftly.

Very swift, vertiginous shifts of perspective in his poems. He can go from a dramatic scene to a philosophical meditation.

CH: One of my favorites in that regard is still "To Mrs. Professor in Defense of My Cat's Honor and Not Only," in which he moves from a cat killing a mouse to the Crucifixion and the universe.

RH: He was so pleased by that poem.

CH: I remember when I interviewed him in 2000, I asked him about that poem and his face changed. [Laughter.] I couldn't read the expression because I'd never met him before.

RH [imitating Miłosz]: "Kołakowski is writing an essay about my poem. I thought it was a trifle, in a way."

CH: Kołakowski wrote about that poem?

RH: Yeah. About animals and the origins of human morality, or something.

CH: How often did you see Miłosz?

RH: Over the years, our routine was that we met Monday mornings. Two or three hours. Sometimes we would socialize a bit. He would come to the door and say [imitates Miłosz], "Vodka, Brenda!" We kept vodka in the freezer for Czesław.

CH: I was thinking of something Joseph Brodsky said in his essay on Nadezhda Mandelstam—that she had been more [Osip's] wife in her widowhood, because she had memorized and internalized his poems. You had something of the same role vis-à-vis Miłosz. It's not the man but the essence of the man, in the same way that attar of roses is not the rose but . . .

RH: In this case, it's a pretty big jar.

CH: So what do you miss? What kinds of things come to mind on a daily basis?

RH: His humor.

In a way, he was a bit isolated. As he grew older, colleagues of his own generation fell away. He never really felt at home in California or in the English language entirely. I think when he came back from Carol's funeral he felt some terror that he would not get back to Poland, he was so happy to be back there. He felt hatred and anger for . . . it's interesting, because of the intensity and volatility of emotions for someone who tried to have a consistent worldview. When he first came here, he didn't much like California. Then you follow, in some of his writings, he's become a Californian and is quite loyal to it. As soon as he got back to Poland, then he could hate and resent his time in California.

CH: He did? Why? Just because it was not Poland?

RH: Yeah, to be back in the Polish language. And he was very lonely here, for a long time. He felt like a stranger.

CH: I remember Morton Marcus's memoir [in this volume], where he recalls Miłosz openly weeping at a reading to find someone who appreciated his poems.

RH: It's not how he saw himself. It's interesting. He has that line in "Orpheus and Eurydice," that poets have a certain coldness of heart.

CH: So he came to hate his time in America. How did he express that? What did he say?

RH: I was surprised, too. It's very hard to call it up exactly. It was such a sad time.

CH: His forty years in America?

RH: No, after Carol's death. He did say something like, [whispering] "I'm afraid this place will *catch* me!"

CH: California does. I wasn't expecting to live here.

RH: Yes. His young wife had died. He had made this life that he really loved—the apartment in Kraków, right off the great square in the middle of the city. I just think he had some years of bitter loneliness, and what came back to him, when he came here to California again, was *that*. The isolation.

CH: I remember asking you about her eight years ago. She seemed such an unexpected companion for him, in many ways. I remember wondering what it must be like to marry someone so much older, knowing he would die. One never dreamt . . . I tried to find someone for *An Invisible Rope* who knew her well; she seemed to be such an important part of his life.

RH: A friend and I were talking about this, whether Carol ever had a confidante. I don't think she did. I'm not aware of who it is, if there was one, which is quite amazing, because it wasn't her mother or her brother. I got to know them a little bit.

CH: In any case, he did return to Kraków. He didn't get "caught."

RH: And his brother died, not long after he got back. So he really lost everything in his world. And he just kept working. His hearing was weak, he had to stop drinking, he had inner ear dizziness.

CH: Did he drink a lot?

RH: Yeah, he loved to drink a lot. He could be quite "in that way" of Europeans. He could be quite disciplined about it. I forget what year it was, but it was after he moved back to Kraków; there was one of those literary festivals, with a bunch of Russians—they literally carried him home. This was when he was ninety.

CH: Between my first and second interview with him in 2000, I went to Egypt. I brought back some dates for him. To my amazement, he tore the box open and finished them on the spot!

RH: There's that poem, "A Confession":

> . . . For they saw
> How I empty glasses, throw myself on food,
> And glance greedily at the waitress's neck.[7]

CH: Yes, but I thought he was exaggerating!

RH: He would finish a meal before anyone had started, and then look up, vaguely startled. Carol would tease him about it. "Czesław, if you eat that fast, you're going to have to sit there, and if the conversation isn't about you, you will fall asleep!"

CH: I know some feel at the end, in his spiritual battle between "yes" and "no," the weight came down finally for the "no." The spiritual despair won. I had felt the opposite—at least after reading the poems of *Second Space*.

RH: There's a wonderful essay by Ira Sadoff that takes your view.
      One of the issues that haunted him was about faith. On the one hand, he had the ordinary trouble of people who want to believe in the one God and the nature of evil. Every time he thought about that, however, it inclined him toward the Manichaean split toward some notion of a daemonic earth,

in which people were trapped and had to suffer, and some free realm of spirit beyond it, such as [Emanuel] Swedenborg and his Uncle Oscar and Blake and others describe. It's what *Land of Ulro* is about. Part of him was driven toward strict theological dualism, or Manichaeism, or Gnosticism, by his meditation on the nature of evil. That was a problem for him because in other ways, the idea of a world without hierarchy and a world in which there was no final justice and one in which we just perished, the world he writes about in the Norton lectures, the worldview of modern biology and physics, was intolerable to him. He is really all over the place on this subject at the end of his life.

So I think he had a view of himself as a closet absolutist and Catholic wrestling with his doubts, and he felt faithful to . . . [Breaks off.] I remember being surprised in those years seeing him, when I would occasionally go with my wife and children to mass, at Mary Magdalen [in Berkeley]. One time I saw Czesław on one side of the church and Seamus Heaney on the other. I thought this was a pretty good parish! But there are many of these late poems and places in the prose writing where he feels loyalty to the wishes and hopes and dreams of people who go someplace to pray, to pray to some emblem of whatever story is going to make everything all right, make the suffering all right, make life comprehensible and make sense.

I remember one time in conversation he was talking about how he couldn't stand Simone de Beauvoir—I think partly because she cut him completely after 1951, because she was a Stalinist in those years. She was also quite arrogant, and he was this outsider Polishman. I think at some point, when we were talking about the shiny, worn stones of churches that had been polished by the knees of hundreds of generations— or he would say in Poland, with the old women praying—he said, "I couldn't bear if they were wrong and that bitch de Beauvoir was right!" Part of him felt an appropriate humility in not being able to understand and simply going to church. And then, one of these last poems is about a priest who can no longer believe, and he sees all these people with their scabs and their losses and their suffering, and he gives them comfort that he can't give himself. That's one of the portraits. Another is the "Treatise on Theology," in which he says, "Here's why one needs to believe." Then there's the poem in which he says, if there is no God, a person is still "not permitted to sadden his brother / By saying that there is no God."[8] More powerfully, there is the poem in which he says, "If a thrush on a branch is not a sign, / But just a thrush on the branch," there will still be one voice that "runs and runs / Through interstellar fields, through the revolving galaxies, / And calls out, protests, screams."[9]

So on the one hand, his whole being revolted against a world in which there was no God and therefore no meaning, and no place for people to believe things would be made good. I also think that he thought—and this came out of the arguments of 1930s and 1940s Catholic Poland soaked in Hegel among the intellectuals and soaked in Marx and in Thomas Aquinas—the great argument, as he saw it, in the twentieth century, was between "being" and "becoming." And that "being" was replaced by "becoming." But "becoming" for him meant Darwinism, Marxism—a view of a world never at rest, with no absolutes.

CH: And no memory.

RH: Yeah.

CH: Didn't he just want something simpler from himself that was simply not in him? He wanted the divine ship to sail the divine sea *for him*. And he was watching these figures in Polish history who were much more fundamentalist, much more intellectually primitive, and yet the crown fell on them and not him.

In "Awakened," he seemed to realize he'd played his role, that "everything happened just as it had to."[10] That *was* the divine ship, and it *was* for him.

RH: He was never at peace with that answer. It was one he tried out.

CH: But we're back to those layers of consciousness: was he ever at peace with the realization that he would never be at peace?

RH: There's a sort of coyness about him to my ear—pleading an absence of vanity around these issues in some of the late work. But I think what he was sort of able to say to himself in his torment of conscience, which was considerable, was that he'd been a good fighter. He'd not rested on these questions.

CH: I think that's so much why we're drawn to him. He appeals to the part in us that's a good fighter.

RH: Finally, to me, the amazing thing about his work was [that] he [found it] just unbearable if experience could be lost. If poetry could only do a small amount to recover the naked present, then he was going to do it relentlessly. He said this many times.

CH: And yet, to get back to a theme in your own poems—"The Dry Mountain Air," for example—there's an acceptance that the moment when your grandmother brought out the chocolate may never have happened. That you may be giving reality to things that never had any reality at all. Miłosz was trying to preserve the hairstyle of the librarian—and you're preserving the dream of a . . .

RH: Of course, I think that moment absolutely happened . . .

CH: But that happens all the time in family arguments: "I remember you were wearing your red jacket!" "No, it was blue!"

RH: In a way, bringing in the other witness allows an escape from the subjectivity of the single-person lyric, which *he* was able to do in a bunch of different ways, by a kind of polyphony in his poems.
 I rolled my eyes at the "Treatise on Theology" because it ends with "Our Lady of Fatima." He said, "What I believe is that she appeared," and he says she hovered ten centimeters above the tree. He does the magician's trick.

CH: And you rolled your eyes at the . . .

RH: I understand that you can't resolve these issues by returning to the stories that the nuns told you in the fifth grade. That's not going to do. But it's as probable as Pound's Venus, or anybody else's deity.

CH: There's a part of us that wants the stories the nuns told us in the fifth grade to be true.

RH: There's an argument for—as Blake said—radical innocence. He finds a way to set it down here and take it away over here, and put it over here. Like the end of *From the Rising of the Sun:* "the form of every single grain will be restored in glory / I was judged for my despair because I was unable to understand this." On one hand, he has the answer, and on the other, he can't believe the answer that he has.

CH: I think part of him wanted the radical innocence—but his role was instead to be a spokesman for all the people who wanted a radical innocence and weren't going to get it in this lifetime.

RH: We were marching along the streets of Kraków that morning. It was thronged. The Fox News of Poland unleashed this terrific attack on Miłosz because the archbishop or cardinal of Poland had agreed to officiate at the service. And the right took this as an opportunity to attack whatever political position they thought Czesław represented by dredging [up] lots of evidence that he was anti-Catholic and anti-Polish, and it was so strong that the cardinal said that he would be at the funeral but he would not go to the graveside, where [Czesław] was being buried, at the church some blocks away. Czesław had written a letter, sending the Polish version of *Second Space* to John Paul, saying—I don't know what it said—

CH: I believe the letter has been lost—

RH: "You probably won't approve of this, but I send it to you anyway with affection and admiration"—or something like that. The pope wrote him back a letter saying, "I think you have served God as a great artist"—something like that. Anyway, this drumbeat had been going on for two weeks— attacks on Miłosz in the press. On the Thursday before the Saturday funeral, the Vatican released the pope's letter. So when I arrived on Friday morning in Kraków, in sweltering heat of the end of August, the headlines all said the pope says Miłosz is a good man.

CH: Which jerked the carpet out from under all those . . .

RH: So the cardinal did go on to the graveside ceremony.

CH: The pope was a much more nuanced person than many people gave him credit for being.

RH: I don't think you get much more nuanced.

CH: I think he recognized that Czesław Miłosz spoke for a lot of people who look at the suffering of a mouse at the paws of a cat and simply cannot be reconciled. Or can only be intermittently reconciled.

RH: The right-wing counterdemonstrations that were supposed to be happening—there was a lot in the paper about them—

didn't happen. I was walking with Adam Zagajewski and Seamus Heaney down the middle of this jammed medieval street, following the casket from St. Mary's in the Square to the Church of St. Peter on the Rock, where he was going to be buried in this crypt—it gives me the creeps to think he's buried in the basement of the church. So we're going along, and Adam pointed over to a couple of ambushed little old ladies on the corner. He said that one of them said to the other, "I don't know what all the fuss is about, I hear he was a bad Catholic." And the other woman said, "Yes, but the Holy Father forgave him." That was the Polish resolution of the two sides of the argument.

Notes

1. Czesław Miłosz, "Theodicy," *New and Collected Poems, 1931–2001* (New York: Ecco, 2003), 445.
2. "Throughout Our Lands," *New and Collected Poems*, 182–88.
3. "Meaning," *New and Collected Poems*, 569.
4. "Magic Mountain," *New and Collected Poems*, 335–36.
5. "Dedication," *New and Collected Poems*, 77.
6. *Time and Materials* received a National Book Award in 2007 and the Pulitzer Prize in 2008.
7. *New and Collected Poems*, 461.
8. "If There Is No God," *Second Space* (New York: Ecco, 2004), 5.
9. "Meaning," *New and Collected Poems*, 569.
10. "Awakened," *New and Collected Poems*, 693.

A Selected Miłosz Bibliography

Poemat o czasie zastygłym [Poem on frozen time]. Wilno: Koło Polonistów Słuchaczy Uniwersytetu Stefana Batorego, 1933.

Antologia poezji społecznej, 1924–1933 [Anthology of social poetry, 1924–1933]. Wilno: Koło Polonistów Słuchaczy Uniwersytetu Stefana Batorego, 1933.

Trzy zimy: Poezje [Three winters: Poetry]. Warsaw-Wilno: Związek Zawodowy Literatów Polskich, 1936.

Obrachunki [Reckonings]. 1938.

Wiersze [Poems]. Warsaw: 1940. Under the pseudonym Jan Syruć.

Pieśń niepodległa: Poezja polska czasów wojny [The invincible song: Polish wartime poetry]. Warsaw: Oficyna Polska, 1942.

Ocalenie [Rescue]. Warsaw: Spółdzielnia Wydawnicza Czytelnik, 1945.

Murti-Bing. New York: American Committee for Cultural Freedom, 1951.

Zniewolony umysł. Paris: Instytut Literacki, 1953. Published in concurrent English, American, and French editions. Translated by Jane Zielonko as *The Captive Mind* (London: Secker and Warburg; New York: Knopf). Translated by A. Prudhommeaux and the author as *La pensée captive* (Paris: Gallimard).

Światło dzienne: Poezja [Daylight: Poetry]. Paris: Instytut Literacki, 1953.

Zdobycie władzy [Seizure of power]. Paris: Instytut Literacki, 1955. Originally translated into French as *La prise du pouvoir* for La Guilde des Livres, 1953.

The Usurpers. London: Faber and Faber, 1955. In America, published as *Seizure of Power* (New York: Criterion Books, 1955). Translated by Celina Wieniewska.

Dolina Issy [Issa Valley]. Paris: Instytut Literacki, 1955.

Traktat poetycki [Treatise on poetry]. Paris: Instytut Literacki, 1957.

Kontynenty [Continents]. Paris: Instytut Literacki, 1958.

Wybór pism [Selected works], by Simone Weil. Compiled and translated by Czesław Miłosz. Paris: Instytut Literacki, 1958.

Rodzinna Europa [Native realm]. Paris: Instytut Literacki, 1959.

Człowiek wśród skorpionów [Man among scorpions]. Paris: Instytut Literacki, 1962.

Król Popiel i inne wiersze [King Popiel and other poems]. Paris: Instytut Literacki, 1962.

Gucio zaczarowany [Bobo's metamorphosis]. Paris: Instytut Literacki, 1965.

Postwar Polish Poetry: An Anthology. Selected and translated by Czesław Miłosz. Garden City, N.Y.: Doubleday, 1965.

Wiersze [Poems]. London: Oficyna Poetów i Malarzy, 1967.

A Selected Miłosz Bibliography

Selected Poems, by Zbigniew Herbert. Translated by Czesław Miłosz and Peter Dale Scott. Harmondsworth, U.K.: Penguin, 1968.
Native Realm: A Search for Self-Definition. Translated by Catherine S. Leach. Garden City, N.Y.: Doubleday, 1968.
Miasto bez imienia: Poezje [City without a name: Poetry]. Paris: Instytut Literacki, 1969.
Widzenia nad zatoką San Francisco [Visions from San Francisco Bay]. Paris: Instytut Literacki, 1969.
The History of Polish Literature. New York: Macmillan, 1969.
Prywatne obowiązki [Private obligations]. Paris: Instytut Literacki, 1972.
Selected Poems. Translated by several hands. New York: Seabury Press, 1973.
Gdzie wschodzi słońce i kędy zapada [From the rising of the sun]. Paris: Instytut Literacki, 1974.
Utwory poetyckie: Poems. Ann Arbor: Michigan Slavic Publications, 1976.
Emperor of the Earth: Modes of Eccentric Vision. Berkeley: University of California Press, 1977.
Ziemia Ulro [Land of Ulro]. Paris: Instytut Literacki, 1977.
Mediterranean Poems, by Aleksander Wat. Edited and translated by Czesław Miłosz. Ann Arbor, Mich.: Ardis, 1977.
Mój wiek: Pamiętnik [My century], by Aleksander Wat. Czesław Miłosz, interviewer; edited by Lidia Ciołkoszowa. 2 vols. London: Polonia Book Fund, 1977.
Bells in Winter. Translated by the author and Lillian Vallee. New York: Ecco Press, 1978.
Księga psalmów [Book of Psalms]. Translated from Hebrew to Polish by Czesław Miłosz. Paris: Éditions du Dialogue, 1979.
Ogród nauk [Garden of knowledge]. Paris: Instytut Literacki, 1979.
Wiersze wybrane [Selected poems]. Warsaw: Państwowy Instytut Wydawniczy, 1980.
Nobel Lecture/Odczyt w Akademii Szwedzkiej. New York: Farrar, Straus and Giroux, 1980.
Księga Hioba [Book of Job]. Translated from Hebrew to Polish by Czesław Miłosz. Paris: Éditions du Dialogue, 1980.
The Issa Valley. Translated by Louis Iribarne. New York: Farrar, Straus and Giroux, 1981.
Pieśń niepodległa = The Invincible Song: A Clandestine Anthology. Edited by Czesław Miłosz. Ann Arbor: Michigan Slavic Publications, 1981.
Rozmowy z Czesławem Miłoszem. Aleksander Fiut, interviewer. Kraków: Wydawnictwo Literackie, 1981.
Księgi pięciu megilot [The Books of Five Megiloth]. Translated from Greek to Polish by Czesław Miłosz. Paris: Éditions du Dialogue, 1982.
Visions from San Francisco Bay. Translated by Richard Lourie. New York: Farrar, Straus and Giroux, 1982.
Hymn o perle [Hymn of the pearl]. Ann Arbor: Michigan Slavic Publications, 1982; Kraków: Wydawnictwo Literackie, 1983.
The Witness of Poetry. Cambridge, Mass.: Harvard University Press, 1983.
Ewangelia według Marka; Apokalipsa [The Gospel of Mark; The Apocalypse]. Translated from Hebrew to Polish by Czesław Miłosz. Paris: Éditions du Dialogue, 1984.
The Land of Ulro. Translated by Louis Iribarne. New York: Farrar, Straus and Giroux, 1984.

Nieobjęta ziemia [Unattainable earth]. Paris: Instytut Literacki, 1984.

The Separate Notebooks. Translated by Robert Hass and Robert Pinsky with the author and Renata Gorczynski. New York: Ecco Press, 1984.

Poszukiwania: Wybór publicystyki rozproszonej, 1931–1983 [Explorations: Selected articles, 1931–1983]. Warsaw: Wydawnictwo CDN, 1985.

Zaczynając od moich ulic [Beginning with my streets]. Paris: Instytut Literacki, 1985.

Happy as a Dog's Tail, by Anna Swir [Świrszczyńska]. Translated by Czesław Miłosz, with Leonard Nathan; with an introduction by Czesław Miłosz and an afterword by Czesław Miłosz and Leonard Nathan. San Diego: Harcourt Brace Jovanovich, 1985.

Unattainable Earth. Translated by the author and Robert Hass. New York: Ecco Press, 1986.

Kroniki [Chronicles]. Paris: Instytut Literacki, 1987; Kraków: Wydawnictwo Znak, 1988.

Conversations with Czesław Miłosz. Ewa Czarnecka and Aleksander Fiut, interviewers. San Diego: Harcourt Brace Jovanovich, 1987.

Exiles. Photos by Josef Koudelka; essay by Czesław Miłosz. New York: Aperture Foundation, 1988.

The Collected Poems, 1931–1987. New York: Ecco Press, 1988.

Metafizyczna pauza [Metaphysical pause]. Kraków: Wydawnictwo Znak, 1989.

Poematy. Wrocław: Wydawnictwo Dolnośląskie, 1989.

With the Skin: Poems of Aleksander Wat. Translated and edited by Czesław Miłosz and Leonard Nathan. New York: Ecco Press, 1989.

Rok myśliwego [Year of the hunter]. Paris: Instytut Literacki, 1990; Kraków: Wydawnictwo Znak, 1991.

Beginning with My Streets: Essays and Recollections. Translated by Madeline G. Levine. New York: Farrar, Straus and Giroux, 1991.

Provinces. Translated by the author and Robert Hass. New York: Ecco Press, 1991.

Dalsze okolice [Farther surroundings]. Kraków: Wydawnictwo Znak, 1991.

Szukanie ojczyzny [In search of a homeland]. Kraków: Wydawnictwo Znak, 1992.

Na brzegu rzeki [Facing the river]. Kraków: Wydawnictwo Znak, 1994.

A Year of the Hunter. Translated by Madeline G. Levine. New York: Farrar, Straus and Giroux, 1994.

Facing the River: New Poems. Translated by the author and Robert Hass. New York: Ecco, 1995.

Legendy nowoczesności [Legends of modernity]. Kraków: Wydawnictwo Literackie, 1996.

A Book of Luminous Things: An International Anthology of Poetry. Edited by Czesław Miłosz. San Diego: Harcourt Brace, 1996.

Striving towards Being: The Letters of Thomas Merton and Czesław Miłosz. New York: Farrar, Straus and Giroux, 1997.

Życie na wyspach [Life on islands]. Kraków: Wydawnictwo Znak, 1997.

Piesek przydrożny [Road-side dog]. Kraków: Wydawnictwo Znak, 1997.

Abecadło Miłosza [Miłosz's ABC's]. Kraków: Wydawnictwo Literackie, 1997.

Inne Abecadło [Further ABC's]. Kraków: Wydawnictwo Literackie, 1998.

Road-side Dog. Translated by Robert Hass. New York: Farrar, Straus and Giroux, 1998.

Zaraz po wojnie: Korespondencja z pisarzami, 1945–1950 [Immediately after the war: Correspondence with writers, 1945–1950]. Kraków: Wydawnictwo Znak, 1998.

Wyprawa w dwudziestolecie [Excursion through the twenties and thirties]. Kraków: Wydawnictwo Literackie, 1999.

To [It]. Kraków: Wydawnictwo Znak, 2000.

Milosz's ABC's. Translated by Madeline G. Levine. New York: Farrar, Straus and Giroux, 2001.

A Treatise on Poetry. Translated by Robert Hass. New York: Ecco, 2001.

To Begin Where I Am: Selected Essays. New York: Farrar, Straus and Giroux, 2001.

Druga przestrzeń [Second space]. Kraków: Wydawnictwo Znak, 2002.

New and Collected Poems, 1931–2001. New York: Ecco, 2003.

Przygody młodego umysłu: Pulicystyka i proza, 1931–1939. [Adventures of a young mind: Articles and prose, 1931–1939]. Kraków: Wyadawnictwo Znak, 2003.

Second Space: New Poems. Translated by Robert Hass. New York: Ecco, 2004.

O podróżach w czasie [On time travel]. Kraków: Wydawnictwo Znak, 2004.

Spiżarnia literacka [Literary cupboard]. Kraków: Wydawnictwo Literackie, 2004.

Legends of Modernity: Essays and Letters from Occupied Poland, 1942–1943. Translated by Madeline Levine. New York: Farrar, Straus and Giroux, 2005.

"Mój Wileński Opiekun": Listy do Manfreda Kridla (1946–1955) ["My Wilno guardian": Letters to Manfred Kridl (1946–1955)]. Edited by A. Karcz. Toruń: Uniwersytet M. Kopernika, 2005.

Czesław Miłosz: Conversations. Edited by Cynthia L. Haven. Jackson: University Press of Mississippi, 2006.

Selected Poems, 1931–2004. Edited by Robert Hass. New York: Ecco, 2006.

Wiersze ostatnie [Last poems]. Edited by Agnieszka Kosińska. Kraków: Znak, 2006.

Czesław Miłosz: Bibliografia druków zwartych [Czesław Miłosz: A bibliography of major works]. Edited by Agnieszka Kosińska. Kraków: Krakowska Akademia im. Andrzeja Frycza Modrzewskiego and Instytut Dokumentacji i Studiów nad Literaturą Polską, 2009.

Contributors

BOGDANA CARPENTER, professor of Polish and comparative literature at the University of Michigan in Ann Arbor, received her Ph.D. from the University of California, Berkeley. She is the author of *The Poetic Avant-garde in Poland, 1918–1939* and *Monumenta Polonica: The First Four Centuries of Polish Poetry,* coeditor (with Madeline Levine) of a volume of essays by Czeslaw Miłosz, *To Begin Where I Am,* and—together with her husband, John—translator into English of Zbigniew Herbert, Julia Hartwig, and other contemporary Polish poets. She has written extensively on the work of Polish writers such as Zbigniew Herbert, Miłosz, Wisława Szymborska, Witold Gombrowicz, and others. She is a recipient of the American Poetry Society Award, the American Council for Polish Culture Clubs Award, and the Golden Cross of Merit of the Republic of Poland.

CLARE CAVANAGH is the Herman and Beulah Pearce Miller Research Professor in Literature at Northwestern University, and the author, most recently, of *Lyric Poetry and Modern Politics: Russia, Poland, and the West* (2009). She has translated the work of Wisława Szymborska and Adam Zagajewski and is working on an authorized biography of Miłosz, to be published by Farrar, Straus and Giroux.

ANNA FRAJLICH, émigré poet, scholar, and educator, has taught Polish language and literature at Columbia University for twenty-five years. Her eleven volumes of poetry have been published on both sides of the Atlantic. She was awarded the Cavalier's Cross, Order of Merit of the Polish Republic, in 2002. She has also received literary awards from the Turzanski Foundation and the Kościelski Foundation. She is honorary ambassador of Szczecin and acting president of the Writers-in-Exile chapter of PEN International in the U.S.A. She is the author of *The Legacy of Ancient Rome in the Russian Silver Age.*

267

NATALIE GERBER is an associate professor of English at the State University of New York; she teaches literature at SUNY Fredonia. She was a personal assistant to Robert Hass during his tenure as U.S. poet laureate (1995–97) and afterwards to Miłosz (1999–2000).

GEORGE GÖMÖRI is an emeritus fellow at Darwin College, University of Cambridge, U.K., and the author of many books on Polish and Hungarian literature, including *Magnetic Poles* (London, 2000).

IRENA GRUDZIŃSKA GROSS teaches in the Slavic Department at Princeton University. Her book *Czełsaw Miłosz and Joseph Brodsky: Fellowship of Poets* was published by Yale University Press in 2009.

HENRYK GRYNBERG is an award-winning Polish novelist, poet, and essayist living in the United States since 1967. The main subject of his writing is the fate of the Polish Jews during and after the Holocaust.

DANIEL HALPERN is the author of nine collections of poetry, including *Something Shining* (1999) and *Selected Poems* (1994). He is the editor of numerous anthologies, including *The Art of the Tale* (1987); and two food books, *Halpern's Guide to the Restaurants of Italy* and *The Good Food*. He has received fellowships from the Guggenheim Foundation and the National Endowment for the Arts, as well as the 2009 Poets and Writers Editor's Award and the 1993 PEN Publisher Citation. He published *Antaeus*, founded in Tangier with Paul Bowles; taught at Columbia, Princeton, and the New School; and is now president and publisher of Ecco.

ROBERT HASS has published a number of books of poetry, most recently *Time and Materials* (2007), which won the National Book Award and the Pulitzer Prize. In spring 2010, Ecco will publish *The Apple Trees at Olema: Selected Poems and Essays, 1985–2009* and a collection of selected essays. Hass was U.S. poet laureate from 1995 to 1997. He was awarded the MacArthur "Genius" Fellowship and the National Book Critics' Circle Award (in 1984 and 1997) and was chosen for the Yale Series of Younger Poets series in 1973. Hass, a professor of English at UC Berkeley, has translated many of the works of Miłosz.

CYNTHIA L. HAVEN has written for the *Times Literary Supplement*, the *Washington Post*, the *Los Angeles Times*, the *San Francisco Chronicle*, the *Kenyon Review*, the *Georgia Review*, and other publications. Her previous books include *Czełsaw Miłosz: Conversations* (2006), *Peter Dale in Conversation with Cynthia Haven* (London, 2005), and *Joseph Brodsky: Conversations* (2003). She has received more than a dozen writing and journalism honors, including a 2008 Milena Jesenská Journalism Fellowship with Vienna's Institut für die Wissenschaften vom Menschen.

SEAMUS HEANEY received the Nobel Prize in Literature in 1995. He is a foreign member of the American Academy of Arts and Letters and held the chair of Professor of Poetry at Oxford from 1989 to 1994. Heaney has been a resident of Dublin since 1976, but between 1982 and 1996 he spent part of each year teaching at Harvard University, where in 1984 he was appointed Boylston Professor of Rhetoric and Oratory. His translation of *Beowulf* (1999) won the Whitbread Book of the Year Prize. His most recent volume of poetry is *Human Chain* (2010).

JANE HIRSHFIELD's seventh collection of poetry, *Come Thief*, will appear from Knopf in 2011. Her six previous collections of poetry include *After* (2006) and *Given Sugar, Given Salt* (a finalist for the 2001 National Book Critics Circle Award); she is also the author of a now-classic book of essays, *Nine Gates: Entering the Mind of Poetry* (1997). She has received major fellowships from the Guggenheim and Rockefeller Foundations, the National Endowment for the Arts, and the Academy of American Poets. Her work has been chosen for five editions of *The Best American Poetry* series. A selected poems volume, *Uważność*, translated by Magda Heydel and with an introduction by Miłosz, was published in Poland by Znak in 2002.

AGNIESZKA KOSIŃSKA is a Kraków-based literary critic who graduated in Polish language and literature from the Jagiellonian University. From 1996 to 2004, she was Miłosz's personal secretary. She is currently custodian of the poet's apartment and archives in Kraków, and of the literary rights to his work. Kosińska is the editor of Czesław Miłosz's 2006 collection *Wiersze ostatnie* (Last Poems). She is the editor of *Czesław Miłosz. Bibliografia druków zwartych* (Czesław Miłosz: International bibliography), 2009.

JOHN FOSTER LEICH was a foreign service officer in Poland and Germany from 1947 to 1950; he was assistant director for exile relations and deputy director of West European Operations, Free Europe Committee, 1950–65. In 1998, he was awarded the Cavalier's Cross, Order of Merit of the

Polish Republic, for his Free Europe work. He was the director of international studies and a professor of political science and foreign languages at Louisiana Tech University from 1967 to 1990.

MADELINE G. LEVINE, Kenan Professor of Slavic Literatures Emerita, taught Russian, Polish, and comparative East European literatures at the University of North Carolina at Chapel Hill until her recent retirement. She is a literary translator who also publishes occasional scholarly studies of twentieth-century Polish prose.

RICHARD LOURIE studied at Boston University with Robert Lowell, who awarded him the Sneath Poetry Prize in 1960. That year Lourie also went to UC Berkeley to study Russian and met Miłosz. Gradually Lourie switched to prose: his novel *The Autobiography of Joseph Stalin* was translated into fifteen languages, and his *Sakharov: A Biography* was featured on the cover of the *New York Times Book Review.* Lourie translated over thirty books from Russian and Polish, including Miłosz's *Visions from San Francisco Bay.* Lourie was also quite active in the anti-Soviet underground; some of his adventures are recounted in his memoir of Miłosz. Lourie is now a columnist for the *Moscow Times* and, like Thomas Hardy, is returning to poetry in later life.

ZYGMUNT MALINOWSKI is a New York City photographer and former senior art editor for John Wiley & Sons.

MORTON MARCUS is the author of ten books of poetry, among them *Moments without Names: New and Selected Prose Poems* (2002) and *Pursuing the Dream Bone* (2007). His literary memoirs, *Striking Through the Masks* appeared in 2008, and his translation of poems by Vasko Popa, *The Star Wizard's Legacy,* is forthcoming from White Pine Press.

JADWIGA MAURER, an award-winning Polish scholar and writer, has taught at the University of California, Berkeley and Indiana University Bloomington; she is now a professor emeritus of Slavic languages and literatures at the University of Kansas. She is the author of many articles and essays, both in Polish and in English, and has published a book on the poet Adam Mickiewicz (London, 1990; Krakow, 1996). She is the author of three volumes of short stories, the last one published in Poland in 2002.

W. S. MERWIN, winner of two Pulitzer Prizes (in 1971 and 2009), among many other awards, is the author of more than a dozen books of poetry, as well as a memoir, prose collections, and translations (most notably of Dante's *Purgatorio* and *Sir Gawain and the Green Knight*). His first collection of poetry, *A Mask for Janus,* was chosen by W. H. Auden in 1952 for the Yale Younger Poets series. Over the years, he has received the Lannan Lifetime Achievement Award, the National Book Award, the Tanning Prize, the Bollingen Prize, and the Ruth Lilly Poetry Prize. His most recent collections include *Present Company, Migration* (which won the National Book Award), and *The Shadow of Sirius.* He is the current U.S. poet laureate.

LEONARD NATHAN (d. 2007) is the author of seventeen volumes of poetry. He received the National Institute of Arts and Letters prize for poetry, a Guggenheim Fellowship, the Phelan Award for Narrative Poetry, and three silver medals from the Commonwealth Club of California. His poems have been published in the *New Yorker,* the *Atlantic,* the *New England Review,* the *Georgia Review,* and others. He was chair of UC Berkeley's Department of Speech from 1968 to 1972 and helped its transition into the Department of Rhetoric.

ROBERT PINSKY's most recent book of poems is *Gulf Music.* He recently edited *Essential Pleasures: A New Anthology of Poems to Read Aloud.* In the 1980s, while living in Berkeley, he helped Miłosz create English versions of his poems. He now teaches in the MFA program at Boston University.

ALEXANDER SCHENKER was deported to a Soviet labor camp in 1940, after the fall of Poland in World War II. He left the Soviet Union in 1946 and studied at the Sorbonne, followed by graduate studies in Yale's Department of Linguistics, receiving a Ph.D. in 1953. He taught at Yale until his retirement in 1995. He is a foreign member of the Polish Academy of Arts and Sciences. He received the Scaglione Prize of the Modern Language Association of America and awards by the American Association of Teachers of Slavic and East European Languages and the American Association for the Advancement of Slavic Studies for his contribution to Slavic studies in the United States. His most recent book is *The Bronze Horseman: Falconet's Monument to Peter the Great* (2003).

PETER DALE SCOTT, a former Canadian diplomat and professor at the University of California, Berkeley, is a translator with Miłosz of works by Zbigniew Herbert, as well as many poems by Miłosz. His own books of poetry include the trilogy *Seculum: Coming to Jakarta, Listening to the*

Candle, Minding the Darkness; as well as *Crossing Borders* and *Mosaic Orpheus.* His website is http://www.peterdalescott.net.

MAREK SKWARNICKI—Polish poet, writer, and translator of poetry—was imprisoned in the German concentration camp Mauthausen in 1944. From 1958 to 1991, he was on the editorial board of *Tygodnik Powszechny.* He has written many volumes of poetry and memoirs from his travels with John Paul II, which he covered as a reporter. His correspondence with Miłosz is included in his book *Mój Miłosz* (My Miłosz).

JUDITH TANNENBAUM has worked in the field of community arts for close to thirty-five years. She currently serves as training coordinator for San Francisco's WritersCorps program. Her books include *Disguised as a Poem: My Years Teaching Poetry at San Quentin* (finalist in the Creative Non-fiction category of PEN Center West's 2001 Literary Awards); *Teeth, Wiggly as Earthquakes: Writing Poetry in the Primary Grades;* and as editor, *Jump Write In! Creative Writing Exercises for Diverse Communities, Grades 6–12.* *By Heart: Poetry, Prison, and Two Lives,* a two-person memoir written with Spoon Jackson, was published by New Village Press in 2010. Her website is http://www.judithtannenbaum.com.

ELIZABETH KRIDL VALKENIER, daughter of Polish literary scholar Manfred Kridl, is an adjunct associate professor of art history at Columbia University, where she teaches the history of Russian art. She is the author of *Russian Realist Art: The State and Society; Valentin Serov: Portraits of Russia's Silver Age; Ilya Repin and the World of Russian Art;* and other works.

LILLIAN VALLEE is an award-winning translator, writer, and scholar who teaches English at Modesto Junior College. She co-translated Miłosz's *Bells in Winter* with the poet, as well as Witold Gombrowicz's three-volume literary *Diary* and Aleksander Wat's *Lucifer Unemployed.* Her dissertation examined primordial tradition in the work of Miłosz. She has received a Fulbright Fellowship, a National Endowment for the Humanities Translation Grant, the Konstanty Jelenski and Alfred Jurzykowski Foundation translation awards, and MJC's Purdy Award for Excellence in Teaching.

TOMAS VENCLOVA, a former Lithuanian and Soviet dissident and currently a professor of Slavic languages and literatures at Yale University, is an internationally known poet. He has authored more than a hundred scholarly publications as well.

Helen Vendler is the A. Kingsley Porter University Professor at Harvard University. She is the author of books on Yeats, Stevens, Herbert, Keats, Shakespeare, Heaney, and Dickinson and has written several essays on the poetry of Miłosz.

Reuel K. Wilson, professor emeritus at the University of Western Ontario, has written on Polish literature and translated from it. He is the author of *Poland's Caribbean Tragedy* (1986), with Jan Pachonski, and *To the Life of the Silver Harbor* (2008).

Joanna Zach is on the faculty of Jagiellonian University. She is finishing her second book on Czesław Miłosz.

Adam Zagajewski lives in Kraków amd teaches one quarter a year at the University of Chicago. His most recent book is *Eternal Enemies,* a collection of poems published by Farrar, Straus and Giroux.

Index

INDEX

Forché, Carolyn: "The Colonel," 192
Frajlich, Anna, 3, 171, 173
Frost, Robert, 211; "Design," 244
Frye, Northrup, 201

García Lorca, Federico, 74
Gazeta Wyborcza, 39
Gerber, Natalie, 2
Gerould, Daniel C., 26, 140
Giedroyć, Jerzy, 19, 25, 26, 32n, 135, 147
Gilbert, Erin, 56, 94, 149, 151, 173
Gilman, Teresa, 183–84
Gimbutas, Marija, 136
Ginsberg, Allen, 51; "Howl," 241
Głowacki, Janusz, 171
Glusman, John, 180
Goethe, Johann Wolfgang von, 125
Goldwater, Barry, 23
Gombrowicz, Witold, 21, 140, 142, 162,
    191, 249, 267, 272; Diary, 115–16
Gömöri, George, 6
Gomułka, Władysław, 89–91
Gorczyńska, Renata (Ewa Czarnecka),
    115, 139, 143, 144, 147, 166, 167,
    169, 237, 238; Conversations with
    Miłosz, 143
Gore, Joseph, 147–48
Grass, Günther, 110
Gregg, Linda, 243; "The Gnostics on
    Trial," 243
Gromada, Tadeusz, 168
Gross, Feliks, 168, 171
Gross, Jan, 118
Grossman, Joan, 130
Grynberg, Henryk, 147
Gumilev, Nikolai, 130
Gurdjieff, G. I., 128

Halpern, Daniel, 156, 236
Hamlin, Jesse, 117n
Hardwick, Elizabeth, 150
Hass, Robert, 5, 6, 7, 76, 102, 108n, 109,
    164–65, 185, 203–4, 214, 223
Heaney, Seamus, 73n, 184, 222, 257, 261
Heart Sutra, 191
Hegel, Georg Wilhelm Friedrich, 258
Hemingway, Ernest, 158
Herbert, Zbigniew, 5, 21, 23, 24, 35–36,
    39, 40–41, 65–66, 69–70, 72n, 73n,
    74–75, 105, 120, 145–46, 150, 158–
    59, 165, 178, 184, 190, 224, 241, 242,
    244; "Pebble," 69; Selected Poems,
    71; "Two Drops," 71, 73n

Hertz, Zygmunt, 105
Hillman, Brenda, 254
Hirsch, Edward, 78, 125, 220n
Hirshfield, Jane, 7, 242
Hitler, Adolph, 121
Holub, Miroslav, 242
Homer, 136, 194
Howe, Irving, 49
Hoyem, Andrew, 185
Hughes, Robert, 64, 130
Hughes, Ted, 73n
Hungarian Quarterly, 6, 28, 32

Illg, Jerzy, 3
Instytut Literacki, 26, 113, 138, 238
Iribarne, Louis, 5, 147
Ironwood, 183, 237, 238
Issa, Kobayashi, 190
Ivask, Ivar, 115
Iwaszkiewicz, Jarosław, 24, 230

Jagiellonian University, 60, 123, 230
Jarniewicz, Jerzy, 209
Jaruzelski, Gen. Wojciech, 135
Jastrun, Mieczysław, 26
Jeffers, Robinson, 4, 25, 35–36, 63, 66, 70,
    244
Jeleński, Konstanty, 105, 124
Jeziorański, Jan Nowak, 144,
Job, 225–26
John, Gospel of, 204
John Paul II, 7, 36, 39–40, 42, 53, 55, 84–
    85, 141, 156, 167, 190, 206, 260, 261
Johnson, Ronald, 96
Joyce, James, 5, 110

Kahan, Arcadius, 140
Kalm, Chet, 147–48
Kantor, Tadeusz, 167
Karkowska, Julita, 173
Karlinsky, Simon, 130
Karpowicz, Tymoteusz, 147, 150–51
Keats, John, 205
Keliuotis, Juozas, 132–33
Kennedy, John F., 23, 226
Kertész, André, 167
Keyserling, Eduard von, 110
Khrushchev, Nikita, 34
Kielce, 92, 95n
Klots, Yasha, 137
Kochanowski, Jan, 66; Laments, 184
Koczorowski, Stanisław P., 33
Kohn, Hans, 13